T0352958

SEMIOTEXT(E) FOREIGN AGENTS SERIES

Originally published as *L'inconscient machinique*.
© Éditions Recherches, 1979
This edition © 2011 Semiotext(e)

Published by Semiotext(e)
PO Box 629, South Pasadena, CA 91031
www.semiotexte.com

Special thanks to Bernard Schutze and John Ebert.

Cover Art: Walead Beshty: *Six Color Curl (CMYRGB: Irvine, California, July 17th 2008*. Fuji Crystal Archive Type C), 2008.
Color photographic paper. 50 x 91 inches.
Image: Fredrik Nilsen
Courtesy of the artist; Regen Projects, Los Angeles; Wallspace, New York; and Thomas Dane Gallery, London.

Design by Hedi El Kholti

ISBN: 978-1-58435-088-0
Distributed by The MIT Press, Cambridge, Mass. and London, England
Printed in the United States of America

10 9 8 7 6 5

THE MACHINIC

UNCONSCIOUS

ESSAYS IN SCHIZOANALYSIS

Félix Guattari

Translated by Taylor Adkins

\<e\>

Contents

I

THE MACHINIC UNCONSCIOUS

1

Introduction: Logos or Abstract Machines?

Does the unconscious still have something to say to us? We have saddled it with so much that it seems to have resolved to keep silent. For a long time it was believed to be possible to interpret its messages. A whole corporation of specialists worked away at this task. Nevertheless, the results were hardly worthwhile, for it seems likely they have all gone astray. Would the unconscious definitively speak an untranslatable language? It's quite possible. It would be necessary to start again from the beginning. First of all, what is this unconscious really? Is it a magical world hidden in who knows which fold of the brain? An internal mini-cinema specialized in child pornography or the projection of fixed archetypal plans? The new psychoanalysts have worked out more purified and better asepticized ideal models than the older ones: they now propose a structural unconscious emptied of all the old Freudian or Jungian folklore with its interpretative grids, psychosexual stages, and dramas copied from antiquity... According to them, the unconscious would be "structured like a language." Yet, it goes without saying, not like everyday language, but like a mathematical language. For example, Jacques Lacan currently speaks about the "mathemes" of the unconscious...

We have the unconscious we deserve! And I must acknowledge that the structuralist psychoanalysts are even less appropriate in my view than the Freudians, Jungians, or Reichians. I would see the unconscious instead as something that we drag around with ourselves both in our gestures and daily objects, as well as on TV, that is part of the zeitgeist, and even, and perhaps especially, in our day-to-day problems. (I am thinking, for example, of the question of "the society we choose to live in" that always resurfaces around the time of each electoral campaign.) Thus, the unconscious works inside individuals in their manner of perceiving the world and living their body, territory, and sex, as well as inside the couple, the family, school, neighborhood, factories, stadiums, and universities... In other words, not simply an unconscious of the specialists of the unconscious, not simply an unconscious crystallized in the past, congealed in an institutionalized discourse, but, on the contrary, an unconscious turned towards the future whose screen would be none other than the possible itself, the possible as hypersensitive to language, but also the possible hypersensitive to touch, hypersensitive to the socius, hypersensitive to the cosmos... Then why stick this label of "machinic unconscious" onto it? Simply to stress that it is populated not only with images and words, but also with all kinds of machinisms that lead it to produce and reproduce these images and words.

We are accustomed to think of material and social facts in terms of genealogies, archaeological residues, and dialectical progress or in terms of decline, degeneration, and rising entropy... Time goes on toward better days or plunges blindly toward unimaginable catastrophes; unless it simply starts to vegetate indefinitely. We can bypass these dilemmas by refusing any sort of causalist or finalist extrapolation and by strictly limiting the object of research to structural relations or systemic balances. But no matter how one goes about it, the past remains heavy, cooled down, and the future seems largely mortgaged by a present closing in on it from all sides. To think time against the grain, to imagine that what came "after" can modify what was "before" or that changing the past at the root can transform a current state of affairs: what madness! A return to magical thought! It is pure science fiction, and yet...

In my view there is nothing absurd about attempting to explore these interactions, which I would also qualify as "machinic," without initially specifying their material and/or semiotic nature. Neither transcendent Platonic idea, nor Aristotelian form adajacent to an a-morphous matter, these abstract deterritorialized interactions, or, more briefly, these *abstract machines* traverse various levels of reality and establish and demolish stratifications. Abstract machines cling not to a single universal time but to a trans-spatial and trans-temporal *plane of consistency* which affects through them a relative coefficient of existence. Consequently, their "appearance" in reality can no longer claim to be given all in one piece: it is negotiated on the basis of quanta of possibles. The coordinates of existence function like so many space-time and subjective coordinates and are established on the basis of assemblages which are in constant interaction and incessantly engaged in processes of deterritorialization and singularization causing them to be decentralized in comparison to one another, while assigning them "territories of replacement" in spaces of coding. This is why I shall oppose territories and lands to *machinic territorialities*. By distinguishing them from set logic, a "machinism" of the assemblage will only recognize relative identities and trajectories. It is only on a "normal" human scale—i.e. that which pertains neither to madness, childhood, nor art—that Being and Time will seem to thicken and coagulate to a point of no return. Having considered things from the angle of machinic time and the plane of consistency, everything will take on a new light: causalities will no longer function in a single direction, and it will no longer be allowed for us to affirm that "everything is a foregone conclusion."

Following René Thom,[1] it even seems possible one can "take back one's throws," since, according to this author, the logos of the biological species would be able to operate a sort of "smoothing of time" in the direction of both the past and future. Due to the definition of these *logoi* and so long as "space-time figures, as well as their variations, conform to a principle excluding discontinuities and angles," the phenomena that refer to them would be able to influence their predecessors and their successors. Here as well, all in all machines become independent of their immediate manifestations while "smoothing" a plane of consistency that authorizes every intersection possible! And yet, these *logoi* inspire only a relative confidence in me. I fear that they merely have an irresistible inclination to escape from the physico-biological world in order to rejoin the mathematical universe of their origin! What particularly worries me is that they can only be factored in, as René Thom explains, so that the most abstract are arranged with the most elementary and the most concrete with the most complex. This simple fact seems to condemn them to definitively fail to maintain their hold on reality. The difference between Thom's *logoi* and abstract machines, such as I conceive them, stems from the fact that the former are simply carrying abstraction, whereas the latter in addition convey singularity points "extracted" from the cosmos and history. Rather than abstract machines, perhaps it is preferable to speak of "machinic extracts" or deterritorialized and deterritorializing machines. In any event, I consider that they should not be comparable to entities attached once and for all to a universe of forms and general formulas. By preserving the expression "abstract machine" in spite of its ambiguity, it is the very idea of abstract universals that I aim to dispute. Abstraction can only result from machines and assemblages of concrete enunciations. And since there is no general assemblage that overhangs all of them, every time we encounter a universal enunciation, it will be necessary to determine the particular nature of its enunciative assemblage and analyze the operation of power that leads it to lay claim to such a universality.

The ideal of order—the systematic formalization of every mode of expression, the control over semiological flows, and the repression of the lines of flight and lines of dissidence—that dominates university research and the practical fields of the social sciences can never be completely attained, primarily because it is the stake of political and micro-political power struggles, but, perhaps more basically because, as we shall see, languages drift in all parts. Scientific formalization fortunately does not make an exception to this rule. The exhaustive dichotic analysis, binarist reduction, and radical "digitalization" of every semiotic practice, whose model has been elaborated by information theory, seems to function today (in league with behaviorism and Pavlovian theories, with which it also has certain affinities) as a sort of instrument of contention in the field of linguistics and the social sciences. We believe that such a method could in principle be applied to any type of social phenomenon. And if we manage to implement it through some sort of sleight of hand, we are then convinced to have grasped the essence of the phenomenon in question: we can stop and pass on to something else. Unless, while pushing things to the extreme, we come from that position to no longer consider any event except in terms of its probability of occurrence, and then, in the name of the sacrosanct second principle of thermodynamics, to proclaim that everything must tend towards a state of equilibrium or that every structural phenomenon must necessarily evolve towards a reduction of tensions and disorder.[2] A few universal principles hang over contingencies and singularities, precisely with respect to probabilizing events on a diachronic axis and structuralizing them on a synchronic axis: this is what the ambition of the various structuralist schools is reduced to! In fact, I believe that this kind of operation always turns up in order to "sweep under the rug" the socio-machinic assemblages which are ultimately the only effective producers of rupture and innovation in the semiotic fields that interest us here. Chance and structure are the two greatest enemies of freedom. They induce the same conservative ideal of the general axiomatization of the sciences that has invaded their field since the end of the 19th century. And since they have furthermore become inseparable from the philosophical tradition as a pure subject of knowledge inaccessible to historical transformations, they return us very quickly to the meddlesome and sclerotic discourse of epistemology. It is always the same juggling act: through the promotion of a transcendent order founded upon the allegedly universal nature of the signifying articulations of certain enunciations—the Cogito, mathematical and scientific laws, etc…—one endeavors to guarantee certain types of formations of power, simultaneously consolidating the social status and the imaginary security of its pundits and scribes in the fields of ideology and science.

Two attitudes or two politics are possible with regard to form: a formalist position that begins with transcendent universal forms cut off from history and which are "embodied" in semiological substances, and a position that begins with social formations and material assemblages in order to extract some (to abstract some) of the semiotic components and abstract machines from the cosmic and human history that offers them. With this second path, certain "accidental" conjunctions between "natural" encodings and sign machines will affirm themselves, will "make the law," during a given period. However, it will be impossible to consider them independently of the assemblages that constitute the nucleus of their enunciation. It is not a question, as one could be tempted to say, of a re-enunciation. Indeed, there is no meta-language here. *The collective assemblage of enunciation speaks "on the same level" as states of affairs, states of facts, and subjective states.* There is not, on the one hand, a subject that speaks in the "void" and, on the other hand, an object that would be spoken in the "plenum." The void and the plenum are "engineered" by the same deterritorialization effect.

Connections are only possible at the point where abstract mechanizations and concrete, dated, and situated assemblages enable a connection to their deterritorialization. Also, assemblages are not delivered randomly to the axiomatic of universals: the only "law" they uphold is a general movement of deterritorialization. The axiomatic returns to the assemblage more deterritorialized in order to solve the impasse of previous systems of enunciation and untie the stratifications of the machinic assemblages that correspond to them. Such a "law" does not imply a pre-established order, a necessary harmony, or a systemic universal of anything.

René Thom, who knew how to denounce the "dream of information theory" with humor, or rather the dream of those whose hopes depend upon a set of formal systems and morpho-genesis,[3] perhaps did not come to the end of his intuition. Does he not lend himself to the brunt of his own criticism when he sets out in search of a system of algorithms that would be able to give an account of *every* morphogenetic change, of *every* "catastrophe" capable of affecting an assemblage?

He rightly considers that the "abstract *logoi*," immigrants of the physical and biological world, never stop "invading" the cerebral world. But there are many other continents from which such "invasions" develop, beginning with the world of socio-economic assemblages and that of the mass media. According to him, every interaction is brought back to phenomena of formal resonance in the last analysis (page [200]). On the contrary, I will start with the idea that assemblages of flows and codes are first compared in relation to differentiations of form and structure, object and subject, and that the phenomena of formal interaction constitute only a particular case, that of a borderline case, within the machinic processes that work upon the assemblages before the substance-form coupling.

Abstract machines do not function like a coding system stacked on from the "outside" on the existing stratifications. Within the framework of the general movement of deterritorialization that I evoked earlier, they constitute a sort of *transformational matter*, what I call an "optional subject"—composed of the crystals of the posssible which catalyze connections, destratifications, and reterritorializations both in the living and inanimate world. In short, abstract machinisms emphasize the fact that deterritorialization in all its forms "precedes" the existence of the strata and the territories. Not being "realizable" in a purely logical space but only through contingent machinic manifestations, they never involve simple combinations; they always imply an assemblage of components irreducible to a formal description. "Descending" from the pragmatic fields to the assemblages, from the assemblages to the components, and then from the components to the matters of expression, we shall see that we will not necessarily pass from the complex to the simple. We will never be able to establish a final systemic hierarchy between the elementary and the compound. Under certain conditions, the elementary can always make new potentialities emerge or make them *proliferate* and include the remainders within the assemblages to which it is related. Also, rather than starting with the elementary, which is likely to be merely a lure, the analysis will attempt to never simplify or reduce what seems preferable to call a *molecular level*. Machinic molecules may carry the keys of encoding that lead to the most differentiated assemblages. Moreover, the scope of the "most complex" generally seems to depend upon the fact that these molecular machinisms are more deterritorialized and more abstract.

If it is true that abstract machines arise neither from the subject-object phenomenological couple, nor the set-subset logical couple, and consequently escape from the semiological triangle denotation-representation-signification, then how do we conceive the possibility of saying anything about them? What will become of representation when there is no longer a subject to record it? These are a few of the difficulties that will lead us to call the status of the modes of semiotization and subjectification into question. The assemblages do not acknowledge—as of yet—objects and subjects: but that does not mean that their components do not have anything to do with something that is *of the order* of subjectivity and representation, but not in the traditional form of individual subjects and statements detached from their context. Other processes of encoding and "ensigning," independent of a deixis and an anthropocentric logic, will thus have to come to light. Universality will no longer have the discourse of a subject, incarnating itself in a word, a revealed text, or a divine or scientific law, as a compulsory reference. Logical propositions will be crafted according to *machinic propositions*. The singular features of a non-semiologically formed matter will be able to lay claim to universality. Conversely, the universality of a process of coding or a signifying redundancy will be able to "fall" into contingency. While conferring onto singularity points a particular power of crossing stratified fields, the signs-particles conveying quanta of possibles will only equip them for a limited number of universal capacities. Indeed, the assemblages that embody the singularity-abstract machine conjunctions remain prone to being undone for the purpose of opening up other possibles and contingencies. Universalist thought always conceals a reverential fear with respect to an established order—be it religious or natural. On the contrary, the thought of assemblages and molecular machinisms should continue connecting all sorts of practices situated in the perspective of the changes and transformations of the existing orders and the diminishing of their power.

Linguistics and semiology occupy a privileged place in the field of the humanities and social sciences. Many problems that other disciplines in this field are unable to solve are reinvestigated by the linguists and semiologists who are supposed to know the real story. Benefiting from a favourable bias due to their achieving fashionable status, and credited with a high degree of "scientificity," linguistic and semiological theories are frequently used as an alibi for all sorts of pretexts. One refers to them as though they were dogma or holy texts. Several generations of psychoanalysts thus spouted forth an incredible amount of Saussurian "signifying" without any critical distance, and even, for most among them, without really knowing what they were talking about. The attitudes of linguists and semiologists have seemed in my view to coincide perfectly with that of psychoanalysts on an essential point: everyone agrees to avoid any overstepping of their respective problematics regarding political, social, economic, and *concrete* technological domains which are in their common territory. The reflections and suggestions that I devote to questions of linguistics and semiotics at the beginning of this book will focus mainly on a questioning of this shared problematic.

In these essays we will successively approach:[4]

—questions of a linguistic and semiotic nature whose examination, in my view, constitutes an essential precondition for any revision of the theory of the unconscious and in particular the manner in which the problem of pragmatics is posed today;

—questions relative to assemblages of enunciation and pragmatic fields considered from the angle of unconscious phenomena in the social field;

—two fundamental categories of the redundancies of the machinic unconscious: faciality traits and refrains;

—the bases upon which a schizoanalytical pragmatics can be constructed that would be non-reductive with regard to political and micropolitical problems;

—in addition, a "machinic genealogy" of the set of semiotic entities proposed throughout this work which, in my view, seems to be able to function within the framework of a pragmatics that would no longer be exclusively a matter for linguistics and semiotics.[5]

A second essay will be devoted to the trajectory of faciality traits and refrains in the work of Marcel Proust.

In order to help the reader familiarize themselves with a few of the problems and terms that will constantly reappear during this essay, but which will be approached from partial angles, I here present a sort of synthetic glossary of some of the essential conclusions.

Against the model of the syntagmatic tree, analytical pragmatics and schizoanalysis will oppose something that is not a model, but a "rhizome" (or "lattice"). It will be defined by the following characteristics:

—contrary to Chomskyan trees, which start at a point S and proceed by dichotomy, rhizomes may connect any point whatsoever to any other point;

—each trait of the rhizome will not necessarily refer back to a linguistic trait. Every sort of semiotic chain will be connected to a wide variety of encoding modes: biological, political, economic chains, etc... bringing into play not only all the sign regimes, but also all the regulations of non-signs;

—relations existing between the levels of segmentarity within each semiotic stratum will be able to differentiate inter-stratic relations and will function on the basis of the lines of flight of deterritorialization;

—under these conditions, a pragmatics of rhizomes will renounce any idea of underlying structure; unlike the psychoanalytic unconscious, the machinic unconscious is not a representational unconscious crystallized in codified complexes and repartitioned on a genetic axis; it is to be built like a map;[6]

—the map, as the last characteristic of the rhizome, will be detachable, connectable, reversable, and modifiable.

Within a rhizome, tree structures will be able to exist. Conversely, the branch of a tree could begin to send out buds in the form of a rhizome. We will classify the pragmatic components into two categories:

1. *Interpretative components*, which we shall indifferently call generic or generative transformations and which imply a primacy of semiologies of resonance and signification over non-interpretative semiotics.

They will also be divided into two general types of transformations:
–*analogical* transformations depending, for example, on iconic semiologies,

—*signifying* transformations concerning linguistic semiologies.

Each of these types of component will only be able to occupy a dominant position within the framework of a particular mode of subjectification of the contents and formations of power: territorialized or reterritorialized assemblages of enunciation for analogical transformations and individual assemblages of enunciation and capitalist subjectivity for signifying transformations.

2. *Non-interpretative components*, which we shall generally refer to as transformational components due to the fact that the preceding components of formal resonance do not constitute anything other, as I already mentioned, than a particular or borderline case. They will also be divided into two general types of transformation:

—*symbolic* transformations concerning "intensive" semiotics (on the level of perception, gesture, mimicry, etc… but also on the various verbal and scriptural levels that escape from analogical redundancies);

—*diagrammatic* transformations concerning asignifying semiotics that proceed through a deterritorialization relative both to the formalism of content and expression by setting into play mutant abstract machines (systems of signs-particles and quanta of possibles working simultaneously within the register of material and semiotic realities).

At the semiotic level of *coordinates of efficiency*, we shall distinguish two modes of *redundancy*:

—redundancies of *resonance* corresponding to the semiological components of subjectification and conscientialization (faciality, "refrains," etc...);

—machinic redundancies or redundancies of *interaction* corresponding to asignifying diagrammatic components (semiotic or not).

At the level of *existential coordinates*, we shall distinguish three levels of *consistency*:

—the *molar* consistency of strata, significations, and realities such as the dominant (or dominated) phenomenology proposes (complete objects, subjects, individuals, etc...);

—the *molecular* consistency that expresses the degree of manifestation or real machinic embodiment of an assemblage (but on this level we can neither distinguish assemblages from fields nor components);

—the *abstract* consistency that specifies the "theoretical" degree of possibility of the two preceding consistencies. The intersection of these two frames of reference ends in six types of fields of resonance and fields of interaction: cf. table page 51.

Notes:

1. Here, I have obviously not employed the expressions "generative component" and "transformational component" in the same sense as the Chomskyans. According to the latter, the generative capacity of a system stems from a logico-mathematical axiomatic, whereas I consider that the generative constraints (of a language or a dialect) are always intrinsically related to the existence of a power formation. This includes the concept of transformation. The Chomskyans conceive it with geometrical and algebraic analogies (one will say, for example, of the transformations of an equation that they modify the latter's form by preserving the "profound" economy of the ratios

involved). I will use this word in a sense that could be brought closer to what, in the history of the theories of evolution, resulted by opposing transformism (or mutationism) to creationism. In fact, we shall see that it involves only a very small share of the derision and provocation of this "abusive" use of the Chomskyan categories insofar as I have used them as a guide *a contrario*.

2. In opposition to the historic decision of the "International Association of Semiotics," I propose, with the same arbitrariness, to maintain a distinction (and even to reinforce it) between:

—*semiology* as a trans-linguistic discipline that examines sign systems in connection with the laws of language (Roland Barthes' perspective); and

—*semiotics* as a discipline that proposes to study sign systems according to a method which does not depend on linguistics (Charles Sanders Peirce's perspective).

2

Escaping from Language

The Wastebasket of Pragmatics

It is undoubtedly due to the repeated difficulties which linguists and semiologists have come up against in order to determine the status of content that pragmatics today certainly occupies a privileged place in the endeavors of many among them. For functionalism, content primarily remained a tributary of phonological chains reducible, in the final analysis, to a struggle of binary oppositions. The dominant position that information theory occupied at the core of linguistics at that time led to the adoption of a definition of language as merely a means of transmitting messages, the remainder being simply noise and redundancy. Because the question of its interpenetration with the social field was never posed, problems relating to the context of communication seemed to have to remain marginal. Through a sort of imitation of the objectivity of the exact sciences, linguistics was put in a position authorizing it to keep away from any embarrassing social problems. It was mainly a matter of "being" scientific. (Let us note that psychoanalysts employed the same kind of process: after being supported for a long time by concepts of a biological, moreover very approximate, nature, they clung to all the disciplines that appeared "serious" to them, in particular to structural linguistics.)

From the start, generative linguistics wanted to dissociate itself from functionalism while reproaching it for being unable to account for the creative character of language. According to the first Chomskyan model, the phonological machine only intervened in the final formation of statements on a level understood as a surface. Statements were supposed to be generated and transformed on the basis of major syntactic structures without losing any nuance or any semantic ambiguity. But the "semantic question" in the following models only adds to the mystery of these "profound" operations. Whereas orthodox Chomskyans claimed to base the production of semantic compositions only on a single mathematized syntax—a syntactic topology—the dissidents of "generative semantics" instead charged this task to a particular logic called "natural logic" (articulating abstract "semantic atoms," "atomic predicates," and "postulates of sense").[1]

Eager to avoid the reductive nature of structuralism's various variants, a linguistics of enunciation has also pursued the study of the pragmatic components of communication. But, as we shall see, it does not appear to have properly seized the social-political implications of its object. Furthermore, in current semiotic and linguistic research, it is ultimately only a question of an enunciation in general outside of space and time, separated from the real struggles and desires of men and women; in short, it is a question of an alienated enunciation.

At every important stage of their development, linguistic theories will have done nothing but displace the pragmatic "wastebasket"—to renew an expression of Chomsky's.[2] With structuralism's binary phonological reduction, the wastebasket was semantico-pragmatic. With the topology of generative semantics, one takes into account the contents, but still not the social assemblages of enunciation, and the wastebasket is pushed back towards a pragmatics with indefinable contours. With the linguistics of enunciation, one finally starts to treat pragmatics seriously, but one endeavors to constitute it via a restrictive mode. It is treated in the manner of signifying contents; the semantic as well as pragmatic fields are flattened, structuralized and finally forced to remain dependent on syntactic and phonological machines. Admittedly, we are referring to systems much more elaborate than those of Martinet's structuralism, but the pragmatic components are always supposed to fit at one point or another into structural junctions— deep or superficial—without taking into account the contingent socio-historical traits and singularity points that specify them. Everything happens as if the socius were thought to be folded within language. Linguists appear to accept as self-evident that semantic fields and pragmatic fields can be binarizable in a way similar to machines of expression conveying "digitalized"[3] information; they give the impression of being suspicious of contents and context, agreeing to take them into account only on condition of having the certainty that they will be able to rigorously grasp them by means of a systematic formalization supported by a system of universals. Nicolas Ruwet, for example, considers that the semantic creativity of language essentially could not be exerted except within the framework of a syntactic axiomatic system concerning language in its totality. He turns away from the perspective opened by Hjelmslev which consisted in admitting that semantic creativity can discover its origin in the concatenation of figures of expression and figures of contents. Undoubtedly, he does not completely exclude existence from such a type of creativity, but he relegates it to a marginal position, which seems to echo, on the linguistic plane, what mad children, and poets experience on the social plane.[4] How do we make sense of this, since deviants and subject-groups manage to invent words, break syntaxes, inflect significations, produce new connotations, and generate linguistic alterations parallel with other levels of social transformations?

Linguists are imperialists! (It's true that they aren't the only ones!) They claim to dominate all the domains related to language, i.e., in fact, a continent whose boundaries never cease to extend. After having tried to annex semiotics, today linguists tend to exercise their sovereignty over a nascent pragmatics. As form of content, they have long assigned it a marginal place and maintain that they recognize its importance, attempting to minimize its political nature. What the structuralists have done for the signified—a massive operation of neutralization—is recaptured on another plane by generative linguistics and the linguistics of enunciation. Most people today only value the semantic and pragmatic study of contents as secondary, but we intend to manipulate them with tweezers and take them carefully to the deviation of the collective assemblages of enunciation that have effectively produced them.

There Is No Language in Itself

The hypothesis of an abstract machinic phylum traversing language, representation, and the diverse actual and virtual levels of reality presents the incentive to corrode the linguistic edifice from the inside, to render it porous without destroying it as such. In particular, it should allow us to avoid two types of dangers:
  —a pure and simple falling back of linguistic machines onto social structures, like Marr's linguistic dogmatism or certain new psycho-linguistic trends;
  —a structuralist or generativist formalization that separates the production of statements from collective assemblages of enunciation.
  In some way, it is necessary to admit that in order for discursive chains to be in touch with reality they must be disengaged from the constraints of language considered as a closed system. How do we escape from linguistic structures without losing their specificity as such? At minimum, it is the classical break between language and speech [*la langue et la parole*] that a pragmatics of enunciation should call into question. But when one is engaged in such a direction,

it seems impossible to stop in the process. In the particular case of a pragmatics of the unconscious—of a schizoanalysis—it will be inevitable to reexamine a certain traditional conception *of the unity and autonomy of language* as a plane of expression as well as a social entity. In fact, it is the main part of the "conquests" of linguistics resulting from Saussure that will be threatened by such a step in this direction. Language is everywhere, but it does not have any domain of its own. *There is no language in itself.* What specifies human language is precisely that it never refers back to itself, that it always remains open to all the other modes of semiotization. When it is closed again in a national language, a dialect, a patois, a special language or delirium, it is always due to a certain type of political or micropolitical operation.[5] There is nothing less logical, less mathematical than a language. Its "structure" results from the petrification of a sort of grab-all through which the elements come from borrowings, amalgamations, agglutinations, misunderstandings—a kind of sly humor governing its generalizations. This goes for linguistic as well as for anthropological laws, for example those concerning the prohibition of incest: seen from the distance of the grammarian or ethnologist, these laws appear to have a certain coherence, but as soon as one approaches closely, everything is muddled, and one realizes that it is a question of nothing but systems of arrangements that can be taken in every direction, of rules that can be bent in all kinds of ways.

The relations between concrete semiotic performances and structural linguistic abilities, like the relations between languages themselves, are marked by a similar principle of relativity which is equally essential on a synchronic and diachronic level. The unity of a language is always inseparable from the constitution of a power formation. One never finds clear boundaries on dialectal maps but only bordering or transitional zones. There is no mother-language except in the phenomena of the semiotic takeover by a group, ethnicity, or nation. Language is stabilized around a parish, fixed around a bishopric, and installed around a political capital. It evolves by flowing along the river valleys, along the railway lines; it moves through oil spots (example of the Castilian dialect).[6]

We shall be able to found the autonomy of a micropolitical pragmatics only on condition of giving up the traditional separation between the exercise of individual speech and the encoding of language in the socius. Indeed, the fluidity of the performance-competence relation goes well with that of the dialect. It can be considered that each individual constantly moves from one language to another. During the course of a day, she or he will speak to a child as "a father must," or as a teacher or a boss; she or he will speak an infantilized language with her or his lover; while falling asleep, she or he will be inserted into a dream discourse, and will then abruptly return to a professional language when the telephone rings; and each time a whole ensemble of semantic, syntactic, phonological, and prosodic dimensions will be set into play—without speaking of the poetic, stylistic, rhetorical, and micropolitical dimensions of the discourse. Studying linguistic change, Françoise Robert states that linguistic mutations appear "by gradual modification, not from the phenomena themselves... but from their frequency, from their implantation in the language."

Thus, we do not observe the abrupt breaks implied by a distinction between synchrony and diachrony (a point on which Chomsky has not dissociated himself from Saussure, who intended to take account of innovations only at the moment when "the community accommodated them").[7] For Chomsky, as Françoise Robert also notes, the reference to an ideal listener-speaker, pertaining to a completely homogeneous speech community, in fact led to investing the separation between the competence and performance of a normative function. And this norm, in the last resort, reestablishes the linguists themselves.[8] The apparent unity of a language does not depend on the existence of a structural competence. Language, according to Weinrich's formula, is an "essentially heterogeneous reality."[9] In the last analysis, its homogeneity could not establish phenomena of a socio-political order independent of the structural reductions for which it can also be the object. However, what characterizes social-political assemblages is their capacity to be the carriers of these indecomposable historical singularities which an analysis will necessarily decenter onto other dimensions and registers. This also happens in the chemical analysis of a biological phenomenon or in the economic analysis of a social phenomenon: there is no chemical structure of a biological fact or economic structure of a social fact that makes it possible to speak justifiably about a primary competence and a secondary performance. There are no biological, economic, social, linguistic, psychoanalytical universals... but abstract machines that differentiate themselves, on the basis of the plane of consistency of all possibles, and which hook up to the singular crossroads points of the machinic phylum. All this without the promotion of a transcendent formalism, without any sort of fate borne by hereditary encodings, economic infrastructures, psychogenetic stages, or syntactic "categorial foundations"...

Syntactic Markers and Markers of Power

By laying aside the Chomskyans' claim regarding a syntax of all syntaxes, is it perhaps possible to recover something from their method in order to describe the abstract machinisms of particular groups of language? I think less of extended groups, such as the set of what one formerly called inflected languages,[10] than of micro-social linguistic assemblages relative, for example, to groups of children, shantytowns, etc. or, more generally, to languages that Gilles Deleuze and I have qualified as minor. Is a linguistics of the private individual, a linguistics of desire, conceivable? Undoubtedly, but on condition that linguists give up their status as scientists. The fascination that Chomskyan formalization has exerted on them during the two last decades is largely due to the topological constructions to which it led: there one handles trees and symbols while distinguishing ambiguities. Chomsky's first approach certainly touched upon something of the essence of the abstract machine that functions in language. But successive reworkings of the proposed models and attempts by psychologists, semanticians, and logicians to recover his system have dulled the abrupt character of this abstract machinism. Perhaps Chomsky's very first intuitions[11] constitute his best work. Today, the advocates of generative semantics are taking the easy road by disputing the overly artificial character of the opposition between underlying/superficial structure and by restoring a continuity between syntax and semantics. All in all, they try to bring Chomsky back to his senses! But insofar as they conduct this operation without themselves ever leaving the semiological framework, it is probable that they will only engulf themselves, following the orthodox Chomskyans, in a linguistics that is more distant than ever from a micropolitical pragmatics. It would be better to return to Chomsky's starting point, but by considering that his first models of abstract machines remained too marginalized from the signifying articulations of language. The grammaticality that he sought to grasp, far from having to alienate itself in a "semantic logic," could on the contrary be understood as one of the modalities of the *abstract power* set into play by the most decoded capitalistic flows[12] (asemantic and asignifying diagrammatic flows). What is grammaticality? With what does this categorial symbol correspond, this S[13] that dominates all the sentences, this primary axiom of the generative structure of Chomskyan syntagmatic trees that forces all derivations to trace back to a single point of origin? Does it simply have to be considered as the elementary nucleus of the first grammatical significations or as one of the most fundamental traits of the pragmatics of a *certain type of society*, as the expression of an abstract machinism that guarantees the consistency of *a certain type of social order*? Does it participate in these two dimensions unquestionably? S is a mixed marker: it is initially a *marker of power* and secondarily a *syntactic marker*. To form grammatically correct sentences constitutes, for a "normal" individual, the precondition for any submission to law. No one is supposed to be ignorant of the dominant grammaticality, failing which they are to be placed in institutions set up for sub-humans, children, deviants, the insane, the misfits; they are sent back to subsystems of grammaticalization; they will be interpreted, translated, adapted...

Generative linguistics has presented competence as a sort of neutral instrumentation subordinated to a creative production of discourse. One would comply with universal linguistic mechanisms apart from any social and historical contingency. But how can we conceive grammaticality in itself and competence in itself? Competence and performance are indissociable. Any crystallization of competence as a standard and as a framing of concrete performances is always synonymous with the establishment of a position of power.[14] Theories of the universality of competence rest on the simple idea that the linguistic production capacity of an individual exceeds her effective production of speech—her performances—in other words, that the individual arranges a machine of expression bringing into play general designs which can produce much more than a simple accumulation of already memorized statements. Undoubtedly, but the relationship between this "machine of competence" and the productions that it "performs" can be reversed. The machine *itself is produced by its production*. How could it be otherwise? How else would one like to bring it about? Do we always return to the same point, to an innate faculty of language?[15] Competences and performances are in constant interaction. At any given time, competence—the machinic virtuality of expression—conceals the keys to unlocking the deterritorialization of stratified and stereo-typed statements; at another time, it is a particular semiotic production which will deterritorialize a syntax that has grown too rigid. A competence territorialized on a given social space—a group, an ethnicity, a profession...—could be relegated to the rank of sub-competence which will cause the devaluation of the various types of performances associated with it.[16] Because of the modifications of power relations in the presence of or from a transformation of local micro-politics, this same competence will be able, on the contrary, "to seize power" over a larger social space and become a regional, national, or imperial competence... A style imposes itself, a patois becomes aristocratic, a technical language contaminates vernacular languages, a minor literature takes on a universal importance... Let us under-stand that such processes of mixing do not relate only to the diffusion of morphemes but also bring into play all the resources of language.

There Are No Linguistic Universals

There is no universality of language nor is there a universality of speech acts. Every sequence of linguistic expression is associated with a network of various semiotic links (perceptive, mimetic, gestural, imagistic thought, etc...). Every signifying statement crystallizes a mute dance of intensities that is simultaneously played out on the social body and the individuated body. From language to glossolalia, all the transitions are possible. If absolutely necessary, one can admit a "relative universality" of certain semiological structures such as the morpho-phonological organization known as double articulation. But from there to account for the heredity, for example, of the speed of apprenticeship in language is a path that certainly leads to a total impasse.[17]

The theory of semantic universals appears even more fragile than that of phonological and grammatical universals. The organi-zation of contents, the constitution of a homogeneous field of representation, obviously depends on the crystallization of power formations such that no category or mode of categorization could be regarded as universal and programmed by a hereditary code. The overcoding of the separation of contents always pertains to a social and micropolitical field. Heredity could only intervene here on strata extrinsic to language and, moreover, nothing establishes that it is itself bound to a system of universals—unless one only considers a system of genes as such which would now imply the ignorance of the role played by the other physico-chemical strata. The relative stability of a system of genetic code has nothing universal about it except the structure of matter. The stratifications that it generates, its mechanical redundancies, the fact that life "returns" there, and that one finds it in the most various species imply nothing but the exhaustion of a transcendent formalism. Under these conditions, why call upon universals if their existence depends, in fact, on contingent relations between heterogeneous layers?

Recently, certain linguists such as John Searle, Wunderlich, etc. have endeavored to broaden the Chomskyan perspective while turning to the study of speech acts. Herbert E. Brekle, emphasizing the role of pragmatic dimensions which he calls, after Habermas, "communicative competence" (or "idiosyncratic performance of competence"),[18] is brought to oppose this to the Chomskyan type of "systematic competence." The latter is viewed to be contingent on abstract structures that would crystallize (after setting rules of formation and transformation) into phonetic chains, while the former would be bound, according to relations of dynamic self-regulation, to a whole set of linguistic, psychological, and sociological factors. This theory of communicative competence should be articulated, according to this author, on three levels:[19]

—that of a "faculty of language,"
—that of language as system,
—that of speech ("idiosyncratic performance of competence").

Such a project would at least have the advantage of releasing the performance/competence relationship from the traditional oppositions between language and speech and between expression and content. The analysis of these levels could perhaps put linguistics on the track to elucidating real speech acts in all their concrete dimensions, which would inevitably lead them to the abandonment of the Chomskyan technology of dichotic trees and, moreover, to the abandonment of the pseudo-mathematization of language. Unfortunately, the pragmatic components which Brekle mentions, and which should bridge the gap between syntax and semantics on various levels, are still designed as resting upon universals. The existence of the latter, which has seemed at least to stem from a misinterpretation of the level of syntax and semantics, frankly appears absurd at the level of pragmatics. Concerning the alleged "universal faculty of language," Brekle nevertheless returns to Habermas's idea of a "universal pragmatics" that would have to account for the general structure of every speech situation and the constitution of every possible speech act. To these pragmatic universals ("universals of dialogue"), one should always oppose, according to Habermas, a particular class of speech acts which would not belong to them but which would be useful, on the contrary, for "representing the actions or behaviors institutionalized in a certain culture or regulated by social norms." The examples proposed to us as the universals of the "general structures of discourse" are:

—personal pronouns with a performative and deictic function: I, you, he/she/it…,

—vocative or honorary forms,

—spatio-temporal deictics, demonstratives, etc…,

—performatives like: affirm, ask, order, promise…,

—intentional or modal expressions like: believe, know, necessarily, and examples of speech acts not belonging to pragmatic universals:

—sentences introduced by verbs such as greet, congratulate, thank, baptize, curse, name, condemn, acquit…

What a curious conception of universality: why would 'I,' 'affirm,' or 'know' be more universal than 'greet,' 'name,' or 'condemn'? Then again, what place will we reserve for the non-individuated assemblages of enunciation, for the transitivism of infancy, for modes of semiotization disrupting the dominant coordinates (madness, creation, etc.)? The investigation of the only part that seems interesting in this project—that of the idiosyncratic performance of competence—should lead its adherents to give up on dusty categories such as the "faculty of language," which was inherited from Saussure, and to finally demolish this obsession with "universals" reactivated by Chomsky. It is not simply a question of linguists contributing to psycholinguistic and sociolinguistic problematics in the analysis of the pragmatic dimensions of "linguistic behaviors," but equally a question of accepting without reservation the full acceptance of problematics pertaining to a micropolitics of desire and all sorts of of macropolitics.[20]

Semiological Subjection, Semiotic Enslavement[21]

What is a crystallization of power in the linguistic field? We can understand nothing of this question if power is again represented as being uniquely an ideological superstructure. Power is not something that simply concerns well defined social ensembles. Power formations do not engage in "human communication." Consequently, they imply a whole complex of "extra-human" semiotic machines. They are the power of the ego and the superego, what make us stammer with fear and what generate somatizations, neuroses, and suicides, etc... The stability of a "state of language" corresponds to a balance between these diverse levels of power. But each level is not disposed towards the others in any important way. In any case, we are not dealing with an amorphous matter. We will thus only be able to account for the stabilization of a "layer of competence" on the condition of precisely articulating domains nevertheless as different as these:

—activities of individual human semiotization (from internal perceptions up to the modes of communication related to the mass media);

—semiotic operations relative to social machines, economic machines, technical machines, scientific machines, etc.;

—machinic indexes and abstract machines (related to the machinic phylum and the plane of consistency);

—systems enabling a correspondence between the preceding domains (deterritorializing lines of flight, components of passage, etc...)

We have seen that an opposition between competence/performance, aside from naturalizing the foundations of language, bypasses the collective assemblages of enunciation—i.e. the true creative groups concerning language—to make way for an alternative: individuated subjectivity or universal subjectivity. But we can approve the position of psycholinguists like T.G. Bever, who consider that judgments of grammaticality are "behaviors like any other" (cit. Hypothèses, Change, 1972, p. 203), without similarly falling into a systematic "psychologization" of linguistics. It is by no means a matter of denying the systematic characteristics of modes of signifying grammaticalization which are guaranteed, for example, by the control of the ensemble of capitalistic pragmatic fields, but only a question of refusing the abstract categorizations upon which one claims to found them. In reality, we are witnessing the same types of process of universalization that every power formation has utilized in order to be given the appearance of a legitimacy of divine right, and, in particular, ones that have sought to "justify" the expansionism of capitalism. Based on the fact that we can always "structuralize" performances that are monetary, linguistic, musical, etc., that we can always discourse on them and binarize them, we then come to consider that they have *always already been there* as a potential, that their elements carried *the seeds of* the beginnings of the form of Capital, the Signifier, Music... But the real processes of power and machinic mutations, which have fixed and stabilized a form, arranged and delimited a type from creative potentialities or metastable equlibria among assemblages, are *absolutely indecomposable*. Abstract machines can always be complexified; they can never be decomposed without losing their mutational specificity.

Also, we must take them in their entirety. It is impossible to comply with them in little pieces, by training or conditioning. Abstract machines, built up from scratch, hook on to a process; they are co-opted by an assemblage and transform its "destiny," or they stay silent and return to a plane of pure machinic virtuality.

Before being stabilized in the form of a language, dialect, etc., pragmatic fields of power formations must first be "tested" by virtue of a collective performance: every intermediary, every degree of fluidity is thus conceivable in the passage from an individual semiotic performance, be it marginal or even delirious, up to encodings that are completely sclerotic, whether they be related to a dictionary definition, academic grammars, religious or political credos...; the efficiency of these encodings depends on the dominant mode of semiotization that they set to work and particularly whether or not diagrammatic components mobilize certain abstract machines (financial, scientific, artistic, etc...). A micropolitical pragmatics will have to concern itself with these semiotic assemblages overflowing it from all sides—from the "infra" side towards corporeal intensities and from the "supra" side towards the socius—personological linguistics.[22] The crystallization of signifying powers corresponds to a particular mode of overcoding the libido:

—via semiological subjection within fields of resonance,

—via semiotic enslavement within interactive fields of machinic redundancies.

The abstract machinic level of a signifying assemblage is specified by the fact that it assures the congruence of these two types of encoding and that it thus presides over the installation of:

—imperatives of the *dominant grammaticality* of expression (redundancy of asignifying figures of expression);

—"ideological" assemblages of semiological *subjection* at the level of content (redundancies of resonance);

—diagrammatic assemblages of *enslavement* to decoded capitalistic flows at the level of the "referent": flows of abstract labor as the essence of exchange values; flows of monetary signs as the substance of the expression of Capital; flows of syntagmatized and paradigmatized linguistic signs adapted to standardized inter-human communications.

Standardized agents of production are mobilized before the transformation of each individual into a speaker-listener capable of adopting a linguistic behavior compatible with the modes of competence that assign us to a particular position in the society of production. In fact, semiotic components of enslavement constitute the fundamental tools that allow the dominant classes to assure their power over the agents of production. The "miracle" of capitalism is that it has succeeded to direct language, such that it is spoken, taught, televised, dreamt, etc. in a way that ensures it remains perfectly adapted to its own evolution. Thus, this operation always appears to be self-evident: the syntagms of power, its presuppositions, its threats, its methods of intimidation, seduction, and submission are conveyed at an unconscious level, a little like those "subliminal" images that advertizing companies insert into a film. If it is an urgency that motivates a feverish search for a new model of the unconscious, it is justifiably to account for such a phenomenon. Refusing the idea that syntactic markers of capitalistic language are the expression of the fundamental exigencies of the human condition and considering that they are only, on the contrary, the result of semiological transformations dependant upon a given context within a power system increasingly intolerant towards intrinsic modes of code are seemingly inoffensive stakes that actually singularly surpass the traditional framework of linguistics and semiotics. The set of machines that are social, technical, desiring, etc... can no longer avoid the overcoding of statist signifying machines. In fact, the signifying power of national languages tends to coincide with the multiform power of States and the networks of community Institutions. Molecular chains of expression are substituted for ancient segmentary structures of the socius in order to constitute a homogeneous plane of content which always conveys the categorical imperative of Kantian moral law, the "necessities" of class consciousness, the demands of the repressive habits and customs of a majoritarian consensus, and, above all, the persecuting refrains of the ubiquitous Superego. It is through the exhaustion of this design that the intensities of desire become unglued from their ancient territorialities and receive their polarity of subject and object. Mediatized, watched over, they become social need, demand, necessity, and submission. They no longer exist except to the extent that their expression resonates with the significations of the mass media, or when, folded onto themselves, they are able to be translated, i.e. when they renounce their capacity of nomadic flux.

Unquestionably, the threat of a power takeover by decoded flows existed before capitalism and already in the most "primitive" societies (in this respect it is appropriate to distinguish, among the latter, between what Pierre Clastres called State societies and Stateless societies, which do not adopt the same attitude of "defense" against a possible accumulation of power in a State apparatus).[23] Undoubtedly, ancient societies were already traversed by literal capitalistic flows which they endeavored to control. But one must admit that a series of causes, circumstances, and accidents proper to the Middle Ages and the Western "Renaissances" resulted in the fact that social structures definitively lose a certain type of control over decoded flows and engage in a sort of generalized Baroquism—economic, political, religious aesthetic, scientific, etc...—leading to capitalist societies strictly speaking. The semiotic and machinic enslavement of the flows of desire and the semiological subjection upon which capitalistic societies rest are founded in reaction to an incoercible dispersion of territorialized codes. They are correlative to the installation of new types of division between sexes, age groups, divisions of labor, relations of social segementarity... A new use of languages, signs, and icons leads to the fact that the most minimal effect of sense—even the most intimate, most unconscious—passes under the control of social hierarchies. Capitalistic powers do not cease to "rethink" in detail every significant relation, to differentiate and specify every semiological "affectation." During the apprenticeship of language, a child will be called upon, for example, to model her first intensive infinitives[24] in order to subordinate them to pragmatic predicatives and fundamental deictic strategies of power (encoding of hierarchical position, mutability of roles, sexual division, etc...). "Becoming a sexuated-body" will be negotiated in one's relation with "becoming a socialized-body" through the regime of pronominality and genders that will axiomatize the subjective positions of feminine alienation. Despite appearances, in a capitalistic pragmatic field, the various social categories of the same linguistic community—men, women,[25] children, the elderly, the uneducated, immigrants, etc...—*do not speak the same language*. National languages, those spoken in the French Academy or on television, are metalanguages. Their "distance" compared to the languages of the earth and the arbitrary forcefulness of their overcoding are the guarantors of their efficiency and paradoxically of their degree of internalization. This semiological economy of power and its implications on the modes of generation and transformation of the syntactic, lexical, morpho-phonological, and prosodic components of language is even in the foundation of the pragmatic fields of enunciation, which Ducrot indicates as the "polemical value" (in the etymological sense) of language.

Return To or Detour Through Hjelmslev

The systematic ignorance of the political and the social that characterizes current linguistics and semiotics can be breached only at the price of reevaluating the question, even of dismembering their basic categories. In this sense, a return to Hjelmslev, or rather a detour through Hjelmslev, could be fruitful. It is by no means a question of renewing his project of the radical axiomatization of language, but of setting out from some of his categories that appear to be the only ones to come from a truly rigorous examination of the ensemble of semiotic problematics, while drawing, in particular, on all the consequences of his calling into question of the status of content and expression.

"The similar terms plane of expression and plane of content have been selected according to everyday use and are completely arbitrary. From their functional definition, it is impossible to support that it is legitimate to call one of these magnitudes 'expression' and the other 'content' and not the reverse: they are only defined as interdependent with each other, and neither one can exist without the other. Captured separately, one can define them only by opposition and in a relative way, as functives of the same function which are opposed to each other."[26]

One can certainly consider it regrettable that the Hjelmslevian double of expression and content in fact coincides with the Saussurian couple of the signifier and the signified, which causes the entirety of semiotics to fall under the dependence of linguistics.[27] In any event, at the most essential level of what the glossematicians call the "semiotic function," the form of expression and form of content contract in order to constitute a "solidarity" that radically relativizes the traditional opposition of the signifier and the signified.[28] This opposition will discover its laws only at the level of substances, namely, the "meaning" of the content and the "meaning" of the expression. This should quite naturally lead us to only consider the existence of forms insofar as they are expressed or enacted by particular substances. This point is paramount because, as I will try to show, it is only on the basis of nonlinguistic or asignifying linguistic semiotic assemblages that such substances can be produced. In other words, "before" the constitution of signifying redundancies and without being able to confer on the latter a primary or hierarchically superior status in relation to other semiotic productions (symbolic, diagrammatic, etc...). It is by semiotizing the most basic materials that this solidarity or this congruence of forms—which coincides here with the abstract machinism of language[29]—constitutes the substances of expression and content. Thus, the formalism of substances is constructed on matters that must be, as Hjelmslev emphasizes, "scientifically formed"[30]—at least to a sufficient degree—to enable substances to be "semiotically formed." Let us finally notice that the distinction this author establishes between the system and the process of syntagmatization does not imply that the latter remains captive to autonomous forms. No form could subsist by itself independently of its process of formation. This will encourage us to consider that the process does not return to universal codes which are self-enclosed, but that it is indissociable, on the one hand, from the assemblages which support it and, on the other hand, from the basic materials which it brings into play (what Christian Metz called, following Hjelmslev, the *pertinent traits of matters of expression*).[31]

We rediscover here the problem of the genesis of formalism. What confers on a semiotic component a creative function and what takes it away? Languages, as such, do not have any privilege in this domain; as encodings of standardization, they can even slow down or prohibit any semiotic proliferation, and it often remains for nonlinguistic components to catalyze mutations and break the conformist shell of the dominant linguistic significations. It is neither at the level of the formal units of content nor at the level of distinctive elementary traits that we will be able to seize the resource of semiotic creativity, but at the pragmatic level of the assemblages of enunciation and at the level of molecular matters of expressions and the abstract machines that these materials bring into play. The linguistic overcoding operation of semiotic processes "in a free state," which tends to reduce these processes to the state of signifying components or to a dependence on language, primarily consists in extracting from each of them the traits and redundancies recoverable by power formations and to neutralize, repress, and "structuralize" the others. This permanent sorting, this systematic politics of "good semiotic choice," supposes the existence of assemblages that not only effectuate it but also components that *manufacture* the signs, symbols, indexes and icons which it is about. The following chapter will be devoted to the production of these components.

3

Assemblages of Enunciation, Pragmatic Fields and Transformations

Assemblages of Content and Expression Are Not Heaven-Sent

Content and expression are not attached to one another by virtue of the Holy Spirit. In the "beginning" of assemblages of enunciation, we find neither verb, nor subject, system, nor syntax...; instead, there are components of semiotization, subjectification, conscientialization, diagrammatism, and abstract machinisms. Whether on a synchronic or diachronic level, systems of correspondence and translation between states of language and states of culture are never self-evident. When they seem to partake in common sense it is because they have been treated in a way suitable for this purpose. Every mode of signification and semiotization must be related to its assemblages of enunciation. These assemblages depend on a degree of autonomy from the plane of content upon which they are inscribed and the readjustment of their angle of signifiance in relation to the local conditions of the semiological triangle,[1] i.e. in the last analysis, their semiotic capacity of "holding" a given subset of the world, setting in motion both the representation and the morphemes of the referent, all the while preserving their own functional cohesion within the framework of dominant syntaxes. Thus, the status of the subject does not rest upon a play of the signifier as structuralist psychoanalysis would have it; it is assembled by a set of heterogeneous components, the latter of which even semiotizes what I have called "dominant realities." The individuation of the process of enunciation and the process of semiotically discernibilizing oneself from another person are themselves inseparable from a certain mode of social organization. The split between the subject of enunciation and the subject of the statement is inseparable from the split between good and bad objects of the unconscious, in other words, the libidinal topics of the social field. The limit between the "received" ego, the semiologized ego, and the extracted ego is constantly manipulated by the socius.[2] The disentanglement of the subject, the other, the law, and the plane of content always correspond to particular objects of power. Thus, content does not crystallize a universal world but a worldliness marked by contingent fields of force centralized around very precise systems of subjective resonance. Phallic redundancies, for example, do not concern a universal symbolic function but male dominance, authoritative institutions, and extremely particularized traits of repressive faciality.

To bring the production of signification back to the concrete ground of micropolitics and matters of expression nevertheless does not assume that its access to deterritorialized systems is prohibited. It is not a question of extracting the assemblages of enunciation and the assemblages of desire on the side of the concrete and the "natural" in order to keep them safe from the abstract and the artificial! This is first of all because deterritorialized desire promotes capitalistic subjectification to a large extent (the ideal of a power essentially based upon semiological subjection and semiotic enslavement), but also because no "molecular revolution" could economize the implementation of deterritorialized assemblages of enunciation.[3] The contingent nature of enunciatory power formations does not at all imply that they "adhere" to the most material realities and abandon the most complex modes of semiotization.

An assemblage draws its greater or lesser degree of freedom from the formula of its *machinic nucleus*, but this formula is basically metastable. As such, the abstract machines that compose it do not have any "real" existential consistency; they do not have any "mass," their own "energy," or memory. They are only infinitesimal indications hyper-deterritorialized from crystallizations of a possible between states of affairs and states of signs. We could compare them to the particles of contemporary physics that are "virtualized" by a theory that only preserves their identity for a negligible time; this identity is nevertheless unnecessary to concretely demonstrate since the theoretico-experimental complex can function in a satisfactory way by simply presupposing their existence. It is this metaphor which has led me to coin, in regards to the diagrammatic effect, the expression signs-particles:[4] abstract machines "charge" themselves with redundancies of resonance (signification) or redundancies of interaction ("real" existence) depending on whether they are fixed and rendered powerless in a semiological substance or whether they inscribe themselves upon a machinic phylum.

Until now, we have not focused on the criteria that would enable us to precisely define an assemblage in relation both to its components and the field in which it evolves. We will be able to clarify this question only on the condition that we better characterize this concept of existential consistency. Indeed, the modalities of existence of abstract machines are radically different from those of concrete assemblages. Existence as a fundamental machinic coordinate concerns three general types of consistency:[5]

1) *Molar consistencies*
Here redundant elements are strongly crystallized and stratified, allowing flows of redundancies to develop:
1. effects of weak resonance (signifying effect, e.g.: pure formal translation);
2. effects of weak interaction (surplus value of stratified codes).
Later we shall reconsider the fact that the molar/molecular

opposition cannot be identified with a type of large/small or macro/micro spatial fitting but arises from an alternative of a micropolitical order, an alternative choice of consistency. (It exists, for example, in the microscopic refrains that follow molar *or* molecular politics independently of the fact that they function on the basis of redundancies of resonance *or* redundancies of interaction.) What characterizes the molar politics of stratification is the constitution of a world of stratified, identified, or hierarchized objects and subjects, singularities and abstract machines there being held by systems of coordinates that authorize only the minimum degree of freedom necessary for the survival of the assemblages.

The exercise of what will later be defined as generative schizoanalysis will remain circumscribed in this low level of molar consistencies. It will consist in operating displacements of consistency within the assemblages, reducing the effects of resonance on behalf of weak diagrammatic interaction.

2) *Molecular consistency*

Elements of redundancy are conveyed by substrates less stratified than the preceding, allowing flows of redundancy to develop:

1) effects of strong resonance (the semantic field as a whole, the imaginary field, effects that are poetic, mystical, etc.);

2) effects of strong interaction (components of passage, such as faciality, refrains…).

It is impossible at the level of molecular interactions to tell the difference between what forms a part of a component, an assemblage, or a field. All machinic interactions count, all redundancies overlap, and all sign-particle trajectories cross. Here we are dealing with the actualized aspect of abstract machinisms. The assemblage, insofar as it represents the dimension of "foreign relation" and the manifestation of abstract machinisms, coincides with its field effects. We are in the order of "degrees of reality" and "degrees of abstraction" without any noticeable absolute demarcation. This type of inter-assemblage, inter-component, and inter-field consistency is a fundamental micropolitical stake for schizoanalysis, so that the degree of flexibility of the assemblages to give in to the various powers of subjection and enslavement—in other words, regarding everything that pertains to social power struggles and the molecular metabolisms of the machinic unconscious.

3) *Abstract (or absolute or intrinsic) consistency*

Here machinic elements escape systems of redundancy. (They are outside coordinates, being themselves in the foundation of systems of coordinates.) We will distinguish:

—the consistency of capitalistic abstractions (Capital, Power, Music, etc…) as a cornerstone of signifying resonances and semantic fields, a sort of lethal level of abstract machinisms, but which does not model the universe of representation;[6]

—the consistency of signs-particles that specifically defines the irreducible nuclei of the abstract machinic possible.

Whichever possible is manifested by the consistency of molecular fields, this type of nucleus holds in reserve a "potential possible." This nucleus never dissolves into the universe of fields and components. This non-manifested possible is contained by the singular traits of matters of expression and "stored" in the abstract machines' general plane of consistency. (Example: given a politics of signifying overcoding, it is not inconsequential that it is implemented by a particular matter of expression. Thus, the fact that certain writing-machines or certain computer machines are used as instruments of social control can radically change the modalities of the latter.)[7] What will later be defined as transformational schizoanalysis is primarily located in these two extreme levels of strong molecular and abstract consistency. It will consist in performing displacements of consistency within the assemblages on behalf of the dissemination of components of passage and the launching of new machines of diagrammatic signs-particles to the detriment of semiotic fields and capitalistic abstractions.

In sum:

The machinic *nucleus* that specifies an assemblage is located at the crossing of two types of diagrammatic consistency:

—the fuzzy set of molecular consistencies (component—assemblage—field);

—the undecidable[8] abstract machinic set of intrinsic abstract consistency.

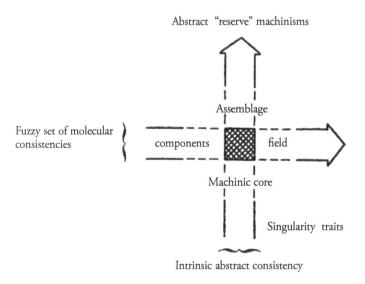

Pairing the existential coordinates of consistency (molar-molecular-abstract) and the coordinates of efficiency (redundancy of resonance-redundancy of interaction) thus leads to six general types of fields of consistency.

	molar	molecular	abstract
redundancy of resonance	signifying fields	semantic fields	capitalistic abstractions
machinic redundancies or of interaction	stratified fields	components of passage	constellation of sign particles (abstract machines)

Let us underline the dissymmetrical nature of these six types of fields. Indeed, if we have on one side the components of the assemblages and the fields that can "swell" in resonance to a point of total powerlessness, on the other side we never find pure nuclei of diagrammatic interaction. Asignifying components develop to some extent on the manure of signifying components; they proliferate like microscopic parasites on modes of subjectification and conscientialization. Even in the case of a pure computer machinism, at the end of the chain somewhere there always remains some semiological terminals that are human.

Before taking up the mixed semiotic (diagrammatic and semiological) assemblages, we shall return to some characteristics of the extreme cases that represent the transformation of abstract machines into signifying abstraction within the framework of assemblages of capitalistic power.

The Signifying Abstraction of Capitalistic Assemblages

A phenomenon of reverse deterritorialization appears at the "end" of the machinic genealogy of semiotic components. A world of simulacra replaces intensive flows through a set of interferences between the different kinds of semiological redundancies. In fact, this world of representation is not more "unreal" than another. It is not representation, the morphemes of the referent, or the figures of expression that have a characteristic of simulacra but the means of passage between these entities.[9] Abstraction could be defined as a conceptual isolate that *simulates* diagrammatic relations at the precise point where they are powerless. It absolutely declares the order of material and moral things in a world where all creative freedom has disappeared. It incarnates Life, the Spirit, and Change only when we are no longer in the presence of death, insanity, and paralysis.

An abstraction will impose itself more like a synthetic a *priori* category so that the capitalistic assemblage that supports it will be able to confer an arbitrary character on its relations of denotation and an unmotivated character on its relations of signification. The ideal of such an abstraction would return us to the case of "extremist" religious assemblages—such as Kierkegaard's "religious sphere"—but ordinary capitalistic abstractions will proceed through reterritorializations of this arbitrariness and this apathy in the form of law codes, orders from above, State imperatives, etc... Resonant-reasonable abstraction is determined primarily for the objective of "framing" subjectivity and objects of desire: a superego responds to an ego, an exchange value responds to use value, an imaginary museum responds to the proliferation of art... The capitalistic use of abstraction, different from that of other despotic systems which were satisfied with an absolute reference, consists in relativizing anything compared to a standard (affects, perceptions, thoughts, human relations, machinic "growth"...). Today its function is to deploy *coordinated systems of power* in every field. The ensemble of lines of flight must come together as a vanishing point—in a pictorial sense—an internal framework point whose position is perfectly determined. Lines of dissidence belong to the normal play of institutional abstractions: they confer on the marginal system of the "weak" a better capacity of adaptation and recovery. This has nothing to do with an arbitrary and unmotivated "gratuity," like that of the powers of divine right, but with an exacerbation of the politics of suppression, distancing, autonomization, and alienation from an increasingly domesticated plane of the signifier. The homogenization of processes of signifying formalization never develops alone.[10] Capitalistic abstraction must unceasingly recreate the void, reproduce the splitting and isolation of an individuated subject in relation to assemblages of enunciation; the signifier must be incessantly reproduced by consciential components and signifying simulation "selected" to be transformed by diagrammatic components. Speech and writing, for example, are never powerless in themselves but always due to a syntagmatization and a paradigmatization that overcodes them. Nevertheless, this powerlessness is always in some part secretly defeated because of what deterritorialized machines of expression—on the level of the "profound" articulations of their figures of expression—themselves tend to escape.

Abstraction is not a "cooled down" abstract machine but an active system of neutralization and recuperation of machinic indexes and lines of flight. Thus, it has always remained bound to key institutions of power. Religious abstractions have long served the grounds for personological, sexual, ethnic, or national identity and modulated the signification of the feeling of *belonging* to a territoriality of reference. All these functions have been captured in relay by a system much more fragmented, much more diversified, and at the same time more molecular and more susceptive to power apparatuses, public infrastructures and facilities, and mass-media machines, so that today all instances of semiotic production and all systems of value weave a gigantic net composed of points of potential signification from which it is impossible to escape without a radical reevaluation of every assemblage of enunciation. Religious overcodings were less malleable, more "passive" than the instruments of this capitalistic network. Every system of redundancy is now constantly altered and recalculated so that the tolerable thresholds of deterritorialization are precisely determined for the established order. Every coding will have to pass and continually pass again through the ordering mega-machine of molecular infrastructures. All intensities will be forced to give up connections that would be established apart from the "coherence" of abstractions and dominant coordinates. Thus, the perspectives open to lines of flight and machinic assemblages will be perfectly delimited: the former will have to be retained on this side of an abstract horizon, and the latter will have to constantly return to the universal contents for which they will become the apparent foundations. If abstract machines are regularly pinned to the heavens of universal abstractions, then assemblages of desire are put to the service of a world order, which is an all too terrestrial fact.

Four Mixed Types of Assemblages of Enunciation

We have not done away with abstract machinisms of language by renouncing formal syntaxes; following Hjelmslev, by relativizing the signifier/signified opposition, we do not abandon the content/expression dyad, whose usage, on the contrary, we will extend to all the various assemblages of enunciation. As Oswald Ducrot suggests, the identification of semantic reality with signification is not absolutely obvious, insofar as the pragmatic dimensions of content exceed signification in its usual sense.[11] Under these conditions, we would benefit from reserving the use of the notions *semantic content* and *semantic field* to a particular case of transformation, namely, analogical interpretations. Certain contents are dominated by redundancies of resonance, others by redundancies of interaction. An assemblage of enunciation will be derived sometimes from the side of signification and sometimes from the side of diagrammatism depending on the transformations of its composition. In fact, all the assemblages of enunciation involving the human world are mixed. Abstractions of power and personological poles close off intrinsic codings, lines of destratification, and diagrammatic processes. Thus whatever the consistency of the vectors that manifest them, abstract machines are never definitively bound to fixed and universal coordinates; they can always "pull out" and re-emit quanta of possibility.

Let us turn to the classification of the pragmatic components announced in the introduction. This will enable us to differentiate four general types of mixed assemblages of enunciation according to the way in which their content is predominantly ensured by:

—*analogical generative transformations* whose *semantic contents* maintain relations "of envelopment" with the referents that they interpret and are generated from semantic fields or *fields of interpretance*. Their mode of enunciation concerns territorialized collective assemblages (for example, clannish assemblages or transitivist assemblages during childhood "before" language acquisition);

—*generative linguistic semiological transformations* whose interpretation stems from a syntagmatic "upholstering" of the plane of content (*field of signifiance*). Here the referent is distinguished from the *signifying representation* by a mode of enunciation that concerns *individuated subjective assemblages* that are relatively more deterritorialized than the preceding (function of the ego);

—*intensive symbolic and asubjective transformations* whose contents index referents and coordinates of enunciation (*machinic indexes, lines of flight*, the *illocutionary function*[12]) and *components of passage* (faciality, refrains...). These contents desubjectify or "machinize" the enunciation and deterritorialize personological strategies without necessarily forcing sign machines to catalyze processes of diagrammatic deterritorialization. They proceed by reassembling semiotic components without, strictly speaking, setting out from new ones (example: mystical or aesthetic desubjectification). Here we shall speak of collective assemblages of enunciation even if only one individual expresses himself, because he or she will be considered a non-totalizable intensive multiplicity;

—asubjective *diagrammatic transformations* whose *asignifying* contents deterritorialize not only the assemblages of enunciation but also the machines of expression and semantic formalisms while simultaneously establishing a direct connection with intrinsic modes of encoding in the various stratifications of the referent (that which implies a "reference" common to another nature at the most deterritorialized level: that of the *machinic plane of consistency*). Here we shall speak of *machinic assemblages of enunciation*.

Notes:

1) Collective assemblages of enunciation are mixed in that they more or less always overflow the box assigned to them in our table: they can be territorialized and arise from a signifying component (example: groups of educated children); they can inject asignifying sense into intensive symbolic components (example: the conjunction drugs-transcendental meditation or diagrammatic writing in repetitive American music); they can alternate depending on an individuated economy of enunciation (sliding from subject-groups toward subjugated groups), etc... Generally, the terms of this quadripartition should not be regarded as the nuclear elements of a "machinic" semiotics. This is only because each of them implements a specific diagrammatic function in order to reach its own point of efficiency (even in the case where it is a matter of a signifying point of powerlessness) and to one degree or another develops an indexical semantic and/or signifying function. Here it is a question of the prevalent accent of a micropolitics of semiotic assemblages. Thus, assemblages of poetic enunciation will produce symbolic concatenations and modes of various subjectification associating regimes of signs which are simultaneously semiologically formed and asignifying, although they are partially agrammatical[13] and carry precoded contents.

	Semiotic components	Functions of content	Semiotic components	Articulations of content and expression
Interpretive generative transformations	A. Analogical	Semantic	A. Analogical	Field of interpretance
	B. Semiological linguistic	Signifying	B. Semiological linguistic	Field of significance (double articulation)
Non-interpretive generative Transformations	C. Symbolic intensive	Illocutionary, indexical and of passage	C. Symbolic intensive	Illocutionary, indexical and of passage
	D. Diagrammatic	Asignifying sense	D. Diagrammatic	Asignifying sense

2) Also let us remark in connection with this table that it could make it possible to transpose Benveniste's linguistic categories of interpretance and significance on a semiotic level, which correspond respectively to the paradigmatic and syntagmatic axes, but on condition of disjoining them from each other. Interpretance would take its autonomy following a transformation relating to the preceding transformations (transformations to the second degree).

We would have as follows:

—if *C transforms into A*: a tendency for the paradigmatic and syntagmatic axes to uncross, inspiring a paradigmatic "flight," what I called elsewhere "a paradigmatic perversion." An asubjective collective assemblage of enunciation is reterritorialized through a field of interpretance. Example: a fascist group constitutes itself on the basis of mystical components;

—if *D transforms into B*: a tendency for the paradigmatic and syntagmatic axes to re-cross, which generates a signifying "retention" and a reinforced squaring of sense. An asubjective machinic assemblage is subjectivized (or resubjectivized) through a field of signifiance. (Example: a crazy writing machine is "brought to its senses," or a "bad author" is inducted into the Académie Française.)

3) Here the degree of grammaticality proposed by Chomsky would have to be the function of the interpretance/signifiance relation or, in other words, the relations of dependence and counter-dependence established within the framework of a signifying linguistic assemblage, between:

—on the one hand: a) "latent" semantic fields of analogical components and b) illocutionary and indexical contents of the symbolic components which are implicated there,[14]

—in addition: "potential" diagrammatic contents of the concatenations of the asignifying figures implemented there.

4) A signifying discourse can be transformed into an asignifying discourse according to two modalities:

—*B transforms into C*: at a morphemic level, it manages to circumvent the despotism of signifying formalisms and is enriched by new indexical "charges," for example, by polysemous or homonymic proliferation which opens it in various directions;

—*B transforms into D*: at the "glossematic" level of its figures of expression (phonemes, graphemes...), it manages to form part of a semiotic assemblage dominated by a diagrammatic transformation whose contents will escape from every system of analogical representation and every signifying overcoding. It is unsettled from its semiologically formed substance and invests the matters of expression's relevant traits which are constitutive of asignifying chains that are "scientifically formed," "musically formed," etc.[15]

5) The distinctions established in this table should make it possible to remove the ambiguity of the concept of icon derived from Charles

Sanders Peirce. Here images concern *semantic and indexical contents,* while relational icons concern *contents or diagrammatic sense* (or moreover oppositions between lexical signification/grammatical signification or relational signification, insofar as the latter would equally depend on diagrammatic components suitable for language).

This *diagrammatic sense* could be close to the *operatory sense* that G. Klaus opposes to *eidetic sense.*[16] For this author, operatory sense brings into play assemblages of signs that represent continuations of phonemes or semantic configurations, while eidetic sense remains captive to the semiological triangle. But, in my opinion, he excessively valorizes eidetic sense from which he makes a sort of secret reference to operatory sense. He justifiably considers that concatenations of symbols in abstract calculations are operations equipped with a certain type of sense, but he adds that it is a question of a "diminished" sense of possibilities for the possible management of the objects they represent. On the contrary, I assert that only *sense without signification* produced by a diagrammatic economy of signs is able to thwart the dead ends specific to semiologies of signification, insofar as it introduces into semiotic assemblages an additional coefficient of deterritorialization allowing sign machines to simulate, "duplicate," and "experience" the relational and structural nodes of material and social flows precisely at the points that would remain invisible to an anthropocentric vision.

Three Limiting Fields

Let us examine in more detail certain "elementary" concatenations of the components and assemblages that lead to the production of three particularly important limiting fields. (I cannot stress enough that a monographic access to real situations would not necessarily make a transition from the "simple" towards the "complex" but, on the contrary, would "discernibilize" the "elementary" components within the complex only insofar as this would enable it to explore more thoroughly certain singular traits of these components and in order to enrich and complexify its experimental exploration. The triadic presentation of the following table is thus not at all comparable to that, for example, of Charles Sanders Peirce. The association of five, seven, or *n* components has certainly been more profitable. Nevertheless, it should enable us to see lines of passage between these assemblages, which anthropologists, historians, or economists have undoubtedly made into typical cases and archetypal structures.)

	assemblage of enunciation	semiotic components	pragmatic fields
Field a	territorialized	icons and indexes	symbolic
Field b	individuated	semiological triangle	signifier
Field c	machinic collective	sign particles	diagrammatic

—Composition a: *Territorialized symbolic fields*

Pragmatic fields of this type—those of childhood, madness, archaic societies—are inseparable from the existence of stratified territorialities. At first they do not rest upon a substance of expression that would cross and unify their various modes of semiotization. They result from the articulation of modes of encoding and from an inexhaustible formalization of a substance of universal expression. For example, we will find in the territorialized assemblages of certain "primitive" societies an activity of mythographic formalization developing itself from the traits of matters of expression that do not correspond with and are unable to be translated into those semiotics which are gestural, perceptive, economic, etc... This does not mean that these various modes of semiotization lack any relation to one another. But what effectuates this relation will precisely be the type of territorialization of the group and its own topology, its translations of itself and those outside its territory. Here the territorialized group assemblage occupies the place which will become that of the signifying substance in the despotic systems of enunciatory individuation. By warding it off, "primitive" societies refuse the implementation of a signifying substance; their politics is that of collectively *acting out* semiotic conjunctions. There it is a question of a sort of pragmatic rhizome, but of a rhizome that seeks to contain and dominate every deterritorializing escape route. Systems of indexes represent precisely the inscription of such a threat upon this rhizome, of such a refusal of falling into signifying abstraction or deterritorialized machinic assemblages. (Example of such an index: the fact that the death of a cow initially calls for the recourse to practices of geomancy, then secondly, if one did not obtain good results through such a process, sacrificial practices and, finally, the means of sorcery in order to thwart a possible "maraboutism," etc... Every moment a "signifying synthesis" comes to crown the entirety of these various steps, while each paradigm only stabilizes its general signification.) The group assembles semiotic components; it does not interpret, it experiments... This *real* passage takes place by respecting *the singular traits of each matter of expression*. Moreover, and here is an essential difference with rhizomes that pertain to a deterritorialized mechanical phylum, these territorialized assemblages do not treat different planes hierarchically. Deterritorialized machinisms are tolerated (example: a fragment of writing), but they are treated on the same plane as territorialized assemblages. It's as if these processes actively and systematically ignored the powers of deterritorialization that hide certain indexes and certain machinisms. This type of field thus excludes neither the existence of the signifier nor diagrammatism but is simply opposed to a power takeover from an instance of overcoding or a machine of universalizing deterritorialization. A religious machine[17] could be carrying abstraction, but it will be prohibited from leaving its totem or its territory. Its eventual aspirations will be repressed because of a general translatability inherent in capitalistic religions. All of this will be done in order to prevent symbolism from being degraded to the "equivalent" of analogical and signifying systems of translatability. Differential coefficients of deterritorialization do not have to be extracted from their original strata. These societies are organized in particular against the deterritorialization of a "higher signifying object" under the form of a capitalization of power at the level of chiefdoms or under the form of a concentration of systems of semiotic enslavement within technical and writing machines. These societies are invested in keeping all systems of deterritorialization within (or returning them to) the state of indexes and encysted machinisms that will neither be quantified nor systematized. It is only in passing through societies dominated by signifying semiologies and asignifying semiotics that this type of quantification and accumulation of the effects of deterritorialization will be employed. Here, deterritorializations still remain in direct contact with the intensities of desire, the body, the group, the territory... Thus, for a long time certain systems managed to resist the pressure of monotheistic religions based on the exclusive domination of semiologies whose content-expression relation is structured according to rigidly fixed syntagmatic and paradigmatic axes. The hasty "structuralization" of ethnographic data has resulted in keeping this phenomenon poorly understood. It is by true interpretative *coups de force* that ethnologists have introduced relations between parents, myths, political anthropology, etc. into their structural grids. This introduction of invariant significations and stable relations of exchange does not develop on its own.[18] These levels of content within symbolic components are connected to one another without being organized in a rigorous way on a structured plane of the signified. It is only with the accomplishment of the hegemony of capitalism in the 19th century that the "absolute stability of the signified, under the proliferation of the relations of designation (...) in order to ground the comparison of forms"[19] definitively imposes itself. A certain type of dictatorship of the signifier is inseparable from a certain historical context and, consequently, it should neither be considered immutable nor universal. Inverse transformations can neutralize it, even reverse it. This is what happens today, for example, in many African societies where "fixations" with modes of tribal solidarity or partial "returns" to animistic practices counterbalance the expansion of Western semiologies. On an individual level, we witness a similar phenomenon when dream semiologies "take precedence" over perceptive semiotics, linguistic semiologies, etc. under the effects of sleep, drugs, passionate exaltation, etc.

Up to what point can signifying components tolerate such attempts at reversing relations of force on behalf of iconic components? Every monotheistic power has had its iconoclasts. And even today the worship of images is attacked by psychoanalysts in the name of the "primacy of the Symbolic."[20] But is linguistics a monotheism? Should we follow it when it proclaims that iconic components *necessarily* maintain relations of dependence with regard to linguistic components? Has the normal, terminal regime of symbolic semiotics fallen under the dependence of the linguistic machine of expression? Why not consider rather that the world of images only happens within certain conditions under the aegis of signifying transformations and that what one could call the "axiom of structure" (which consists, after Saussure, in separating the language (*langue*) of acts from speech (*langage*) and expression) is only one particular case resulting from a contingent semiotic conjunction? We previously saw that signifying transformations did not have anything inescapable or universal about them and that they were related to a certain type of regime of individuation of the enunciation and inter-subjective communication. Semantic generative fields are thus only variants of transformational fields. Without the support that they take from a certain type of asignifying machine of expression, their *power of evocation would be null.*

—Composition b: *Signifying, individuated, and abstractified field*

This field returns us, essentially, to the previously described regime of the signifying abstraction of capitalistic assemblages (page 51). It develops from a process of the transformation of old territorialities, furrowed on all sides by signifying systems. Indexes are connected and accumulated; in Pueblo societies, for example, with the Hopi (whose "theocratism," according to Lévi-Strauss, evokes Aztec civilizations in a rustic form) we begin to interpret indexes compared to one another; this is the reign of "reassessment," bad conscience, and guilt.[21] Some abstract codes *capitalize* the icons and indexes while the constitution of signifying assemblages is primed. The whole of society has become vulnerable to capitalistic abstractions. Analogy represents only the first stage of the operation of leveling and rendering heterogeneous semiotic links translatable (it would be necessary to speak, in fact, of "degrees of analogism"). Analogy and *signifiance* constitute the two modalities of a similar politics of reterritorialization and subjectification of contents. Whereas analogy organizes them into relatively informal fields articulated by relatively territorialized assemblages of enunciation, *signifiance* and its chains of double articulation arrange them via paradigmatic and syntagmatic coordinates much more strictly articulated with individuated assemblages of enunciations that are directly subjected to capitalistic social systems. Analogical formalization is less rigorous, less deterritorialized, and more molecular than that of *signifiance*; it puts into perspective strata of expression that preserve their own consistency (fields of interpretation). One symbol interprets another symbol which is itself interpreted by a third and so on, without the process ending in a final signified whose sense would be sedimented, for example, in a dictionary and without the sequence compelling us to respect a grammaticality that determines rigorous rules of syntagmatic concatenation.[22] The work of signifying territorialization upon content brings into play an additional degree of deterritorialization of expression; this is no longer founded on analogical motivations but on the "arbitrariness" of asignifying sign machines[23] that phonoligize, graphematize, morphologize, lexicalize, syntaxize, and rhetorize them, etc... It is true that analogical transformations are not specific to a particular type of assemblage of enunciation; they can also be associated with diagrammatic semiotics. But in this case, the same signs will be treated according to two semiotic politics, one generative, the other transformational. On one side, these signs will function as symbols in an analogical mode, and on the other, as figures of expression in a diagrammatic mode. This mixed system corresponds precisely to the mode of signifying representation that renders asignifying machines subservient to *signifiance*. Empty signs without semantic content, for example, the phonic or graphic images of the word "table," are *seen* as a table.[24] Thus the diagrammatic process, while territorializing the analogous field, is closed off again in a world of quasi-objects. But, unlike symbolic representations, this world is "worked on" from the inside by syntax and logic, upon which the formalization of significations and dominant propositions rests; on one side, it invites us to insert ourselves into a reality that "comes of itself," an everyday reality; on the other, it involves us, in spite of ourselves, in the circle of its pragmatic implications, and its signifying chains alienate us with an immense social and technical machinery. The libido is then fully captured, functionalized, and subjectivized according to the requirements of capitalistic economy. A formal subjectivity thus replaces that of the territorialized assemblages of enunciation which has to be spectacularized throughout social rituals much less than the latter. It haunts every intensive system as a differential value; it functions as the *capital of differences*; it is the matrix of every abstract capitalization of power.

With the installation of a State machine, signifying power really acquires its autonomy. The double escalation of machinic deterritorializations and the reterritorializations of power find with the state machine if not its point of equilibrium, at least its point of negotiation: its stock market. State machines function simultaneously as a molar structure of re-enclosure and as a molecular mega-machine, a sort of semiotic cyclotron that articulates and controls all the cogs of the economy and society. On its molar side, it secretes a collective semiological substance. It is never intensities as such that are retained by this substance, but differential relations, correlative relations of powerlessness due to an incriminating consciencialization, a Manichean phallic power, etc... On its molecular side, it emits signs-particles allowing it to cross, transform, and recuperate old territorialities. Thus, it converts the "time of use values" and the "time of desire values" into the "time of work values," dutifully quantified. Capitalistic abstraction incarnates these two aspects of the signifying substance: it hangs over the intensities, pinning them like butterflies in a collection, reducing them to the state of fixed indexes; but it also implements them by inserting them into a process of the linearization and "flattening" of old territorialized rhizomes. All material intensities contributing to the formalization of the expression must be aligned, "returning single-file." It becomes inappropriate to sing or dance while one speaks; what counts, at present, is simply the assemblage of differential characters of the overall system as it contributes to the operation of new deterritorialized powers. The prosodic components concerned with song, mimicry, gestures, posture, etc. of "primitive" speech can do nothing but degenerate. We shall pass from one element to another according to a *syntactic order* and no longer in the apparent disorder of territorialized assemblages. The coefficients of deterritorialization of each of these formal exhaustions will be compared and measured. Layers will have to be subjected and hierarchized at the time of this passage; the remaining semiotic rough edges will be smoothed out to the benefit of these linear sequences which constitute the most economic means of effectuating such comparisons and such hierarchization. Anything that fails to be caught in the neutralization of non-linguistic components conserves the possibility of the system of intensity's going out of control. As we saw, in order to ward off such a threat, these pragmatic fields can only call upon diagrammatic machines, whose action is likely to exacerbate machinic processes even more severely. The maintenance of their homeostasis implies the multiplication and indefinite growth of a whole network of semiotic operators (institutions, infrastructures, media) charged with setting into resonance, normalizing, abstractifying, and syntaxizing all systems of redundancy. Their role is to control the entry of abstract machinisms and diagrammatic signs-particles, which will be tolerated only in so far as it appears compatible with the dominant systems of abstraction and formal syntax. Example: the introduction of polyphonic and harmonic components of writing into the history of music, but on condition that it is composed with "temperament" and not according to an uncontrolled Baroquism of flows. The fixation of a universal syntax inseparable from the formations of "classical" music is charged with controlling musical enunciation (lessons, academies, patronage, concerts, etc.). It is only when other more deterritorialized components enter the scene, calling into question the compromise that represents this music prematurely qualified as "Baroque," that the process will begin the continuous explosion that characterizes the evolution of modern music. This deterritorialization of musical semiotics stemmed from the same abstract machinisms as those that have worked upon the representations of the world in the religious, philosophical, and scientific domains. Here as elsewhere abstraction has functioned as a reflective surface, a stopping point for components capable of being organized according to a machinic rhizome. It is the same dualizing[25] substance that secretes abstractions and fixes intensities on reductive and dichotic trees of implication. Thus, the transcendent formalism of signifying fields, their "paradigmatic perversions," constantly remains exposed to a double danger: on the side of content, a proliferation of uncontrollable machinisms; on the side of expression, the installation of a sclerotic syntaxization that can lead to their disappearance.

—Composition c: *Diagrammatic, collective, machinic, and asignifying fields*

It is impossible to conceive the assemblage of a scientific experiment apart from a field that generates plans and descriptions which are topological, mathematical, axiomatic, digital, etc… But sign-machines can also function directly within material and social machines without the mediation of significative processes of subjectification, something which has become more obvious each passing day. The fact that the common essence of semiotic machines and material or social machines stems from the same type of abstract machine is the decisive step we must take in order to base a political pragmatics on something other than good intentions.

The oppositions figure/ground or matter/form in territorialized assemblages and the dualism of the signifying substance of individuated assemblages stops being relevant here. Seemingly, we return to a polyvocal expression similar to that found in territorialized assemblages. Yet it has nothing to do with the personal, technical, mythical, assemblages etc., rightly located within the actualization of bodies, organs, and territories on the basis of a system of signifying subjection; we are confronted by machinic "populations" and non-human machines within which the overcodings of despotic abstractions will no longer establish order in the same way. What hangs over this pragmatic field is no longer a territorialized assemblage or a formal subjectivity but the *plane of consistency* of the entirety of machinic potentialities. The machinic assemblage of enunciation re-articulates the machinic indexes on an intensive level, and not merely on a differential level. Moreover, it orients systems of stratification toward deterritorialized "solutions." We have thus left the register of the autonomy of territorialized assemblages or the differential dualism of the signifying substance of individuated assemblages. The machinic rhizome is vectorized (and vectorizing) according to its multipolar, multisubstantial, multideictic coordinates.[26] *A vectorial field of processes of destratification* replaces the global hierarchies. One is no longer in the presence of an autonomized machinic substance; the machinic components escape stratification; in their actualization they progressively develop a *phylum* implying both their actual position as well as the historical and logical sequences which have led to it and their diagrammatic potentialities. The "virtual," the "theoretical," and the "experimental" all contribute to integrating this phylum.[27] It is no longer necessary here to maintain a distinction between material deterritorialization and semiotic deterritorialization. Indeed, matters of expression are themselves "treated" within diagrammatic processes as experimental matters. It is therefore not advisable to group, for example, energetic, physico-chemical, biological, libidinal intensities, etc., on one side and, on the other, emotional, aesthetic, revolutionary, scientific intensities, etc… Systems of intensities are combined, "rhizomized" upon themselves; machinic assemblages connect conjunctions among "scientifically formed," "aesthetically formed," "revolution-arily formed," and "semiologically formed" materials without privileging these latter. There no longer exists any absolute primacy of one system over another; material components are not necessarily more territorialized than semiotic components. What counts here is not the existence of a particular differential index, that of a coding, or a sign-machine: it is the "action" of a set of quanta of deterritori-alization. Certain intensive assemblages are quantitatively higher than others. A machine of mathematical signs can become tem-porarily overpowered by an assemblage. The indexes of field "a" and the abstractions of field "b" remain in field "c" but pass to the second position. Instead of remaining virtualized in an index, attached to an abstraction, or put into orbit around a black hole, as was the case with semiological components, in this type of field, abstract machines fully exploit their capital of possible. All this occurs in spite of codings and molar stratifications. "Feelings," private life, and inte-riority do not escape their action. That a scientist, for example, goes insane and/or falls in love and/or becomes perverse will play a part in his research. An erotic line of flight or a mutant libidinal charge can thwart the effects of a black hole or produce new ones, divert state-ments, unlock experimental assemblages, or ruin them irreversibly. But conversely, the fact that the signs-particles carried by a mathe-matical or physical formula strikes the subjectivity of this same scientist can upset the functions of his faciality, refrain, or everyday life and make him fall in love or insane or perverse. "Specialized" passions, those of artists and scientists, but also *all* passions, must not be separated from the actions and productions of public life. It is not a question of relating the work to "intimacy" but of dissolving the lure of "intimacy." In its beginnings, psychoanalysis made us take some steps in this direction, but it quickly stopped along the way.

Pragmatic Inter-Field Transformations

Pragmatics does not simply pertain to communication.[28] For there to be communication, it is necessary that things and signs are in a position to communicate. Semiological assemblages constitute only one means of communication among others, which are specified by the fact that they produce fields of redundancies of resonance on the basis of sign machines. Only these fields can connect themselves with other fields of redundancy. Semiological assemblages are one thing; fields of semiotic interaction are another.

This leads us to divide the pragmatic fields into four principal categories, which, moreover, never cease interfering with one another. Two *generative fields*[29] dominated by semiological components: *fields of interpretance* (semantic fields) and *fields of signifiance*. Two *transformational fields* dominated by non-interpretive semiotic components: *symbolic fields* and *diagrammatic fields*.

The following table is inscribed in the prolongation of the preceding table (page 55) relative to assemblages of enunciation. It illustrates the mode of formation of the four types of pragmatic fields that result from the "intrusion" of non-interpretive transformational (symbolic and diagrammatic) components within interpretative generative (analogical and signifying) fields. It goes without saying, however, that pragmatic fields of enunciation (just like the semiotic components they bring into play) will not be reduced to the composition of standard elements, for example, to universal subjective positions like those in Lacanian theory (discourse of the Master, the Hysteric, Knowledge, the Analyst). Thus the classifications suggested here are all relative: any methodological necessity is only imposed to consider that none of the pragmatic fields enumerated here have any priority over the others whatsoever.[30] A "rhizomatic" analysis could just as easily be brought about from less classically semiological components such as those tied, for example, to psycho-somatic black holes, faciality and refrains, power formations, etc…

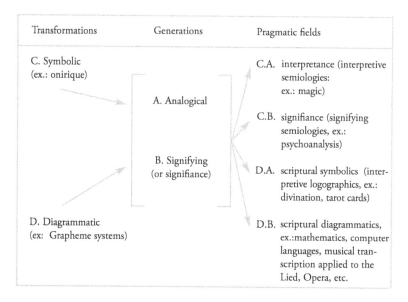

Transformations	Generations	Pragmatic fields
C. Symbolic (ex.: onirique)	A. Analogical	C.A. interpretance (interpretive semiologies: ex.: magic)
		C.B. signifiance (signifying semiologies, ex.: psychoanalysis)
	B. Signifying (or signifiance)	D.A. scriptural symbolics (interpretive logographics, ex.: divination, tarot cards)
D. Diagrammatic (ex: Grapheme systems)		D.B. scriptural diagrammatics, ex.:mathematics, computer languages, musical transcription applied to the Lied, Opera, etc.

Let us illustrate this relativity starting from three cases:

—Territorialized fields of enunciation do not correspond to only one *dominant* type of analogical transformation; they can easily bring into play symbolic, diagrammatic, and signifying transformations (example: the speech of primitive societies as it "refuses" the reductive effects of generative signifying components is based upon relatively symbolic interpretative techniques; but this refusal "emptily" implies the threat of a signifying economy).

—The individuation of the enunciation, while being specific to the dominant type of signifying transformation, also brings into play deterritorialized symbolic transformations (similar to the Gestaltist Figure/Ground) and a machine of diagrammatic redundancy organizing the symbolic formalisms according to a plane of content coming to fill the effects of the black hole of subjectification to some extent. Certain components can be specialized in this function of reterritorialization of subjectivity (transformation of faciality and refrain; transformation of the "double"; transformation of the couple; transformation of paranoic knowledge, etc...). It is in reaction to subjective deterritorialization, which is "steered" either by a consciential transformation of resonance or by a desubjectivizing diagrammatic transformation, that a system of a collective appreciation[31] of sense will be able to stabilize.[32]

—The pragmatic fields dominated by diagrammatic pragmatic transformations remain haunted by subjects of enunciation that have been exhausted in the signifying individuation of the enunciation. The representation of a listener-speaker as the fictitious pole of the production of statements becoming increasingly abstract to them and the fact that "one continues to speak" through the mouth of individuals nevertheless takes on an increasingly relative scope. The statement is emitted and received by complex assemblages of individuals, bodies, material and social machines, semiotic, mathematical, scientific machines, etc., which are the true sources of the enunciation. In any event, this type of semiotic field cannot be absolutely dissociated from the artificial reterritorializations of the enunciation correlative to it, so that we can affirm that these diagrammatic fields always appear throughout assemblages that preserve a minimum of "mixture."

4

Signifying Faciality, Diagrammatic Faciality

Facialized Consciousness and Reflexive Consciousness Without Object

There always exists a time in the ordination of social space when the dimension of the face intervenes to delimit what is legitimate from what is not. This occurs not only through explicitly significative traits of faciality (of the "wide-eyed" variety) but also on the level of significations more difficult to encompass: such and such a manner of speaking will spark the feeling that we are dealing with someone of "good intentions," a foreigner, or even someone strange, odd, or dangerous.[1] The feeling of signification, previously defined as redundancy to the nth degree, although empty, is nonetheless territorialized: this feeling is embodied in signifying substances, which include stereotyped contents as well as types of accent, intonation, timbre, rhythm, faces, and, we shall return to this, refrains. A voice is always related to a real, imaginary, or composite face...

One of the essential activities of the reterritorialization of consciential redundancies[2] within the framework of capitalistic fields resides in the facializing eye-nose-forehead triangle that collects, formalizes, neutralizes, and crushes the specific traits of the other semiotic components. Psychologists have adequately described the sudden appearance of this "gestalt-sign."[3] But they have considerably reduced its scope in treating it as a fixed[4] ethological imprint either by making it an identifying mechanism or by conferring it a role in the matrix of the entry of the 'I' into the symbolic system.[5] Neither the symbolic entry into the order of faciality nor transcendent symbolic facialities exist. Faciality can oscillate to the side of serial identification, but it can also operate on behalf of desiring machines.

A certain module of faciality, with its tolerated deviant-types, loses or gains control over the entirety of contents and traits of expression. This decides whether or not a gestalt-sign of faciality succeeds in operating a systematic framing of all perceptions and all behaviors while determining the strategies of the subjection of desire. This module is established in the middle of the face like a third eye, an eye immanent to every signifying representation whose movements of scanning and continual re-centering develop a general surface of reference. The "asperities" of the matters of expression are neutralized one by one while a circular white screen divides the effects of resonance between the semiological triangle, the ego, and the object. Thus, a *facialized consciousness* is centrally constituted in the resonance of the set of black holes that can emerge from various semiotic components and operates a semiological capitalization around an individuated subject of the enunciation while identifying a "person" in a fundamentally Manichean way: either the person's foundation is this face-voice or nonsense, either the massive and global acceptance of the ego and its dominant personological coordinates or the "end of it all" and the abolition of every socius. The answer, always tautological, corresponds to what Ulysses replied to the Cyclops when he asked him for his name: Nobody—it's nobody in person![6] An abstract faciality speaks at the heart of speech, dressing up subjective black holes, masking semiotic collapses, deploying personological structures of power. Thus the consciential subjection of faces ends up excavating a binarist figure-ground referent as the support of the universal translatability and responsibility of statements. All flows and objects must be related to a subjective totalization; all modes of subjectification must be situated in relation to *my* consciousness as the impossible tangent of the reception of all contents through the void or as the ideal pole of all reterritorializations and reifications without object. The machinic sense of faciality does not at all "signify" this *micropolitics*[7] of closure and permanent reference of contents to dominant significations. The ultimate paradigm of faciality is an "it's just like that," an expression of a semiological *coup de force* establishing that, once and for all, "that" will always mean something. The "thing" is identified, located on various abstract coordinates, grasped, prevented from fleeing or escaping the system of significations, and kept from threatening the reigning socio-semiotic order.

Such a *coup de force* is inseparable from strategies of power carried out on all planes (socio-economic, sexual, etc.). I am stressing here the redundancies of faciality that shape the body to the signifying politics of a certain type of capitalistic field. But they cannot be isolated, on the one hand, from different types of redundancy of faciality and, on the other, from different consciential components, like, for example, those refrains which can also carry out, as we shall see, all kinds of two-dimensional (three-dimensional, *n*-dimensional) interactions between heterogeneous pragmatic fields. In particular, faciality occupies a determining place within pragmatic fields that are developed on the fringes of "sexuated-body becomings" and "social-body becomings." Faciality then generates an optional micropolitical subject constantly moving between two states:

—that of facializing, globalizing, binarizing, phallicizing forms in constant resonance with social roles and the capitalistic Imaginary;

—that of singular faciality traits which, on the contrary, are likely to interact with machinic redundancies conveying new quanta of the possible while crossing the faces, being connected to other singularity traits of all kinds, circumventing micro black holes of anxiety and culpability...

Here we could reintroduce the distinction established by Charles Sanders Peirce between sign-types and sign-occurrences and speak about *face-types* and *face-occurrences*. "Normally," the feeling of everydayness that is indispensable to all of our perceptions of the world is constantly modulated by a faciality-type which indicates that "nothing happens." It functions as an indicator of "normality." One of the reasons behind the fascination for everything "retro"[8] seemingly involves some sort of maladjustment to the recording of everyday life, but only so as to consolidate it with the current faciality-type: "Well, at that time, they found it *normal* to have this kind of face circulating among horse-drawn carriages; there were Germans, rickshaws, wooden clogs..." The normality of yesterday supports that of today. The traits of everyday life that inhabit the Imaginary of a generation—either through childhood memories or through "delegated" memories attached for example to crystal sets, antiquated telephones, and old postcards—are themselves secretly inhabited by these constellations of faciality traits. Thus normal or normalized faciality constantly becomes encrusted and superimposed upon the normal landscapity. This is what sparks the feeling of signification in the belonging to a territory and gives it the seal of *appropriation*. Even if this territory is reduced to something trivial, even if it is completely unimportant: the important thing is that it wards off the black hole of senselessness. There is signification: that's what's essential! And this facialized signification cannot allow any matter of expression to escape that would allow it to leak. While endeavoring "to absorb" a paradigm in order "to capture" it, a witch-doctor runs the risk that this signification will escape, return to the heavens, or simply become incarnated in a dangerous animality. Within the framework of capitalistic assemblages, such an escape hardly has any chance to happen—except in rare moments of childhood, passion, madness, and creation. The individuation of the enunciation—as the relay of permanent social control over the production of statements—is literally obsessed with the threat of semiotic collapse. What would happen if this obsession stopped? It would be anarchy, the end of social etiquette, the collapse of the bourgeois bureaucratic order, the incoercible resurgence of the Freudian "primary process..." In order to conjure these new figures of hell and damnation, but in small amounts and slowly, modern intersubjectivity is now primarily founded on a vacuous faciality, a blind face-to-face between two absent gazes.

The operation of detachment from a machinic faciality, starting with the eyes-nose-forehead triangle, leads to two types of micropolitics which we shall examine in the following subchapters:

—a molar politics of facialization through the promotion of a general faciality of reference that crowns all the faciality-occurrences and *subjects* them to the broadest significant consensus;

—a molecular politics of the emission of faciality traits on the basis of this same faciality-occurrence that thwarts signifying traps and whose stakes are decisive for the introduction of diagrammatic processes of semiotic control (for better or worse).

In fact, these two micropolitics are complementary: they are distributed in the functions of opening and reclosing signifying assemblages. General faciality only installs its systems of neutralization and equivalence of faciality-occurrences against individuals insofar as they prove to have faciality traits incompatible with the capitalistic economy of flows. There are certain heads that do not pass in the system. It is necessary to hide them, cut them off, make them over, or better yet transform them from the inside.

CAPITALISTIC FACIALITY
A Faciality for "Dressing Up" Decoded Flows

The individuation of the mode of consciential subjectification primarily rests upon the capacity of capitalistic faciality to function as a universal resonator, unifying the heterogeneous modes of subjectification, rendering local significative redundancies translatable, and hierarchizing paradigmatic coordinates specific to each power formation. Redundancies of faciality develop an empty semiotic screen upon which reflexive consciousness begins to be reterritorialized. All the systems of re-enclosure and arborescence combine and enter into resonance in order to block the potential rhizomatic "pressures" of asignifying semiotic components. This screen of reflexivity constitutes the homogenizing substance of significations, an intermediate substance between the plane of consistency of abstract machinisms and the machinic phylum of the matters of expression adjacent to their territorialities "of origin." Here faciality functions as the inverse of the phallus. The face, the phallus, and self-consciousness revolve around the same abstract machinism of reterritorialization of decoded flows that endeavors to construct a *feeling of appropriation*, a *"power over"* being delimited from a *"power against."* One cannot say that there is a consciousness *of* faciality or a consciousness *of* the phallus. The three modalities of the same separating power that convey these three instances—standard deviations of faciality, intentional objectification of consciousness, phallic dichotomies—do not, however, stem from the same universal mechanisms. When they are found to be similar everywhere, this is because they have been standardized by the action of power formations with a hegemonic inclination. They could also, if these powers were reversed or circumvented, differentiate themselves or take different paths. Particular facialities are bound to power formations which are themselves inseparable from all the interactions in the social field. "Montages" of faciality take on a greater or lesser importance due to the micropolitical options of the assemblages of enunciation pertaining to them. The world and its faciality never cease intertwining their relations. A face is always tied to a landscape as its foundation in such a way that it shuts off in itself, shrivels away in the grips of an apparatus of power, or reopens on a line of flight in order to provide an exit toward other possibles. During the course of a day, I travel from one faciality to another. My typical expression at present is no more "my own" than any other. It is perhaps even that of another; not necessarily that of another *person*. But also that of an animal, a plant, a constellation of objects, a familiar space, an institution—for example, the "a priori" faciality of the doctor, the robotic face of the "insane" or the police, or a landscape-faciality, or a professional, ethnic faciality etc.

On their side of deterritorialization, capitalistic powers put forth a phallic function, enslaving all the affects and contents of the sexuated body to an operative asignifying system founded on the social division of the sexes—phallus/non-phallus—while, on their side of reterritorialization, they present constellations of faciality traits that "personalize" and "humanize" this reductive operation by restoring desire to tiny territorialities, either the derisory refuge within asmile, a wink of an eye, or in the micro-bastions of power in a repressive grimace of the father, the teacher, or the internalized superego. The personological faciality "attributed" to individuals by the socius does not remain "external" to them. Thus, it is not legitimate to bring faciality back to a theatrical mask, as the Etruscan etymology of "persona" would wrongfully result in doing. This would suppose that a profound, authentic, originary, inalienable faciality would continue to exist behind the superimposed masks. Facialized consciousness, all worldly intrusion, and the reflexive consciousness in which all intersubjectivity appears "to come up against" merely constitute components among others: they can even be regarded as particular types of semiotic equipment assembled from machines of capitalistic abstraction. Let me repeat that the ideal of a pure *a priori* form for every formalism, of a machine of pure consciential redundancy, and of a transcendent referential faciality does not arise from a mode of universal subjectification but out of a set of systems of representation, social structures, and productive machines based upon an economy of decoded flows.[9]

Faciality is established with the intersection of subjective consciential individuation and the set of material, social, and semiotic flows taking part in capitalistic "modes of production." Beyond the redundancies of faciality, phallic binarization, refrains, beyond even the ultimate invisible becoming of subjectivity, nothing else is profiled... except a hopelessly empty consciousness (the Sartrean "being-for-itself"). Consciousness, even in its movement against black hole subjective reterritorialization, no longer arrives within these modes of production except to cling to the hyper-deterritorialized objects that tend to radically escape them. We are thus in the presence of two polar modalities of consciousness: that of pseudo-territorialities of resonance and that of an irrevocable deterritorialization; that of tranquilizing (and re-assuring) faces and significations and that of anxiety without object, or rather, of an anxiety which aims at the *reality* of nothingness. Capitalistic economy thoroughly exploits the Manichean apparatus that results from the play of these two consciousnesses. In particular, the all powerfull political and micropolitical forces of the media reside in their capacity of developing a collective facialized consciousness that acts as a counterpoint to the globalization of anguish.

The primary function of facial capitalistic conscientialization is to mask the fact that there is nothing inescapable in the mobilization and sequence of operations that contribute to the processes of semiotic subjection. The facialization of an ego, self-consciousness and the feeling of belonging to a "mother-language" are one and the same thing, even though we never cease passing from one mode of subjectification to another and from one idiolect to another. At each moment, the assemblages that control the capitalistic pragmatic fields attempt to recuperate the semiotic components that would try to regain their freedom of action. These assemblages repel certain faciality traits while changing the disposition of others, imposing prefabricated icons and refrains in order to neutralize desire's points of turbulence. Once upon a time, they transfigured or were banished into some animalistic facialities from childhood on behalf of mommy and the fairy, the dwarf and prince charming, daddy and the king, etc. Today, after the total retreat of territorialized[10] assemblages and the capitalistic hegemony of decoded flows, it it is now up to the mass-media to produce substitute ritual and totemic facialities that no "natural" assemblage is in any position to secrete on its own. It is no longer a territory, a clan, or an ethnicity, but the whole of visual and auditory space which is implied by the standardized models of an essentially functional faciality. This utilization of certain prototypes of faciality by capitalistic societies does not imply, let me emphasize this, that these prototypes can be reduced to a system of reified icons as the support of an alienating identification. The manipulation of the imaginary by the media cannot be brought back to a simple "sedative" function in order "to calm" instinctual representations. Fundamentally, its intervention develops from the diagrammatic that specifies the mode of capitalistic subjectification. This manipulation aims at the installation of operators of the enunciation capable of concentrating and minimizing the semiotic components implied by power formations. It is a question of neutralizing, by reducing them, the "n" animal, vegetal, and cosmic eyes of the rhizomatic possible which could subsist within residual territorialized assemblages. By "purifying" representations of the polyvocality of its contents, the media install a vanishing point behind every glance at the intersection of dominant coordinates, beginning from which all local significations enter into resonance.

Faciality as Binary Signifying Machine

The investigation of the concrete role of faciality in capitalistic pragmatic fields will only further highlight the absurdity of the path that consists in reducing speech and language to a simple transmission of messages. This essay began with the question: "how do we escape from language?" But it is primarily through its facial substance that language escapes itself, fleeing in all directions. Every proposition only receives its social weight of truth insofar as a "service" faciality takes charge of it. Every segment of signifying discourse is a tributary of faciality traits that "manages" its morphemes, that supports them in relation with dominant significations or deprives them of their sense. Iconic faciality does not depend on signifying binary machines that would have to account for it; it is on the contrary signifying linguistics that comes to be stabilized by calling on the binary machine of faciality.

The system of transposition and hierarchization of semiological productions instituted by capitalistic assemblages of enunciation rests upon the efficiency of a system of sifting through faciality traits that make it possible to extract *a dual option matter*, a matter of the possible from which every semiological asperity has been eliminated. Both the possible to come and equally the "past possible" are "retreated." Nothing that has happened would be possible otherwise; the possible has never had any other choice but to submit to signifying recording. The signifying possible and the seemingly arborescent possible are thus definitively imposed to the detriment of all rhizomatic possibilization. One is here dealing with the very workings of the signifying binarization of statements. Through the bias of consciential components of faciality, a semiotic production can always be reduced to the state of normalized signification. Signifying power nods its head; that's ok for a signification! It raises its eyebrows: this means that there is a danger of nonsense, or that of a previous meaning being annulled. The set of paradigmatic equivalences and axioms upon which the domain in question was up till then founded must again pass through the machine.

In order to take on this central indicative role within dominant significations, faciality: 1) must be *detached* and taken separately from other components; 2) its functionality must be *neutralized* in a way that does not interfere with that of the components from which it records standard deviations and passages at the limit. Should it happen that it would begin work for itself, it would immediately lose its power of capitalistic regulation. In that case, a "primitive" polyvocity of matters of expression would resurface, the kind one "finds again " in schizophrenics with its grimaces, its mannerisms, or in "autistic" children. But these passages at the limit do not simply concern those whom one could call "professional deviants," but also every faciality-occurrence threatened by facial transgressions to one degree or another. It would be necessary here to return to the studies performed on the history of memory in order to better discern the evolution of the modes of discursive territorialization, in particular the periods that precede the "mechanization" and informatization of memories, when mnemotechnic montages based upon the domestic environment were used as a mental space of reference.[11] The deterritorialization of iconic supports has displaced the apprenticeship of memory toward systems of dichotic deduction. Some current university examination techniques rely on a statistical control of memory. What emerges from the student is an average judgment, a satisfactory recognition frequency rate of the *profile* of a question: "how does it sound," and "can it pass." What such examinations select, in the last analysis, is less an accumulation of knowledge than the aptitude of an "elite" for cutting a "brave figure" in all circumstances. Machinic memories and complex productive assemblages take care of the rest. (But there is nothing fundamentally new here: all practices of selection have always relied on specialized facial syntaxes which also must be compatible with the most general political and social semiotic syntaxes, beginning with basic grammar.)

The mini-cyclotrons of language-face integration which, at the level of collective semiotization proper to each institution and each agency, return statements to the circuits of legitimation or directly throw them into black holes of nonsense, do not work simply within the sense of the specified categories of individuals: redundancies of the faciality of hospital, education or military institutions equally concern all the people in a population, and contaminate all the nooks and crannies of the collective Imaginary. At the most general level, this social, mass-mediated faciality has the function of controlling the entry and regulating the intensity of the set of semiotic components employed by semiological systems.[12] Faciality constitutes a sort of "superego" entrusted with *making the enunciation responsible*. But unlike the Freudian superego, it is a question here of a component that is installed following a pragmatic capitalistic transformation and that individuates listeners and speakers essentially such that they "respond" from the dominant discourse, and thus, in no way from an intra-psychic authority that would proliferate in the decline of a universal and symbolic castration complex.[13] A child, who doesn't stop going from one activity to another or a "pervert" from one sex to another, is considered by the social authorities of facial regulation as being outside the range of dominant adulthood and falling under the dependence of social formations responsible for "assisting" him. One can blame a deficit or an immaturity, for the fact that he feels he is "not responsible" for his actions, that he does not identify in a stable way with a role or a function, that he does not reintegrate the set of his semiotic productions in a single and unique facial consciousness of reference. But one can equally regard that such an attitude is the consequence of a resistance to social learning, of a rejection—this would only be a provisional title—of power[14] coordinates. In the framework of territorialized assemblages of a primitive, insane, infantile or poetic enunciation, the world of contents is never homogeneous: the polygon of significations has its center everywhere and nowhere, while its circumference spans the entire universe. In order to "discipline" the multiplicity of points of signifiance, *facialized consciousness* brings these points back to the invariant overcoding constellations that gravitate around it. We are now in the presence of a double movement:

—of a constitution of a *landscape-face*, deterritorialized from the inside, focalized in a black hole, simultaneously a vanishing point and a centralizing point, a point of arborescence and closure whose translation engenders the illusion of a homogeneous world of signification;

—the emplacement of *facial syntaxes* which engender the illusion that the universe of abstract machines, including their own, relies on centralizing structures, a monosubjectivism and a monotheism (correlative to a degeneration of the polycentrism of animalistic and animistic cosmologies).

Smoothing in the Single Direction of Faces-Landscapes

This faciality-landscapity tends to dissolve the territorialized limits of natural sociality and to neutralize the "excessive" machinic effects that could be engendered by a systematic decoding of flows. The whole order of the possible has to be inscribed upon this substance of the signifier. No intensive matter of expression can be organized according to rhizomatic connections. The multitude of the eyes of the cosmos and becomings-animal and -vegetable disappear on behalf of a central eye from which all spatial, rhythmic, moral, deictic coordinates radiate, etc.

This empty eye that haunts capitalistic faciality knows of only one thing, which is that nothing could exist independently of the dominant worldliness, nothing could escape the signifying contamination that "aligns" the cosmos and every form of life with a *mechanized*[15] society, nothing could frustrate the systems of formal equivalence guiding behaviors by remote control, and finalizing productions of all kinds in a blind perpetuation of normative abstractions. No point of mystery can resist the inquisitorial gaze of the signifier: all spaces are overshadowed by a basic faciality which, though not necessarily as "spectacular" as that of Big Brother, Amin Dada, or the Ayatollah Khomeini, is nonetheless omnipresent. The facialization of landscapes can take extremely subtle forms, borrowing from very indirect semiotic means. Even in the extreme case of an abstract painter, a faciality of this type will be able to crystallize: "Look, there's a table that has to be from the time of Dewasne or from the time of the Denis René gallery…," and this faciality will itself be interpellated by a certain style of faciality proper to that epoch, emanating from even the texture of the canvas: "It is good that I have known you in these last years, you who pretend at present to 'situate' me, you yourself have remained the same in order to judge me and measure me in this way." When the Narrator of *In Search of Lost Time*, on the shores of Balbec, renounces his first idea which would consist in emptying the maritime landscape of all human presence in order to no longer be attached to anything but the passionate study of "Young girls in flower," this does not mean that he has changed his opinion, but that he returns to a human faciality from which he has long departed.[16] At each moment, he was never truly disengaged from the facial systems of dominant classes within which these modes of semiotization are deployed. He simply changes course; he abandons a fixed politics, too classically literary, romantic, or symbolic in relation to landscapity-faciality for a more virulent and corrosive one in order to finally grasp "the nascent state" of the movements of desire, of the ruptures with popular "ways of seeing" the world to which he still remains captive. The Proustian procedure which consists, for example on the basis of certain faciality traits, in unleashing processes of semiotic germination modifying the reigning coordinates of literary space, should be compared to a drug experience but only in the domain of internal perceptions and sensations liberated, beginning with a noise, from speech or gesture, an efflorescence of intensities of desire which alters the "hierarchies" that preside over the organization of the ordinary world.

The "objectification," "subjectivization," and "alterification" of the enunciation are never given once and for all. They stem from particular contexts and micropolitics. Their stakes involve the eyes of desire, everything *we look at* in the cosmos, the socius, and interiority, everything that *makes us "look at that."* When the capitalistic regime of enunciation focalizes all the vanishing points, all the lines of desire, all the openings, and all the possible connections onto a central point of significance, it creates an echo effect within the set of semiological black holes and submits all the modes of subjectification to the regime of a general culpabilization. The stratifications and segregations then support one another, switching places throughout a cumulative operation of inhibition and powerlessness. Everything that evokes a non-subjected desire within the dominant faciality is suspicious and threatening for an order founded on the preservation of its limits, the status quo, and the blockage of everything that could be developed outside of the norms of the system. The promotion of a strong ego by the traditional psychoanalysts, each in his or her own way, illustrates such a politics of the enslavement of subjectivity to the imperatives of social control and the normalization of collective labor power. Whether identification is ruled by fundamental images or by symbolic structures amounts to the same thing: constellations of the faciality of power establish their law upon libidinal economies and impose a rigorous delimitation between the sphere of production values of use and exchange and the sphere of the values of the representation of desire (desire that is marked, culpable, repressed, quelled, castrated). Thus, the "four-eyed machine" of the Anglo-Saxon psychologists ("eye-to-eye contact") in appearance effectively functions as a collective micro-agency charged with scanning the subjectivity of a child beginning with consciential redundancies of the dominant faciality, along with modeling and hierachizing her being-for-alterity and her being-for-interiority.

Territorialized pragmatic fields could separate an inside and an outside in a way that opposes a reassuring possible and a menacing possible (free so that part of this outside invests the inside and, conversely, so that a reassuring inside is installed outside the territory and organizes its own circuits). It is upon the collective territory of social, religious, sexual, and ludic activities that all the animalistic, cosmic, and subjective forces were inscribed. Within capitalistic fields, this break passes to the interior of signifying chains. The signifying break, potential everywhere, aims to impose the devices of dominant significations everywhere. At any time, a prototypical face can emerge from the landscape: the face of the Christ-King or the Virgin-Mother through the clouds of the Imaginary of a certain time or, today, the face of "our President" on TV. The various figures of immanent faciality in the socius lose their polyvocality a little more each day—for example their animality traits—and their territorialities of origin. The ideal of capitalistic subjectivity implies a systematic deterritorialization of the supports of expression—free so that they are reterritorialized on functional substitutions, such as the nuclear family, the ideal of social standing, etc. It is no longer in an ethnic group, an elected people or even in God's own son on the cross that the multiform intentions of deterritorialization converge, nor even towards an empty surface, but in this third dull eye that haunts the gaze of the white man of affluent countries and in which all creative powers of desire come to die out and to be tied to the investments of desire.[17] "Digital" faciality traits have been substituted for the emblematic faciality-landscapity that delimited a territory making it possible in theory to simultaneously read all face-occurrences, past and present. Traditional ethnic antagonisms which were quite localized[18] have been commuted in a universal racism that has become inherent to white capitalistic faciality. The discriminating function of faciality which appears obvious in certain cases (for example, the faciality traits that oppose a black in the time of "*Uncle Tom's Cabin*" to a "Black Panther") often engages in a series of constellations of institutional facialities much more difficult to decipher. One of the essential tasks of the media consists in continuously adjusting facial formulas, calculating them in order to answer for every possible situation. In other words, these institutional facialities will have to "fit in" with one another: the faciality of the average Frenchman, for example, will have to be opposed to that of the foreigner, without going to the point of a deadly racism, or that of the adult, white, cultivated, integrated doctor… In other words, it will have to be incorporated into that of the nurse, sure to be subjected and maternal, but without complacency…

Facial Syntaxes and Signifying Quantification

It is either x, y, or nothing. And this x, this y, and this nothing, through the play of faciality around a point of redundancy, selects what has to be rejected on the side of nonsense, prohibiting a rhizomatic disposition of faciality traits from leading to the emission of semiotic signs-particles that escape from signifying semiologies (but we affirm that, paradoxically, the agencies of capitalistic faciality which have taken charge of preventing such eventualities contribute to recreating and accelerating such processes). When we have to consider a "judgment of faciality," what I have called, after René Thom, a "feeling of signification,"[19] we have begun to neglect the thresholds of relative acquiescence that precede the passages to significative articulation. The concrete facialities of particular power formations "negotiate" amongst themselves before giving their green or red light to a general faciality of reference. Even in the case where power formations seek to directly manipulate the latter—with, for example, forcing a chief of State onto television who attempts to obtain a "frank and grave" facial acquiescence—an unconscious detour through a fuzzy[20] optional material of the prejudiced judgments of faciality[21] is always necessary. It is only when this "elementary" work of faciality will have allowed the ability to discern stabilized collections of signifying objects that propositional dichotic operations, which basically serve the normalization of messages and eventually their logical quantification, will be able to intervene.

In order to be consumable and subjectivizable by concrete individuals and yet adapted to a standardization of information, capitalistic messages must simultaneously be treated as the particular contents of a general system of content and must be incarnated in social syntaxes and heterogeneous hierarchies of power. The deterritorialization of collective archaic facialities, the subjection of animalistic eyes, the promotion of institutional facialities, and a landscapity-faciality of universal reference constitute so many conditions of such a semiotic "reincarnation" of decoded flows. The junction of these two universes (that of the decoding of flows and that of human incarnation) operates through a setting in resonance of black hole effects—semiotic lacunae—correlative to a reduction of rough edges specific to the various matters of expression and a general flattening of the world of content onto a signifying screen. It is on this level of unifying and reductive fusion that the consciential components of facialities and refrains intervene. Faciality generates a concrete general equivalent that deploys a space which traverses social territories and promotes human signifiance through a claim to universality. As we will see later on, a similar operation aiming at the specific modes of temporalization concerns the components of refrains. The gazes and refrains which thus take possession of these territories and lived rhythms can be qualified as concrete on the side of their incarnation and as abstract on that of their capitalistic functions. These abstract-concrete mixed redundancies gravitate around a nucleus of deterritorialization that prohibits them from being converted into lines of flight and from being integrated into the diagrammatic processes of machinic assemblages. The set of faciality-occurrences and institutional facialities is "attracted" to the empty faciality of this capitalistic conscientialization which, having its center everywhere and nowhere, remains unlocalizable within space-time coordinates. The supposedly essential anxiety of the human condition within its various historical modalities does not have any other foundation but this attraction and the vertigo of semiotic collapse associated with it. They come closer to approaching the invisible faciality limit of the "borderline-faciality" of reference[22] on the boundaries of semiotic black holes of annihilation, while the most concrete and typical facialities are subjected to the tyranny of facial redundancies of symbolic, personological, and Oedipal identification. Thus, the empty and the invisible are masked and populated by simulacra which will convey all kinds of proper names and will be tied up in deathly familial and castration complexes. (On the side of refrains, temporalization will tend to break down in a compulsory repetition which collides with infinity in an abstract, eternal, punitive, and absurd time.) It is with this tangent of the black hole of the individuated enunciation that Capital and the Libido establish their points of junction (on condition of understanding the latter as the most deterritorialized result of the set of the modes of semiotization of power formations and accepting the idea that faciality and refrains can constitute themselves from essential components in the unconscious economy of the socius).

Thus, an entire syntax crowns, hierarchizes, and adjusts to the various normalizing power formations. Signifying coordinates of the "normal" world are deployed and controlled on the basis of calibrated facial formulas (prototypes of men, women, children, etc., normal at such and such a moment of the history, in such and such a country, such and such a social situation, taking into account such and such a fashion, etc.). In capitalistic societies, the world only becomes human, rational, and universal insofar as it manages to be subjectivated around such formulas. The faciality of territorialized assemblages ward off the arborescent possible without either compromising the heterogeneity of the matters of expression or overcoding the components of expression. The faciality of assemblages founded upon the individuation of the enunciation requires a centralization, an arborification, a gridding, and a finalization of all the means of expression over the signifying substance. Any threat against the established order is projected onto a faciality. Conversely, the very setting in question of faciality is an indication of potential social subversion. It is through "behavior" suitable to its features of faciality and through the makeup respecting certain fashion standards that a woman becomes "available" on the market of dominant sexuality, thus expressing her submission to phallocratic powers. But history and its social struggles are also stamped onto faciality: the faces of middle-class men and the workers of the "Belle Epoque" are not the same as those of the Popular Front or the "Occupation." In 1968, a faciality with long hair shook the world. Suddenly, we stopped seeing people in the same way; statements were "turned upside down." Some amazing propositions at that time emerged in every field; long accepted notions were emptied of their meaning in the space of a few hours; the possibility of a new order of things was taking shape on the horizon. We only wanted another relation to work, another relation to the environment that started to appear, and also another childhood, another homosexuality… Certainly, the effect of such changes is not expressed merely on faces; clothing, body maintenance, ways of speaking, etc. also contribute to it. But, unlike what occurs in archaic territorialized assemblages, the set of these "nonverbal" components become pertinent only when they are reframed on the sensitive deterritorialized slab which has become the face and when they concentrate in it their singular effects of sense. Either way, faciality as the substance- relay between materials of heterogeneous expression and dominant significative redundancies always imposes itself everywhere.

When a Yanoami shaman "loses" the animality traits of Hekura which flee toward their rock of origin or the sky, ritual syntax is suspended. A bond with transcendence is broken and a particular quest must be undertaken to reconnect it.[23] From then on, the same does not apply for capitalistic assemblages: everything must be foreseen and made calculable in order to generate infinite syntactic cross-checkings that allow it to systematically arrange faciality traits. Analogical and signifying components of faciality tend to no longer return to themselves; faciality has become a substance that is found both everywhere and nowhere; it even constitutes the substance of semiological fields. Traits of faciality, corporeality, and landscapity are no longer articulated with local components, as was the case with collective territorialized assemblages. They are based upon a pragmatic syntax of bipolar standards and deviant-types. For a "deviant" faciality, crossing certain thresholds has become a veritable predestination to an assumption of responsibility through specialized equipment (centers of readjustment, psychiatric hospitals, prisons, etc.).[24] All the phenomena of communication and exchange are dependant on the laws and jurisprudence governing the dominant faciality.[25] Having thus been focalized and hierarchized on the same facial substance of expression, all significative redundancies will return to the power formations that are in a position to embody a "supreme faciality" and come to a conclusion on the legitimacy of every facial signification and, more still, of their existence as such: "does it pass or not, is it made of signification?" As soon as the empty eye of power ostracizes a faciality which "does not return to it" and which no classification, equipment, or specialist can situate, psychological and legal metalanguages are urgently implemented to escape from the impasse. The universe of dominant significations does not tolerate any escape over which it lacks control. An "evil eye" phenomenon has become almost unthinkable. Every effect of sense, after some passages along the tangent of the black eye hole of the faciality of power, will have to answer without ambiguity, either yes or no, to the questions asked. Reference or vertigo of annihilation, sense or nonsense, it's all or nothing! Such is the fundamental binary break in which consciential components are charged by faciality. The signifying break only comes to impose its univocal truth in black and white, which produces syntactic breaks and feedback loops of faciality. A statement takes on its weight of signification and its value of social truth only insofar as it is validated by this kind of central oscillography constituting facialities of power. If it deviates too much, it spins outside common sense, and then the entire machinery of correction and recuperation is put in motion all at once. At the end of this machinic relay current, it is generally impossible to sustain its violence a second time. Here smoothing takes on a unique sense: "at home" or "not at home"—that corresponds to something or nothing—that can be said or not—that could be valid or not sit well—he is French, or foreign and thus hostile—that lies outside the family or they are "people we don't know." "Before" the hegemony of faciality, some possibilities of polyvocal approximation remained; "afterwards," it is exclusively the alternative. Ambiguity, persuasion, half-lies, and half-truths will now arise from the system of laws, those of language and those of social order.

With the infinite range of facial movements, facialized consciousness will only retain the significative passages in extreme cases, the threats of crossing the deviant-types. For example:

—a smile too marked, beyond a certain limit, will be interpreted like an insane grimace or insolent mockery;

—a too affected submission will become underhanded;

—a pout beyond the standard will become a mark of contempt;

—too old a face or too wrinkled will inspire fear;

—tan skin, beyond a certain threshold, will spark mistrust ("it's a foreigner, an Arab, a Jew, a gipsy"), especially if it is associated with a "deviating" linguistic accent;

—"sexual choice" will also have to be posted clearly on the face: any ambiguity or uncertainty would be felt like a threat to phallocratic power; not only must it be immediately understood that one is dealing with a man, a woman, even a homosexual, but moreover with which kind of man, woman, or homosexual.

The Capitalistic faciality machine does not operate only through total breaks, massive dichotomies and bi-polarizations of contents. Its action of reductive binarization also relates to the texture of matters of expression associated with it, which it converts into signifying substances. The power takeover of linguistic systems founded upon systems of distinctive oppositions and articulated from a finished range of glossemes of expression results in a whole endeavor of eroding the semiotic rough edges of intensive components of expression. The primacy of linearized glossematic chains relatively autonomous with respect to the world of signified contents (because of the elaborate structuration of their phonological, syntactic, lexical organization, etc.) implies a complex process of the subjection of assemblages of enunciation to power formations and, in particular, to local capitalistic faciality machines. If nothing came to oppose its own movement, the consciential component of faciality would end up such that every expressive production would necessarily come to fold itself onto a reduction, onto a translatability in terms of elementary quanta of signifying faciality, i.e. in the last analysis, onto a structured succession of automated binary choices likely to be computerized, along with every other abstract quantity of information.

Signifying facial substances homogenize metabolisms of deterritorialization—for example, those of perceptive or social life. It stratifies them, reducing them to static positions. The inside and the outside become reversible: the event dissolves in the texture of syntagmatic articulations. All of this has always already been there, lurking in a possible corner of the signifier. Nothing can occur outside of the facialized since every idea of externality has become relative.

No new semiotic conjunction is conceivable, no creative nomadism, no "amazing" encounter, no flash of desire. A unique and single event remains in the innermost depths of all that occurs: the threat of annihilation in the black eye hole of the Superego. All the dimensions of singularity and multiplicity—i.e. of desire—relative to every event are threatened by the erection of a supreme iconic marker that imposes its syntactic generations on all of "creation" in the name of an intangible and empty command which could be stated as follows: "everything is redundant with everything else; everything signifies; order will be guaranteed forever, everywhere." The most insignificant event could be the occasion for an intrusion of consciential faciality components. The signifying god of capitalistic societies watches over the subject with the turn of every phrase, word, and phoneme. Its function of semiotic binarization should be conceived as a process opposite from what is described by information theory. Rather than starting from a division of statements in order to reconstruct the meaning of words, the signification of sentences, the rhetorical range of discourses… it would be appropriate to leave aside the concrete options leading to one division rather than another. For information theory, the message in transmission is a subset taken from a set predetermined by other elements. From the beginning it is given within a homogeneous body of messages made up from particular rules of formation (systems of implication, opposition, complementarity, etc.). However, we have seen that the calculation that relates to this body could not itself be held as constitutive of that body itself.[26]

The fact that we can index a statement of a certain quantity of information following a binary treatment of reduction does not imply that it is in itself and as such reducible to this quantity of binary choices. In order to be able to produce such a result, statements must be "prepared" beforehand—in the sense that one speaks of an anatomical preparation. When the quantity of information carried by a message is defined as being proportional to its rarity, what is sought is by no means the originality of the statement that is considered. Rarity here relates to the expression and originality of the contents. Can one admit that what determines the informative character of a message is the way in which the originality of a statement is taken into account—the relationship between what is retained and what is left out—by the machine of binarizing expression? The entire operation of signifying reduction lies in this passage from content to expression, in this crushing, this lamination of the matters of contents by the signifying forms of expression. (It is not appropriate yet on this molecular level to establish a clear-cut distinction between materials of content and materials of expression, insofar as the content-expression opposition is not yet stabilized here.)

Let us try to determine the process behind the facial "treatment" of speech more precisely. The theoretical quantification of a statement consists in bringing a subset of traits of expression back to a perfectly definite set of semiotic objects. As an example, let us consider a message with a response to the question: "Which place does Pierre occupy in this line of eight people?" If a set of references making up eight different letters is constructed, the problem will be reduced to "pulling out" the letter P within this set, representative of Pierre. All the other classifying traits have been "provisionally" abandoned. It is not a matter of sex, age, the reality of existence, etc. The set will be divided into three binary breaks, three successive questions of the type: "Is P in the first half of the set or the second?" The position of P is now identified. The number of these binary choices defines the quantity of information.[27] Which part will take on, in such an operation, a semiotic component seemingly only indirectly concerned with this process, such as faciality? Precisely the one that *creates the conditions* of reduction for the entirety of reference on its arrival. Capitalistic faciality teaches us *not to see it*, to create abstractions of the value of things, to adopt a limiting point of view on the side of which identification becomes impossible.

Faciality "interposes" itself between intensive multiplicities with changing and heterogeneous delimitations such that they are semiotized by asignifying components and the "well coordinated" world of signifying semiologies. It proceeds to the first discernabilizations and the first binarist arrangements that will make propositional operations relating to informational messages possible. It is what, in the last analysis, masks the functions of subjection to dominant semiologies by presenting its operations as being based on invariant logical procedures rather than concrete devices of power.

Thus the technique of reduction suitable for capitalistic facialization which endeavors to produce discretized[28] objects and localizable faciality-landscapities also concerns a dichotic method of opposition. The system of breaks of consciential components depends here:

—neither on a theoretical data-processing quantification bearing upon pre-assembled collections (we should say "ensemblized");

—nor on the high-speed emission of diagrammatic microbreaks, which we shall examine in the subchapter devoted to the molecular economy of faciality traits.

This system operates by putting molar facial sets into circulation. In other words, sets with uncertain boundaries. This is more an operation of "gestaltization" than a logical or diagrammatic one. Its functionality can be compared to that of a game consisting in discovering a name at the end of a series of yes or no questions. What does it do?—Is it an object or living thing?—A man or an animal?—Male or female?—Blonde or brunette?—Someone here or elsewhere?—Top or bottom?—Was it before, now or later (this ternary choice can also be broken up into two binary choices—before or now—and—now or later) etc. It happens in this way only due to synchronic waves of redundancies of resonance which establish the binarism of signifying faciality. I "see" the thing, I recognize his familiar face and a trait, sometimes imperceptible, of my own faciality, coming from this encounter and the "*visa*" of signification it gives him. One faciality responds to another. Every effect of meaning is instituted between two deterritorialized winks.

The margins of uncertainty are thus gradually reduced by this work of discernibilization and normalizing classification until the set of intensive systems are entirely arranged. However, a considerable number of residual contents will continue to escape this facial syntax-ization of content. These will be indexed in particular by the system of modern proper names. Attaching individuated faciality traits onto proper names seems to mark the end of a capitalistic evolution of the modes of semiotization. The hypothesis can be put forth that in archaic languages each substantive functioned like a proper name and that every statement implied a collective appropriation[29] of a collec-tive faciality-landscapity. The ownership or property of a name, the localization of a "proper characteristic" on an individuated territori-ality, actually seems to lose any real consistency with the takeover by consciential components of faciality of the set of semiotic compo-nents. Everything is individuated, but nothing appears proper to any group or any person. (In any event, we shall see further that the modern proper name, a deterritorialized semiotic formation, will take on an essential place in certain diagrammatic operations.)

DIAGRAMMATIC FACIALITY TRAITS

Capitalistic faciality proceeds through redundancies of resonance and binary reduction; diagrammatic faciality traits proceed through machinic redundancies and abstract machines irreducible to data processes. The former works for the subjection of desire, the latter for its release. With them, we leave the world of arborescences, simulacra and black holes of the face-landscape system for that of rhizomes. In machinic rhizomatic systems, we tendentially no longer find circularly aggregated eyes nor signifying layers accumulating in concentric zones as in the territorialized assemblages,[30] an empty eye or a superegoistic vanishing point on every horizon, but lines of flight carrying quanta of diagrammatic possibilities. A becoming-imperceptible effaces every incarnation of the gaze.[31] Having lost its "consistency of referent,"[32] the wall of the signifier can be crossed and a new type of semiotic break can be instituted in direct contact with matters of expression. What characterizes machinic rhizomes compared to territorialized assemblages is this unmediated relation between systems of coding and material flows, which is the fact that points of deterritorialization—the machinic indexes—are no longer neutralized there but are directly articulated in the abstract machinisms that open up new possibilities and create a "machinic future" for them (by destratifying them, by articulating them with one another, and launching semiotic bridges between matters heterogeneous until now).

We have successively passed from a territorialized organization of the figure-ground type to the concentration and interiorization of a signifying break, bipolarizing values and optional matters radiating from an eye over the set of faces and landscapes, then to the emission of signs-particles in a network, which are sorts of probe heads or guiding devices of active deterritorialization that untie their passage from the nodes of faciality and landscapity. But here it is by no means a question of a linear evolution that would allow us to pass without transition from one universe to another. Rhizomatic organizations "already" existed in archaic societies, while arborescent systems never stop developing in societies that rest upon machinic rhizomes. However, archaic rhizomes remained—or endeavored to remain—territorialized, while "modern" diagrammatic machines appear to be carried away by an irreversible process of deterritorialization. In order to remain in place under these conditions, signifying power formations seem to be forced to subject themselves to a sort of incessant monitoring of the adaptation and recuperation of asignifying machinisms. Thus it is undoubtedly advisable to attenuate the opposition that we have established between the sphere of semiotic components pertaining to signifying semiologies and that of diagrammatic components, the former maintaining a sort of "constitutional" dependence vis-à-vis a reductionist theory like that of information, and the latter resisting, on the contrary, any treatment that would make them give up their essential singularity features. In the same proportion, extrinsic modes of *semiotic quantification*, which proceed through detachment from redundancy, transposition and the simulation of an equivalent semiotic, can no longer be radically separated today from modes of *machinic quantification* operating directly within material assemblages, living assemblages, social assemblages, etc.

It is thus impossible to maintain strict boundaries between social faciality and diagrammatic faciality features. This is no more than to claim to protect anything from the "pure thought" of devastations that, according to certain omens, the data-processing revolution would be on the way to accomplish. According to us, it is wrong that a humanistic conception of science would cling to the idea of the ultimate and radical division of labor between scientist and machine, attempting to reduce the possible field of any intervention in informatics to data processing previously worked out by mankind. Today, machinic conscientialization has become inseparable from human conscientialization. The computer, which has remained until now the affair of specialized technicians and which has concerned only a poorly elaborated mathematics, is more and more integrated into the complexes of enunciation where it will become almost impossible to make a distinction between human creativity and machinic invention. As of now, data processing deals with certain problems of mathematics which have remained suspended by a quantitative insufficiency of the means of semiotization (the resolution, for example, of the centenary problem known as coloring a map with four colors, will have taken 1,200 work hours for a computer to carry out the ten billion operations necessary); now it is starting to be able to formulate original mathematical problems.[33] The current proliferation of computers and microprocessors indicates to us to what point, at least in the technical and scientific fields, the "purely mental" modes of semiotization have already lost their independence compared to machinic assemblages. At this point, digital machines deterritorialize sign machines so that the former end up acquiring a sort of asignifying transparency which perfectly enables them to be "molded" in their techniques of representation and recomposition to the singular traits of matters of expression.[34] Let us nevertheless remark that on this purely technological level, asignifying "progress" can still be made from any kind of social assemblage! Informatics can be relegated to the service of the mystifications of the media, polls, the Stock Exchange, etc. as well as to a different politics of the capture of a liberating collective consciousness.

Instead of an "eternal essence" of human faciality, it is in the current nature of informatic language that the limits of a machinic faciality will be found. Data-processing is still poorly adapted to temporal phenomena of rupture, destratification, desire, in other words to processes of deterritorialization which can do nothing but escape the reductions of signifying binarisms. We previously evoked the fact that theorists on different sides wish to do away with the idea that a prediction of the future can be the object of a calculation based on the global "tendencies" of the past or that the most differentiated must necessarily fall under the dependence of the least differentiated, or that productive-expressive assemblages have to be divided into superstructures dependent upon infrastructures.[35] The mechanists, finalists, idealists, dialectical conceptions, etc. of matter and history implicitly idealized the binarization of the possible, a closure of the future through all sorts of processes. Categories of "defacialized" time and space (despite all the critical philosophical theories and physico-mathematical relativists) are imposed in the name of particular instruments of capitalistic modes of thought. A "machinics," breaking with the former, would imply a refusal of the dichotomy between material processes and semiotic processes. It would be brought to consider the deterritorializations of time and space only in connection with a new type of assemblage of enunciation, new types of faciality traits, refrains, relations to the body, sex, the cosmos (it could even, in extreme cases, envision reverse causalities and inversions of time, as astrophysicists who study the interactions inside black holes currently do). In a preliminary phase, it will undoubtedly merely be a question of desubjectifying and deobjectifying assemblages of semiotization in order to begin the ulterior stages of the establishment of another human world. New concrete operators of faciality and refrains will precisely have a function of crossing times and spaces, insides and outsides, and the subjects and objects of the capitalistic universe. They will not manufacture time and space "in general," but *this* time and *this* space lived by a particular assemblage in a *particular* context which is ecological, ethological, economic, social, political, etc. "Internal" deterritorializations—for example, those that widen our vision of the outside world or those that complexify sexual behaviors—are inseparable from "external" deterritorializations working upon the environment and the social field. Because the internal rhizome cannot be considered independently of the external[36] rhizome, a desired face will utilize registers as diverse as those of singular identifying components, power formations with standardized facialities, creative diagrammatic faciality traits…

Concrete machines—refrains, eyes, faces, landscapity traits…— relaying resonances of black holes carried by semiotic components cannot be classified or labeled according to general categories. They are organized only within the framework of particular arrangements specific to each type of assemblage which themselves escape any taxonomic systematization. The components of an assemblage of enunciation do not all have the same importance; their relative weight can vary from one situation to another. Certain components are organized between them in order to form constellations that will reappear in a cyclic mode (example: sleeping, waking, meals, etc.). They are then centralized and hierarchized on particular arborescent points, a particular faciality, or refrains that program the recomposition of the same assemblages, the resumption of "everyday" consistency and the modes of subjectification that correspond to them. Others behave like a killjoy, or rather like a kill-reality, while settling at the edge of a signifying tree of implication by thwarting the effects of resonance, by catalyzing a rhizome, by unraveling the globalizing redundancies of the face, everyday life, and landscape, while making refrains and mutant faciality traits work on their own account. Thus, in the register of "machinic consciousness,"[37] nothing is determined in advance. No type of one-way interaction between the inside and the outside, the before and after, the molar and the molecular, or the supra and infra can be calculated with absolute rigor. The machinations behind a glance can emerge, for example, "on the ground of destruction of the eyes that 'look at me'"[38] but, conversely, the eyes with regard to a for-others cut out from all human gestalt can be installed right in the middle of the world, cracking it open and taking possession of the modes of subjectification which reign there, as is shown by the exploration of a Jean-Luc Parant when he describes the eyes "with the flower of solid SOLID matter" that encircle us and also excavate the emptiness in front of them via "flying machines," birds able to fly over windows and landscapes ("AND THE EARTH AND THE SKY AND THE NIGHT AND THE DAY ENTERED").[39]

5

The Time of Refrains

CAPITALISTIC REFRAINS

Time is not sustained by humans as something that would happen from the outside. There is no interaction between time "in general" and man "in general." Just as space is facialized according to dominant social norms and rituals, time is "beaten" by concrete assemblages of semiotization be they collective or individuated, territorialized or deterritorialized, machinic or stratified. A child singing in the night because it is afraid of the dark seeks to regain control of events that deterritorialized too quickly for her liking and started to proliferate on the side of the cosmos and the Imaginary. Every individual, every group, every nation is thus "equipped" with a basic range of incantatory refrains. The trades and corporations of ancient Greece, for example, possessed their own kind of sonorous seal, a short melodic formula called "*nomos*."[1] They made use of it to affirm their social identity, their territory, and their internal cohesion; because each member of the group "belonged" to the same sound-shifter, the refrain thus took on the function of the collective and asignifying subject of the enunciation. All that we know about the most ancient societies indicates that they did not separate, as capitalistic societies do, components of song, dance, speech, ritual, production, etc. (for example, in African languages known as "tonal," a word will have a different meaning according to whether some of its phonemes are produced with a high tone or a low tone). In fact, in these types of society one is suspicious of overly accentuated divisions of labor and modes of semiotization. Specialists—for example, African blacksmiths—are "localized" within castes; their unsettling *savoir-faire* supposes certain dealings with magical powers.[2] They entrust heterogeneous assemblages (associating the ritual with the productive, the sexual with the ludic and the political, etc.) with the responsibility of effectuating all the phase transitions of social life—at least those with a marked collective importance. Diagrammatism thus does not make an appeal here to a machine of autonomous expression, to hierarchized power formations that dominate it in order to capitalize on all the "benefits" of the socio-semiotic division of labor to their profit.

Capitalistic societies shed this mistrust in regard to the "pure"— the pure specialist of a pure material, such as iron or the thread of speech and writing. It is on the contrary the heterogeneous, the mixed, the fuzzy, and the dissymmetrical that worry them. The paramount importance they place upon scriptural components is correlative to a process of simplification and rationalization for the latter. In the West, the automation of writing, speech, song, mimicry, dance, etc. will consequently bring about a certain deterioration of calligraphic refinements, the quality of prosodic traits, postural etiquettes, in short, everything that gives life and grace to mixed assemblages of expression. Every component has acquired an independence jealously supervised by specialists, watchtowers, champions… In the musical domain these transformations are indicated by a progressive disappearance of complex rhythms and a binarization and ternarization of basic rhythms. This "purification" has also been supplied with a general impoverishment of timbres,[3] if not basic melodic cells.

The simplification of the basic rhythms of temporalization— what I call refrains—contributes to an evolution in the opposite direction of the modes of consistency previously evoked.[4] From the angle of their intrinsic consistency, it leads to an impoverishment, to a serialization of the assemblages that it affects (in the universe of capitalistic refrains, everyone lives in the same rhythm and the same accelerated cadences). On the contrary, from the angle of their inter-assemblage consistency it leads to an infinite multiplication of assemblages of enunciation centered on specialized and highly differentiated refrains starting from elementary traits. The *"nomoi"* of the scientific, artistic, and sporting castes etc. no longer function as signs of recognition but as rhythmic schemata of machinic propositions, as diagrams of every kind. (For example, the mathematicians' discourse will convey complex formulas, relational icons, and epistemological indexes of orientation according to specific sequences.)

Both capitalistic refrains and faciality traits must be classified among the collective micropolitical infrastructures responsible for arranging our most intimate temporalization and modeling our relation to landscapes and the living world. Besides, neither of these can be separated from the other. A face is always associated with a refrain; a significative redundancy is always associated with a face, with the stamp of a voice... "I love you, do not leave me, you are my world, my mother, my father, my race, the cornerstone of my organization, my drug. I can do nothing without you... What you are really—man, woman, object, ideal of standing—in fact matters little. What counts is that you allow me to function in this society, that you neutralize in advance all the solicitations of the components of passage that could derail me from the system. Nothing will be able to happen anymore that does not pass through you..." It is always the same song, the same secret misery, whatever the apparent diversity of the notes and words. As in Baroque times, Western music has claimed to become a universal model, occasionally absorbent and with some "folklorish" condescension. Particular styles of music were no longer related to territories, unless via the mode of exotic seduction. From that point on there has been *Music*. The styles of music played in the courts of European royalty have imposed their laws, their ranges, their rhythms, their harmonic and polyphonic designs, their writing processes, their instruments... Seen from the "outside," this pure—deterritorialized—music seems richer, more open, more creative than the others. But what in it exactly is on the level of "consummated," individuated, or collective assemblages? Weren't the refrains of everyday consumption, which are the by-products of "classical" music, those running through our heads all day, on the contrary impoverished because they were focused on an individuated enunciation and because of their "mass-mediated" production?

Instead of being assembled on the basis of territorialized systems, such as the tribe, the ethnic group, the corporation, and the province, the subjectification of these refrains is internalized and individuated on the machinic territories which constitute egos, roles, persons, loves, feelings of "belonging to." Now initiation into the semiotics of social time no longer arises from collective ceremonies but from processes of encoding centered on the individual that tend to confer an increasingly large role to the media. Thus, instead of the lullabies and nursery rhymes of former times, this initiation takes places under the eyes of a televised teddybear—calibrated to the latest marketing methods—inducing children's dreams while antipsychotic catchphrases are administered in large doses to young boys and girls suffering from love sickness... These catchphrases, these rhythms, these call signs have invaded every temporal mode of semiotization; they constitute this "spirit of the time" that leads us to feel we are "like everyone else" and to accept "the world as it is..." When Pierre Clastres evokes the solitary song of an Indian face in the night, he describes it in an attempt to escape from the processes of the "subjection of man to the general network of signs,"[5] in an aggression against words as means of communication.

Speaking, according to him, does not necessarily imply "putting the other into play." Such an escape from social redundancies, such an "ungluing" of refrains and facialities from the predominant alterity has undoubtedly become much more difficult to attain in societies like ours living under a general regime of inter-subjective mush, mixing cosmic flows and investments of desire in the most ridiculous, the most limited, even the most utilitarian daily newspapers. Can we still even conceive a mode of existence, such as that of the Indians of the Amazon, that never excludes, whatever its degree of social integration, a solitary face-to-face with the night and the finitude of the human condition? It is not completely in vain that structuralist psychoanalysts today value having to base the Subject and the Other on an exclusive relation to the signifier. Indeed, it works well in this dead end that leads us to the evolution of "developed" societies!

The "modernist illusion" could be defined by everything that leads us to appreciate our relation with life, time, thought, art... as being superior to that of ancient or archaic societies simply due to the fact that it is machinically "armed," i.e. because it brings into play innumerable instrumental and semiotic relays and develops what Pierre Francastel calls a "third world" between matter and image.[6] Kafka, in whose work the reader frequently witnesses heroes encountering their own solitude under the pressure of an unbearable hissing and who themselves cruelly suffer from a noisy world, has perfectly described this inanity of responding to capitalistic sound in our relation to time ("...the song existed within us in the old days, our legends mention it: the texts of these old songs even remain within us, although no one can sing them any longer. We thus have an idea of what the song can be, yet the art of Joséphine does not precisely correspond to this idea. Is this song? Isn't this just hissing?").[7]

The collapse of territorialized refrains leads us to the limit of a hissing black hole, as if it were binary music! All Western music could be regarded as an immense fugue developed starting from this single empty note. Clogging the black hole of his madness with increasingly evanescent, increasingly deterritorialized refrains of childhood, making their basic cells proliferate *ad infinitum* through incessant melodic, harmonic, polyphonic, and instrumental creations; was this not, moreover, the destiny of a Robert Schumann who had to incarnate, including up until his final collapse, perhaps the most decisive turning point in scriptural music?[8] When musicologists today transcribe into Western notations music known as "primitive," they badly measure the number of singularity traits that they cannot collect, in particular those concerning the secret relations that bind them to magical statements or religious rituals.[9] For example, specialists who will establish the arrangement of complex rhythms characterizing some of these musical styles will represent a break in rhythm in terms of syncopation or counterpoint rhythm. For them, the base, the universal reference, will be isorhythm. They forget that "primitives" do not necessarily function on the basis of the same abstract machines of rhythm as ours. The standard for some of these societies is perhaps a syncopated time. Their life appears to be arranged by rhythms of great amplitude to which we have lost all means of access, haunted as we are by our own uniformly isorhythmic refrains. Undoubtedly, we could relatively situate this problem better by returning to the rhythms of our childhood with the incessant breaks in substances of expression and temporalization which characterized it and through which we preserve our nostalgia... With the school, military service, and the "entry into life" through large-tiled, bleach-scented corridors, our refrains have been purified, asepticized. A thorough study of this phenomenon would certainly result in establishing a correlation between the rise of the modernist illusion and the progress of public hygiene.

Here we are not preaching any return whatsoever to the primitivism of childhood, madness, or archaic societies. If something is infantile in our societies it is not the children but the reference of adults to childhood. Therefore, what we must aim at from the schizoanalytical perspective are not regressions or fixations on the counting rhymes of the youngest age, but the transference of blocks of childhood that associate refrain redundancies with faciality redundancies into pragmatic fields.

To the extent that "original" territorialized assemblages, like those of the extended family, rural communities, castes, corporations, etc. have been swept away by deterritorialized flows, components of conscientialization also have been attached to and studded with residual objects or semiotic substitutes. (A whole set of elective affinities, or even of direct filiation, could thus perhaps be brought to light between the Lady of courtly love, the infantilism of romantic sentiment, the Nazi fascination with Aryan blood, and the ideal of standing that reigns in developed societies.) This capitalistic deterritorialization of refrains has selected material traits of expression lending itself to the play of what could be called the politics of extremes. The machinic nuclei of assemblages of temporalization in fact proceed in three directions at the same time:

1) towards a hyper-territorialized subjectification, particularly in the domain of the domestic economy, by opening a quasi-unlimited field to power operations taking control of the rhythms of the body, of the most imperceptible movements of the married couple and their children—"What you have, you are not like most, nor is what you think, or what your *jouissance* is made of (or your refusal of *jouissance*)…";

2) towards a diagrammatism that is always more "profitable" for the system through the development of new technologies of the *chronographic enslavement* of human functions. The refrainization of the work force no longer depends on corporative initiations but on the internalization of blocks of code, of professional blocks that

have become standard—everywhere the same type of framework, technician, bureaucrat, supervisor, O.S., etc.—delimiting milieus, castes, deterritorialized power formations;

3) towards a rhizomatic mutation, deterritorializing traditional rhythms (biological and archaic), nullifying capitalistic refrains and opening the possibility of a new relation to the cosmos, time, and desire.

We left off from the idea, along with the idea of faciality redundancies, that refrain redundancies play an essential role in the micropolitics of consciential components. If this is true, we will not have to reconsider questions concerning the molecular consistency of the field of refrains since they are the same as those of faciality.[10] But it remains for us to found the legitimacy of such a parallel. It is nothing extraordinary to confer a determining expressive role on faces and to postulate that they hold a fundamental place in the genesis of the effects of signification. But does it have to be the same with this intangible material of refrains? Isn't this a question of something much more passive? Generally, doesn't everything that concerns our relation to time leave us much more deprived than what concerns our relation to space? We circulate more easily in space than in time. On the contrary, the study of certain traits of the intrinsic consistency of refrain redundancies will show us that not only do the former concern the same type of double play between consciential components (opaque consciousness of resonance and/or diagrammatic hyperconsciousness), but that, moreover, they can have a more powerful deterritorializing action with a longer range than those of faciality. It is at least in this direction that we shall orient our analysis of Proustian refrains. I propose to show in the second part of this chapter that it is first of all and above all in the domain of animal ethology that we shall have to base the existence of a problematics of innovation, creativity, and even freedom concerning the components of the refrain.

THE ETHOLOGY OF SONOROUS, VISUAL, AND BEHAVIORAL REFRAINS IN THE ANIMAL WORLD

The choice of examples presented here attempts to respond to the following preoccupations:

—relativizing the notion of a hierarchy of instinctive components based on a hierarchy of nervous centers such as those developed following the work of N. Tinbergen;

—regrouping a certain number of reference points relative to the emergence of components of passage typical of the refrain between stratified systems and diagrammatic processes, producing mutations in the order of spatio-temporal coordinates, social coordinates, etc...

Ethological Hierarchy or Biologico-Behavioral Engineering

At the center of what we could call the "ethological misunderstanding" prevails a coupling between:

—factors of inhibition,

—and innate release mechanisms.

Every conception ending in arborescent hierarchizations of behavior sequences rests upon this basic binary mechanism (similar in other respects to what grounds the "ideological" uses of information theory). Wanting to specify too rigorously the nature of "what inhibits" or "what impels," one comes to hypostasize the existence of a "soul" inhabiting these sequences. For those having been arbitrarily mechanized from the beginning, it becomes inevitable upon "arrival," in order to give an account of the functionality of the system, to relate them back to transcendent authorities. It is always the same politics of "far-off worlds" or "objects from above" that winds up reconstituting linear causalities and losing the singularity points carried by abstract machinisms along the way. However, the micropolitical consistency of inter-assemblage fields appears to organize aggregations all the more complex and all the more capable of adaptation and creativity than the intrinsic consistency of the machinic nuclei employed by the deterritorialized components contiguous to these singularity points and which are to some extent specialized within the transformations, within the diagrammatic[11] "phase transitions"—(and not just within transcodings without any modification of the assemblage). It is this entire morphogenesis of assemblages through the decomposition of stratified substance-form relations, this rhizomatic creativity that systematically—or by the system—fails to be grasped by mechanical theories, data processes, signifying structuralisms… A rhizomatic conception of inter-assemblage pragmatic fields (and non-arborescent, as Tinbergen proposes with his famous schema) should result in shedding light upon a new dawn of innovative openings in the behavioral programmings of the animal world as well as in the processes of re-enclosure leading to speciation. In this respect the study of refrains deserves special attention because it seems, in fact, that their entry into animal and human assemblages systematically thwarts the rigid oppositions between the acquired and the innate, between a rigorous biological determinism and a freedom of invention. Perhaps this has something to do with systems comparable to those of chemical catalysts and protein enzymes which, without directly taking part in the molecular interactions that they facilitate, orient them in a decisive way. What counts in these "crystallizations" of behaviors seems to be less the intrinsic nature of each one of their components—hormonal, perceptive, ecological, social…—than the spatial and rhythmic devices that they generate and from which diagrammatic strategies and tactics of stratification make it possible to create "interchanges" launching semiotic bridges between parallel universes which seemed to never have to communicate together. This "machinics" and this biologico-behavioral engineering of components of passage, like those of refrains, mimicry, etc. generates sequences of "stigmergy" (each sequence articulating itself with the following one without a "finalized knowledge" or an overall project being implied) as well as modes of subjectification implying an explicit questioning about the "direction" of an intentional arc. The behaviorist prejudice which consists in postulating that a complex behavior could result only from the assembly of inhibiting systems and releasing systems inevitably results in missing the limit states, the "breaks of mechanism," the diagrammatic potentialities, the creative lines of flight through which evolution selects its adaptive paths.

From this point of view, I perhaps bolstered in an excessive way the opposition between inhibition through black hole effects and rhizomatic releases. We shall see that it is starting from such black holes that redundancies are emitted which contribute to deterritorializing stratified systems. In order to be able to activate, certain innovative processes are perhaps held to begin, preliminarily, within black hole impasses which will emerge, during long sequences and apart from any "constructive dialectics," only from "catastrophes" in the sense René Thom[12] gives them (example: invasions, epidemics, the Hundred Years War, etc. at the dawn of the great capitalistic revolutions). The ethological "equipment" of refrain, silhouette, faciality, etc. will not perhaps have had for a million years another function than of controlling new rhythms and choosing new topological figures in order to ward off such catastrophes and to develop new metabolisms of escape from black holes. In any event, it seems legitimate that when in the animal world stases of inhibition are presented in the form of a behavior-crossroads between important options for the survival of a species, every time all sorts of interrogative pauses are found there, "times of comprehending" (according to an expression of Jacques Lacan), or many reiterated systems of gossip, ritual dance, festival, and sacrifice, characterized by the interaction of refrains, traits of corporeity, traits of faciality, etc.[13]

The living rhizome explores potentialities through complex semiotic metabolisms. Selective pressure promotes the integral automation of certain assemblages, while it disaggregates others from them, or while it installs them in intermediate states, sorts of phase transitions, in order to "save time" to some extent. Thus, many assemblages that seem marginal in appearance vegetate as if waiting on the miraculous chance encounter of a line of deterritorialization that would allow them to "set out again." Nothing *a priori* here justifies the negation of an economy of desire, a politics of the "defense of life for life," with anything that involves drama and absurdity. In reality, biochemical causality, strategies of the survival of the species, the tricks and improvisations of desire all incessantly overlap within the same rhizome, and we can only hope to "retrieve" them on condition of accepting the principle of an absolute polyvocality of the paths and means of doing so.[14] Would the difference between animal desire and human desire lie in the privileged relation that the latter—according to structuralist psychoanalysts—would maintain with speech and law, whereas the former would remain fixed within systems of ritual fascination and ostentatious expenditure tied down to a passive Imaginary? Would speaking desire be "freer" than coded desire? Nothing makes it possible to conclude, however, that the modes of semiotization of animal desire are more impoverished than those of human desire. We find there the same rupturing effects of micropolitical black holes or of aphanisis, to borrow an expression of Ernest Jones.[15] During the nuptial parades of birds, abrupt reversals of situation frequently emerge: the courting phase will suddenly be replaced by an aggressive attitude, then simulations of bathing, etc., the various behavioral sequences seeming to be entirely demolished into pieces. Could such examples be used to account for a specific alienation of animal desire? But this same mode of semiotization is found in mankind in "blockages," for example, when a person who was accidentally interrupted during the recitation of a text is forced to "start over from the beginning." Although blockages appear less delimited here and more opened, as though impaired, behavioral stereotypes are found everywhere in human pragmatic fields, as phobic or obsessive reiterations will testify. In fact, we could bring to light all the intermediate behaviors establishing a bridge between animal desire and human desire. Perhaps the single difference that would remain the most difficult to reduce would concern, in fact, these stases of arrest that we evoked previously: in the framework of capitalistic societies, the "time of comprehending"—at least on the scale of the individual—frequently degenerates into passive acceptance of social repression[16] in resigned contemplation of the inanity of the human condition, everything that appears rather distant from the vitality of animal desire.[17]

Multidimensionality of Territories

In humans, the hypertrophy of nonspecific circuits regulating the vigilance of the nervous system, the exacerbation of its individuation of enunciation, the constitution of gigantic heaps of empty reflexive consciential components: these will have been some of the conditions for "launching" deterritorialized refrains and facialities. Undoubtedly, it is impossible to determine if the general bankruptcy of the "originary" territorialities have been the cause or the consequence of these processes. In any event, I believe that the "ungluing" of the collective history of humanity can be characterized by this sort of deterritorializing gangrene that has taken over every domain. Generally, it seems to me that evolution can be called creative only by taking into consideration the general tendency towards the efflorescence of the most deterritorialized forms. But it is advisable to banish at the same time any idea of dialectical progress as well as any unfavorable moral connotation in the appreciation of these successive movements of deterritorialization and reterritorialization, especially in the domain of historical transformations. This is first of all because contradictions are never completely overcome but are generally only circumvented through a displacement of the problems, the old territorialities remaining in place while singularity points become the seat of a "machinic revival."[18] Second, let me repeat, this is because the deterritorialized "solutions" selected by history are neither richer, nor more inventive than those of seemingly more primitive states. Thus, the fabulous acceleration of the contemporary technico-scientific phylum, considering that all is well, does not appear to shed light upon inventions which are intrinsically more "inspired" than those that have been promoted over several million years by the living phylum. The distance between humans and animals does not concern distinct essences but assemblages different from their components of semiotization. The deterritorialization of his *Umwelt* has led man to invent diagrammatic operators such as faciality and refrains enabling him to produce new machinic territorialities. But this kind of evolutionary machinic escape can already be located in the animal world, particularly in the installation of territorialized social assemblages. It is known that these assemblages are delimited by means of extremely diversified techniques—odorous markings through excrements or special secretions, distancing other animals through "territorial songs," intimidating sexual exhibitions, etc. These operators of field consistency considered separately often only appear to arise from innate encodings, functioning as types of reflexes or taxes. Thus, to anticipate an example that will retain us later at a greater length, the function of the very colored ornamentation of mottled Diamonds—Australian sparrows studied by K. Immelmann[19]—seems to be able to be reduced to inhibition relations of vicinity and adjustment of the distribution of individuals in a given space. (If we are dealing with whitish subjects of the same species, we will witness, in fact, a sort of collapse of this "critical distance" and a contraction of groups.) But a systematically oriented examination in the direction of inter-assemblage relations would undoubtedly result in shedding light upon openings that relativize the mechanical character of these encodings. We can put forth the hypothesis that it is precisely in this type of opening that selective pressure is "introduced" (without being able to consider, once again, that there is any irreversible projection towards new coefficients of freedom: an evolution of this kind can perfectly lead to a "totalitarian" specialization of castes, sexes, species…).

Let us return to the principle example of symbiosis between certain species of wasps and orchids popularized by Rémy Chauvin.[20] It is known that the wasp, effectuating a simulated sexual act with a morphological and olfactory lure constituted by the rostellum of the orchid, afterwards releases and attaches the pollen that it transports onto other plants, thus ensuring the cross reproduction of this species. The ensemble of the transcoding systems authorizing these round-trip tickets between the vegetable kingdom and the animal kingdom appears completely closed to any individual experimentation, training, or innovation. Selective pressure has only retained here, starting from encounters which were perhaps in the beginning only accidental and improvised, the sequences that it managed to systematize, control, and encode in the strictest way. Field interactions here depend on abstract machinisms that have been stratified to some extent in the machinic nuclei of the genome of the species and which ontogenesis has only to decipher and transfer mechanically. But, even in such extreme cases, we would be wrong to reduce the inter-assemblage systems to a simple "pooling" of the quantities of information carried by the respective genes of each species. Indeed, it then becomes impossible to apprehend the pathways between the innate, the acquired, and the experienced, between biological encodings, ecological adaptation, and collective semiotizations. In fact, as I shall endeavor to show with the following examples, even (and perhaps especially) when the field interactions utilize such "mechanized" components of encoding, they leave the inter-assemblage interactions in "play," preparing in return the appearance of new mutational components on the scene.

Under these conditions, nothing would be gained by reducing a symbiosis like that of the wasp and the orchid to a simple "attachment" between two heterogeneous worlds. This encounter produces what I called elsewhere a "surplus-value of code," i.e. a result that exceeds the simple totalization of the involved encodings (the sexual purpose of the orchid + the nutritional aim of the wasp). The new symbiotic assemblage actually functions like a mutant wasp-orchid species evolving on its own account and redistributing the genetic and semiotic components selected from both original species according to its own standards (morphological, physiological, ethological components, semiotization of visual, olfactory, sexual lures, etc.). Thus a new evolutionary line of flight is launched on the bio-ecological rhizome which is in other respects immediately masked by the genetic encodings that delimit it the assignment to the species and phylogenetically circumscribed sequences. Everything happens as if the consistency of actualized fields is "hardened" and stratified to the degree that the intrinsic consistency of virtual possibles become more fluid, better disposed with regard to new encounters. The specialization of functions and the speciation of evolutionary clones would thus create the same conditions of an acceleration of the innovative deterritorializations of an invention of new possibles. We shall see that this is what occurs with the components of refrains: the more they are enclosed, ritualized within the pragmatic fields of the species, the more in contact they are with the machinic nuclei where the essential phenomena of machinic mutation are played out. Hence their "superiority," perhaps, compared to faciality traits in the realm of machinic transition power.

Faciality-Corporeality, Sex, Territory, Hierarchy, and Free Will in Baboons

The overly massive oppositions between the acquired and the innate, the biochemical and the "adaptive," the individual and the social, the economic and the cultural... can only be opposed by research that takes on the task of illuminating the "predisposed" components in such a function of passage. Transversalized operators destratify behavioral assemblages on all levels of the animal phylum; but it is obviously easier to locate them in more "evolved" animals. Let us consider, for example, three social types of assemblages in baboons and vervets within which sexual components and components of territorialization are found in a key position:

—The first relates to the internal hierarchical relations expressed by mimicries of intimidation, of more or less simulated combat, etc. and which within the group determines the respective places and rights of the dominant males, marginal males, females, and the young. Ethologists stress that quarrels resulting from this internal regulation must be carefully distinguished from external territorial quarrels. As Eib Eibesfeldt writes, from whom we borrow this example,[21] *"quarrels of hierarchical order are not bound to territorial possession"* because, in effect, "in territorial defense, most often rivals of different hierarchical ranks are united in common action against foreign invaders."

—the second concerns the *collective defense of the territory.* Certain baboon males are posted as sentinels along the periphery of the group with their backs turned, each of them ostensibly exhibiting their very colored sexual organs (sometimes with the approach of an intruder their penis becomes erect and is rhythmically animated). But it has been observed that this collective behavior only functions with regard to the neighboring troops of the *same species.*

—the third concerns an *individual behavior of flight* in the case where predators emerge: "each of them recovers its freedom and

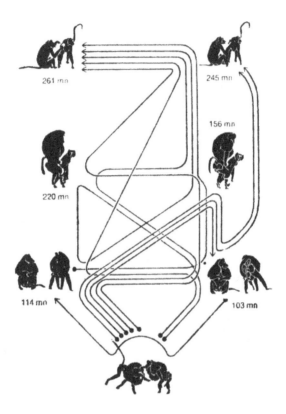

breaks rank as unobtrusively as possible." In sum, it is the inverse
question of the preceding assemblages.

Thus, there is a collective mode of semiotization of the defense
of the territory interconnected with "original," intrinsic sexual components and a field of inter-assemblage faciality-corporeality (we
know in particular the decisive role of the release mechanism of
aggression or submission which in monkeys is played out through
looking or being looked at in the eyes).[22] In other species, other
"formulas" will show us an inversion of this sex-aggression connection
in which the simulation of aggression replaces a ritual component of
seduction. In any case, we can already draw from this example,

against the functionalist's dogmatic good sense, that there are cases where the penis does not relate in a univocal fashion to a stratum of the organism and to a function of reproduction, nor does the hostile grimace always relate to a social tension. Let us underline that the sex organ—in reality the *image* of sex organs—only intervenes as a means of intimidation in the assemblages of spatial delimitation internal to the species (while in sum constituting a "social space") and that the predator/species faciality-corporeality differential proper only intervenes as components of passage rather than in well determined situations. Thus they should not be considered as "partial objects" in the Kleinian sense or as *objets "a"* in the Lacanian sense, but merely as operators, as concrete machines contributing to the collective and individual semiotization *of a certain exterior.* Here they are only points, tunnels of deterritorialization that articulate particular assemblages of internal hierarchy and collective defense (the external delimitation of a territory, the border beyond which there is a cessation of collective semiotization and the black hole effect) as well as diverse individuated assemblages like those of flight.

Adherence to specific silhouette and faciality-corporeality traits is inseparable from belonging to an ethological territory. The image imprint of a group or species member (or the accidental imprint of an intrusive "faciality") in the course of a sensitive period should not be dissociated and opposed to the various modes of apprenticeship with which it is associated, as this is the case with experimental protocols that disorganize the integration of behavioral components.[23] A study endeavoring not to crush the rhizome of socio-biological assemblages would result in speaking of "imprint choices" coexisting with "genetic choices," "choices of apprenticeship," and "choices of experimentation." Until now, fortunately ethologists have not fallen within the trajectory of the majority of ethnologists who cut out their "terrain" in tight sections (parental relations, analysis of myths, politics, economics, etc.). And whatever psychoanalytic tendencies they might have among them (particularly in the domain of the imprint, which they sometimes compare to the "infantile fixations" of Freudian psychogenesis), the idea of a signifying structuralism accounting for all behaviors has not yet been constructed (indeed, we can imagine the strong "interpretation," for example, of the behavior in monkeys called "rage copulation," in terms of more or less repressed homosexual impulses). But until now, the facts in this domain have not been submerged in the theories, and yet it is on the same rhizome of innateness, imprint, apprenticeship, and individual initiatives that we admit that complex behaviors are inscribed, such as in nuptial parades where sexual and rival struggles obviously take part in the same economy of desire and cannot thus be separated into distinct impulses.[24] Therefore, it should not have been so paradoxical to want to articulate within the same "rhizome of choices" components relevant to fields seemingly as heterogeneous as:

—that of the individual with its biological rhythms, its reflexes, its conditionings, its improvisations, its dysfunctions…

—that of the group with its collective devices, its rituals, its ecological regulations, its modes of apprenticeship and initiation…

—that of the species with its mutations and genetic spirals, its techniques of delimitation,[25] its symbolic attachments, etc.

What kind of scandals would arise in affirming that a finality, that an abstract machinism, that a "thought," if you will, governs the evolution of every branch of the animal phylum? Admittedly, not an individually arranged thought, but a thought with "n" dimensions where everything starts to think at the same time, individuals as well as groups, the "chemical" as well as the "chromosomal" or the biosphere. While surmounting many methodological aversions, certain primatologists faced with these kinds of rhizomatic questions are today led to "harrowing revisions." For example, when they manage, while accounting for observational facts, to consider on the scale of the entire species the existence of "altruistic behaviors" in primates, these behaviors become manifest through a sacrifice where the individual "renounces" his own chances to the profit of those of a relative.[26] With "molar" causalities—involving individuals and well delimited functions—the molecular phylum is thus found traversing individuals, species, and milieus.

The question of freedom should not simply concern the domain of the spirit, i.e. that of a semiotization claiming to be independent of material things. Considered independently of the rhizomatic, inter-assemblage play that we evoked earlier, this question is devoid of sense. A certain kind of freedom and even grace exists on the level of the nervous or digestive system. On the contrary, we justifiably notice these systems when their operations are out of order, producing tics, grumblings, stomach pains... A semiotization entrusted to a genetic or automated regulation via a harmonious apprenticeship undoubtedly has advantages over a semiotization that is seemingly conscious and free, yet prone to anguished interrogations or spontaneous blockages preying upon every part of the intentional arcs. Freedom is not created with subjectivity! True "machinic freedom" only starts the moment when annoying or uninteresting things can be made "like themselves" and when, without falling into a generalized and blind automatism, we become able to focus our capacities for life and expression into what moves, what creates, what changes the world and humanity, in other words, into individual or collective choices of desire. The opposition between a pure, signifying, individuated, and culpable subjectivity and a collective, biologico-economic destiny over which consciousness—including social and machinic consciousness—would have to take control is not tenable. The same can be said of the dilemma between freedom and the innate. All these Manichean breaks in the last analysis arise from power formations that use them to divide creative assemblages. Neither absolute deterritorialization of pure self-awareness, nor the automatism of an ant colony: freedom consists in the give and take of quanta of deterritorialization emitted by refrains, facialities, etc. and carried by the *ensemble* of the components of an assemblage, whether these quanta be material or libidinal, individual or group-oriented, private or public... By thus negotiating their free valences, their degrees of freedom relative to times, spaces, the most diverse intensities, and inter-assemblage "optional subjects," refrains and faciality constitute themselves in the privileged places of micropolitical confrontations. We cannot stress enough that these mobilize every molar, molecular, and abstract consistency, whatever its degree of semiotic efficiency. Nothing is played out in advance! The general laws that appear to arise from universal causalities never reign at the local, regional level where their incidence always remains partial and delimited. An intelligence and even a sort of cosmic consciousness can thus preside over the choices orienting the developments of a species. Conversely, a blind and catastrophic fear can seize the most developed human society and lead it to set up systems of subjection and enslavement bringing it closer to societies of hymenoptera (production for production's sake, systematic segregation, generalized gulags...).[27]

The obsessive prudence of researchers who above all dread falling into paradoxes that would lead them to mix "spirit" and "matter" is not simply due to the artificial survival of a whole mess of archaic quarrels. In my view, it conceals a completely essential, political issue. For example, Tinbergen's anthropocentric conceptions regarding a hierarchy of behaviors to me seem to reflect a certain vision of the organization of the socius; they establish a choice concerning the good behavior (the good politics) of animal and human assemblages. They are neither more nor less serious than any other ideology, being situated at their antipode, relative to sexual impulse, transcendental meditation, breathing methods, etc., but they at least have the merit, in spite of their approximations and their confusions, of posing the essential questions concerning more sophisticated methods of non-oppressive semiotic enslavement.[28] The political issue subjacent to these questions appears to us to be the following: is it conceivable that a highly differentiated structuration of behaviors and the socius is not necessarily correlative to a constraint of individuals to oppressive hierarchies and a methodical flattening of their spaces of freedom?

The Refrain of the Blade of Grass

In a certain number of bird species (sparrows, web-footed birds, wading-birds, etc.), the presentation of a blade of grass (or thatch or algae) from the male to the female as an homage appears to play a specific role in the chain of behavioral sequences of the nuptial parade. Example: the mottled diamond. The male sings and dances to attract the female's attention, draws itself up on a branch and, while balancing, holds up a blade of grass in its beak. Then he imitates the characteristic position of the young of his species in search of food, leans his head to the side, and pretends to offer his grass blade without however releasing it.[29] This instrumentation of a grass blade, which leaves little place for improvisation, finds its place in this study insofar as it appears to us to implement a *semiotic index* inscribed upon two registers:

—that of the chain of behavioral sequences;

—that of the bird's silhouette which functions here as an equivalent of faciality.

In humans, ethologists have shed light upon what they call "flirtatious behaviors" and "welcoming behaviors" expressed through extremely fast mimicry (whose details can be grasped only with a slow-motion film) and whose encoding is most probably hereditary.[30]

The ritual of the grass blade in birds obviously does not concern the same components of expression as those of flirting and welcoming in humans. But it seems to me interesting to compare the means producing the *detachment* of semiotic indices assuming similar functions. The human face articulates traits, while the bird forges external signs-tools.[31] This supposes the existence of quite different matters of expression. The heads of birds have not been innervated, deterritorialized like human faces.[32] But such a comparison has interest only insofar as it is admitted as a hypothesis that assemblages of faciality necessarily "precede" the existence of animal mouths and human faces, in other words that the expressive machines "precede" the means of expression (free so that these means interact in turn upon the machinisms in question). The ensemble of the elements of the expressive complexity of human faciality is thus produced, in my opinion, from the same abstract machinism which tends primarily:

1. toward the centralization[33] and the setting in reference on a specific semiotics of non-verbal faciality traits of expression (gestures, postures, attitudes, etc.);

2. toward the "mental" territorialization of effects of linguistic meaning on icons attached to faciality-types.

It is here that by itself this comparison finds its limit. A specific analysis of every assemblage would lead, in effect, to "drawing" our blade of grass far from deictic functions on the side of ecological niches, and to constructing human faciality from the dimension of semiological redundancies characteristic of particular social formations. It would be far too easy to interpret the blade of grass and faciality traits starting from the same psychoanalytical algorithms: phallus, unary feature, bar of castration... (not to mention the partial and transitional objects which are a little outdated today). Contrary to what psychoanalysts with their stereotyped interpretations may claim, it is by "crossing" the differences, i.e. by leading an effective analysis, that we can hope to shed light upon the existence of uncommon abstract machinisms—unlike "complexes," they would belong to no one—which take part in the same processes of deterritorialization, the same adaptive lines of flight, the same types of semiotic solutions. We are thus at a crossroads here. This grass blade, barring the silhouette of a bird, can be put to the service of an animal "becoming-human" by showing us that signs and tools do not merely belong to our own societies after all, along with that of a human "becoming-animal" while enabling us to discover that many seemingly deliberate behaviors actually relate to an ethological montage. In order to try to clarify this latter path and to shed some light upon the "machinic sense" of this ritual of the grass blade, we shall be led in the continuation of this chapter to survey a few phylogenetic landmarks relating to it. Ethologists explain that it is a question of an archaic "residue" referring to a nesting activity. But what does this term "residue" mean? What does it concern, leftover waste, an epiphenomenon, an artifact, or a partial function of representation, a stimulus, a reflex? Rather than the signal or sign, here we would like to speak of concrete machines (machinic indexes or diagrammatic operators) working within machinic assemblages without necessarily returning to the hierarchical systems of reflexive arcs, signifying structures, or explicit assemblages of enunciation. What should be accounted for are not universal topics whose applications would have to "localize" contingent singularities, but a "machinics" bringing into play components very different from one another (hereditary, acquired, improvised...), whose crystallization would escape any general formula. One could object that we displace the problem of "universals" by postulating a universal deterritorialization instead of a rational evolution. But the difference resides in the fact that this deterritorialization does not concern an order "in general," for it does not partake in a progress inscribed in the order of things.[34] The semiotics of the grass blade results from a "purification," from a deterritorialization, from a territorialized nesting behavior. I believe to be able to show that this local deterritorialization led to the "consequence" of a change in the abstract formula which articulates on a much larger level, in the species considered, the modes of semiotization of the territory and those of sexuality. However, this change does not as such involve a "political" progress of the species or a release of desire from the individuals who compose it. Let me repeat that abstraction and deterritorialization are not synonymous with a dialectical transformation "surmounting" the residues; they always remain attached to semiotic asperities, archaisms, stratifications resulting from the interactions between phylogeny and ontogeny, to the ecological and historical "accidents" that *specify* them without however irreversibly attaching them to a context or an evolution pursuing a majestic trajectory. This is particularly obvious for what we could call the abstract mechanization of "increasing-sociability." It implies, as we suggested with the example of finches, a deterritorialization of certain components. But it will be quite difficult to associate such an evolution with any "progress" of the species. Furthermore, this does not mean that we must definitively give up any appreciation concerning machinic progress related to inter-assemblage transformations. Certainly there objectively exists a multitude of undecidable cases, in particular when behavioral stratifications are presented in the form of residues "in waiting." In any event, "progress" does not maintain a univocal relationship with one machinic formula over another. If it exists, it is on the level of the ensemble of a rhizomatic process. It is political and not normative; in other words, it does not concern transcendent criteria (example: individual freedom which is obviously lacking in ants); it must be appreciated according to the expansion of the assemblages' rhizome, the vitality of its creative lines of flight, the elegance of its solutions— to speak like mathematicians—and since I definitively gave up avoiding the charges of idealism, I will also add according to a grace and beauty which are not merely sensible through human eyes.

The semiotics of the grass blade for birds, like that of faciality in humans, does not simply have a function of *representation*, impulse, or inhibition. With other less "spectacular" components in the rhizome of assemblages (hormonal investments—I shall return to this in connection with refrains in birds—emotional investments, perceptive investments, and also "political" investments on the level of the territory and the species) it works directly within the semiotization of a world, within the *production* of a lifestyle. To illustrate the non-representative, asignifying, diagrammatic aspect of this component, let us now examine two series of examples: the first captured in widely different bird species, the second among the varieties of an antiquated species of finches. This list, in spite of its inevitably superficial character, should enable us to open the machinics of the grass blade—i.e. the deterritorialization of a certain type of nesting assemblage—in two directions:

—that of a transformation of the modes of the semiotization of the *territory* in "advanced" species towards the development of gregariousness and the intensification of social life;

—that of a transformation of the role of specific *refrains* which, as they become less territorial, tend to subordinate the most "intimate" assemblages, like those of courting rituals, or tend to even be erased on behalf of solitary performances "for pleasure."

In a word, we shall see this refrain of the grass blade produce an enlargement of the rhizome in two directions: one toward the socius and one toward individuation.

First Territorial Series

In grebes, web-footed birds that live in a small society but nevertheless have a very strict conception of territorial defense, the male constructs a floating nest in collaboration with a female during mating season. The courting ritual, which depends entirely upon this activity, is punctuated by a face-to-face intimidation succeeded by simulated excremental activity and offerings of plant debris. The fact that the latter behavior is "still" not very ritualized can be compared with the relatively slight degree of sociability developed in this species.[35]

In grey herons, wading birds which live in small colonies (though some heronries grow up to 100 nests) and which coexist unproblematically with sparrows as well as with falcons and kite birds, the most elaborate offering ritual already exists. When a nesting place has been chosen—already constructed or about to be—if a female begins to be interested in the cries, the movements, the swaying of the neck, the pointing of the beak toward the sky, and the shagginess of the male's plumage, the male stops its attempts of seduction in order to invite his partner to participate in the construction of the nest. For this purpose, he brings her branches which she will deposit in the work in progress; but the least abrupt gesture, the slightest amount of awkwardness will be able to call everything into question and start a true battle of beaked blows.[36] We thus remain closer to reality than to the symbol here. Let us notice in passing, in order to illustrate our previous remarks on this subject, that the nuptial assemblage is not yet completely constructed upon "genetic rails"; in innate encodings and apprenticeships under the conditions of the imprint it can indeed be associated with conjunctional tactics, with improvisations at every moment.

These two examples already indicate to us certain correlations between, on the one hand:

—assemblages of the opening of the male's *Umwelt* toward the female (courting ritual);

—assemblages of the delimitation of a territory for a couple and the establishment of a protected space for its progeny;

and, on the other:

—the deterritorialization of the offering's machinic indexes;

—and a certain "disposition" for gregariousness.

In Troglodytes, which constitute one of the least sociable families of sparrows (but which are still able to be gathered by the dozen in times of great cold in order to stay warm), the activity of territorial delimitation introduces what Paul Géroudet calls a "music-box refrain," i.e. a very stereotyped song addressed as a constant warning to possible intruders. The male, after having taken possession of his territory, then arranges nests—sometimes up to a dozen. When a female arrives upon the scene, the male lowers the intensity of his song which is then reduced to nothing more than a single trill. "He brings himself to an elevated point in front of one of his nests, sings and stretches, spreads his wings and agitates his displayed tail, then enters the nest, sings while looking outside, leaves and returns several times in quick succession. The invitation is clear: if the female agrees, she will answer with a small cry, jerky bows and scrapings, and will *end up inspecting the nest.* However, the female does not always make up her mind, the nest can appear badly placed or poorly constructed to her; carrying on her way then, she impresses herself upon another male; this one in turn hastens to dedicate the same attentions to her, while the vexed neighbor is confined, by the boundary that he respects."[37] It was necessary to completely quote this description by Paul Géroudet to show the richness of the semiotic interactions of this courting assemblage which, one will have noticed, does not comprise an offering sequence. We are not "yet" within the miming of the construction of a nest, but only with the presentation of a completely built nest. The courting assemblage and that of territorialization remain autonomous compared to one another. But what in my view especially seems to have to be retained in this example is the role of the refrain's *components of passage.* And that with a double meaning because in fact it partakes here in two successive phases of the assemblages, and, by doing so, it perhaps "announces" an additional degree of deterritorialization which will lead to a more pronounced automation of vocal semiotics and to its subjective internalization via a more individuated mode.

Second Series: the Refrain of Australian Finches

In a general fashion, it is considered that finches (pinsons) occupy a unique place in the finch (fringilles) family. In fact they unite with a species that is relatively more "territorialized" than this family which, by contrast, is perhaps the most social of those constituting the sparrow order. Unlike other finches—canaries, bullfinches, etc.—Australian finches only live in bands rather than an annual group; depending on the period of reproduction, components of territorialization are automated and imposed upon components of sociability. Curiously, it seems that the male finch then defends his "district" more ferociously than he would outside this assemblage of sexual territorialization where he abandons himself to an unrestrained gregariousness.[38] The Australian finches studied by K. Immelmann and M.F. Hall allow us to follow the evolution of the blade of grass ritual through the behavioral vestiges that are solidified throughout the entire gamut of the species and constitute, in some way, a series of "living fossils."

In the Bathilda and Aegintha genera, the males can only court a female without effectively holding a piece of thatch in their beak. By contrast, they do nothing but mimic the construction of the nest.

In the Neochimia genus: same scenario, but the male utilizes another material than what is used when it effectively constructs the nest. The semiotization of the offering has thus become automated.

In the Aidemosyne genus, the male only utilizes a blade of grass in the initial courting phases.

In the Lonchura genus, it is only when it has decided to perform the courting ritual that it sometimes carries a blade of grass.

In the Emblema genus, the male picks at some blades of grass, but he does not carry them.

In the Poephila genus, the courting ritual with a blade of grass only appears occasionally and above all in young males.

Parallel to this movement of deterritorialization traversing the evolution of Australian finches and conferring an increasingly symbolic character to the grass blade offering (to the point of making every visible manifestation concerning it disappear), we shall return to the emergence of another type of transformation now concerning components of refrains properly speaking. Eibl Eibesfeldt writes on this subject that "beginning from the transportation of material for the construction of the nest, actions employing the blade of grass are developed in the males; in certain species, the latter have become more and more rudimentary; at the same time, the song of these birds, which primitively serves to delimit the territory, undergoes a change of function when these birds become very sociable. In replacement for the courting ritual of offering the blade of grass, the males sing very softly close to the female."[39]

Genetic Codes, Imprint, Apprenticeship, Improvisation…

We have tried to show that the components of a behavioral assemblage never simply put forms and quantities of differentiation into question. Matters of expression do not play a passive role by filling in a semiotic formalism or transmission channel in the sense that information theory bestows upon it. Through the bias of concrete machinisms, such as faciality and refrains, they actively participate according to all sorts of modalities, catalyses, "choices of rhythm," stratifications, lines of flight… They are "inhabited" by abstract machinisms that "opt" in favor of one connection over another. If some of their specific traits are left aside, they can be called to play a role on the first level due to a new connection. A refrain that has remained "in reserve," territorialized, will take on, for example, as we have seen, an essential diagrammatic function for the development of the sociality of the species. Here analysis can no longer rely upon general systems of correspondence and universal algorithms; these keep it from being applied to grasping irreducible material traits, liberating molecular quanta of deterritorialization, transgressing thresholds of viscosity, mobilizing black hole effects and effects of rupture, deploying scansions, cadences, redundancies proper to the diverse biological, social, and machinic strata set in play. From the moment we are placed in the perspective of concrete machinic assemblages duly situated within the cosmos, history, and the socius, it becomes necessary to abandon the massive, amorphous form-matter opposition on behalf of a deterritorialization working within both forms and matters while generating deterritorializing forms and deforming matters. Certainly, we can always account for quantities of movement and translation of forms on the basis of "purified" spatio-temporal coordinates. But the capture of intensities, mutations, and regimes of deterritorialization invoke the intervention of other coordinates of existential consistency. What characterizes components of passage like faciality and refrains is the fact that they work simultaneously within standardization and within deterritorialization, within form, substance, and matter, and that they enable passing from one assemblage to another. They do not belong to space and time "in general"; they effectuate particular spaces and times.

Because of their own "material" characteristics, the silhouette and refrain traits in birds, even when they assume similar functions within assemblages such as those of courting rituals, still do not maintain the same type of relation with the process of deterritorialization that traverses the former and the latter. Silhouette traits appear to be "maintained" by a phylogenetic deterritorialization conveying nest-building components and offering rituals while tending to be erased on behalf of an indexical semiotization integrated into the other semiotic components (dance, posture, etc.). Here deterritorialization has brought about the dissolution of an autonomous assemblage which was quite plastic from the beginning, which "stuck" to the territorialities of the species pertaining to it, and which constituted a sort of cornerstone of extremely heterogeneous components (morphological, iconic, mimetic, postural, etc.) from a great variety of "tools" and procedures (blade of grass, branch, seaweed, offering of fish, etc.).[40] This happens in the exact opposite direction with the song component in birds. The component, at the "origin," is also territorial; but to the extent that it is territorialized, it is refined, specified, and automated. It has come to play an entirely particular role in processes of evolutionary selection, because it can be considered in certain sparrows, for example, that the emergence of new "dialects" has consequently led to an "ethological isolation" for certain populations and the emission of new species.[41]

The behavioral "catalytic" function of bird songs, besides the fact that it articulates intra-specific refrains—centralized on the territory or the courting ritual—can also return to a much less specific system of alarmed cries. For example, when finches are flown over by predator birds, they will begin to emit calls perfectly resembling those of the other bird species who in addition will not fail to profit from the information if they are found within the vicinity. The mobilization of these slightly differentiated cries is very progressive: it seems "designed" in a way so as not to allow the predator to establish binaural comparisons to help it locate the birds emitting the song (territorial songs or courting songs, different for each species due to narrow frequency variations, are on the contrary easy to localize). The finches' song functions thus on a double register of alarm and territorial frequency-jamming or of specification and localization. It also lends itself to combinations that make of it a sort of asignifying, behavioral language. We have seen that the Troglodyte, in passing from a territorial behavior to a courting behavior, could inflect its refrains—based on intensity, reducing it to a trill—this change of course constituting a system of signalization and mobilization within the same component. We have also seen, this time on a phylogenetic plane, the refrain being substituted in Australian finches for systems of offering. Does this mean that the most deterritorialized component—here, that of the song—tends to be imposed within the rhizome of assemblages? This is what seems to confirm for us Tinbergen's description of courting behavior in the Albatross, whose very specific scenario is almost "crowned" by a song component,[42] or Lorentz's description of grey gooses, where there is also found this same sort of "cry of triumph" in the conclusion of the courting ritual that marks the neutralization of aggressive components and the establishment of a "defensive community" at the level of the couple.[43]

The ritualization of a behavioral assemblage is not synonymous with automation. A semiotization can become machinal without being mechanical for all that. Some approximations, variants, lines of flight, and black hole effects always remain possible. We have evoked the nuptial examinations lacking in Troglodytes or nest-keeping scenes in Storks, but it would also be convenient to include a few "gratuitous acts" like the titmouse's imitation of the vulture song[44] or the unmistakable cackle of a starling at the height of its excitation which, having a real talent for imitation, caricatures in full the songs of blackbirds, orioles, and even farmyard animals.[45] And what should we make of the exhibitionism of the nightingale, which leads it to be dangerously exposed to predators while elevating itself five or six meters off the ground in order to give its extraordinary vocal performance its maximum range?[46] However, this ritualization is no longer synonymous with the appearance of "non-deterministic" components, even in the case where this ritualization emphasizes over-deterritorialized components, like those of bird songs (and, for humans, like that of speech and religious ritualizations). Still, let us borrow a few examples from ethology in order to illustrate this dependence, or rather this system of rhizomatic co-relations between the genetically coded components and components of imprint, apprenticeship, individual initiative... Let us first of all return to our example of the mottled diamond, which, one will recall, associates a "grass blade" component and a "return to childhood" component in the courting ritual. To arrange its territory, it also resorts to two other semiotic components in order to distance the other males: a visual component—a brightly colored plumage[47]—and an auditory component—a stereotyped refrain. But the acquisition of this refrain in young Diamonds is through *apprenticeship* near their relatives. In the case where one of them is raised in a family of striated Munie (which ornithologists call Capucin), it is then the song of its adoptive father which is learned.[48] Since this apprenticeship is initiated during a so-called "sensitive" period a long time before the young bird is able to sing effectively at all, it is advisable to distinguish between a phase of purely auditory semiotization (by "imprint") and a phase of active, phonic semiotization. Moreover, "behind" these two components, other biological components of a completely different nature stand out, as in the fact that a diamond female that "normally" does not have a territorial song acquires one as soon as hormones of the male sex are administered to her. She then reproduces the song of the species with which she has been "impregnated" at the time of the "sensitive period" of the first 35 days of her life.[49]

Therefore, because a component like the refrain is more deterritorialized than the others by no means implies that it has distanced itself from the most "deterministic" components, like those of apprenticeships through imprint or endocrinal transformations. It is perhaps even correct to expect that to the extent that a component deterritorializes, it becomes more "in touch" with the most molecular levels of behavior and life itself. There is no doubt, for example in humans, that linguistic semiotics, parallel to their function of magical conjuration and social subjection, has contributed to a new kind of assemblage of an instrumental and machinic "total-power" over our own behavior, our environment, and other living species. The continuous escalades of deterritorialization, which this unraveling of a "mechanosphere" represents on the biological, linguistic, and social orders, has taken on such an importance that, without it, the survival of humans would be inconceivable today. (In particular, on a biological level, the humans of industrial societies only "hold up" due to their capacity to artificially discernibilize, semiotize, and dia-grammatize the pathogenic agents that attack them.) But what is it on the relatively elementary level, where we have remained until now, within semiotic components like that of refrains in birds? We cannot insist enough on the fact that, even in such a domain, the relations established between biological components and semiotic components do not function in one way. We shall better grasp the complexity of this type of relation by examining a graph like that which R. Hinde proposes in order to account for the interactions between the various factors intervening in the canary's reproductive cycle. With the canary alone, this brings into play:

—physical components, like the length of day and the degree of sunlight;

—biological and morphological components, production of hormones, growth of the gonads, incubating plates, the oviduct, etc.

—perceptive components, iconic "stimuli" emitted by the image of the male and his changes in attitude;

—individuated behavioral assemblages, such as those of laying eggs and social ones, such as those of courting, nest-building, etc.

This author thus explains in four points the "principles" governing these rhizomatic relations:

1. The causes and consequences of sexual behavior are narrowly tied to those of the construction of the nest and *cannot be considered separately*.

2. External stimuli (male, nest) create endocrinal modifications whose effects *are added* to those of these factors.

3. The production of hormones is submitted to *various controls*.

4. Hormones have *multiple effects*.

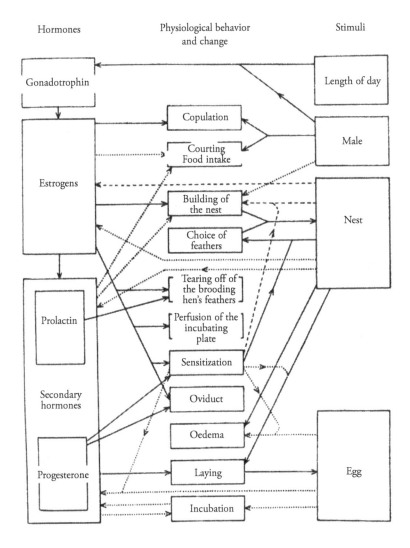

Hormones — Physiological behavior and change — Stimuli

Gonadotrophin

Estrogens

Prolactin

Secondary hormones

Progesterone

Copulation

Courting
Food intake

Building of
the nest

Choice of
feathers

Tearing off of
the brooding
hen's feathers

Perfusion of the
incubating
plate

Sensitization

Oviduct

Oedema

Laying

Incubation

Length of day

Male

Nest

Egg

(The bold lines of the schema indicate the facilitative influences: the indented lines are inhibitive influences and the dotted lines are probable facilitative influences, but not proven.)[50]

The Synchrony of Rhythms and Memory

Demarcations within behavioral rhizomes between assemblages of semiotization and semiotic or encoding components are completely relative and do not imply any priority of one instance over another, nor any *a priori* hierarchy. Some assemblages are stratified, automated, and "reformed" according to the component within another assemblage, whereas some components get to "generate" and produce new assemblages. Moreover, certain hyper-stratifications can involve zones of semiotic collapse, of black holes, which in turn can become generators of over-deterritorialized lines of flight.

Thus the organization of the assemblages and components within a rhizome does not necessarily respect the existence of levels staged according to a pre-established order—for example the order of the "physical," the "chemical," the "biological," the "semiotic..." Some "transversals" connect the "most social" with the "most biological" or the "most ecological" in the animal order. But wouldn't this nonarborescent disposition be "doubled" by this less visible hierarchy, now no longer concerning assemblages and components, but even the texture of the latter, what we have called, following glossematicians: material traits of expression and encoding? Does social faciality, which we are tempted to classify among collective micro-Agencies and which comes to express the delimitations of power between the "acceptable" and the "licit" while being responsible for globally memorizing the "graphs" of binary choices conveyed by the dominant significations,[51] rest upon the innate faciality traits that ethologists of behavior currently study in the last analysis?[52] There is a similar problem in a domain relating to the synchronization of the ensemble of semiotic components: that of memory or *memories*, to be more exact. What relation do conscious memories, if not free memories at least deliberating ones, maintain with involuntary memories (Marcel Proust's searches), unconscious memories, and organic memories? For their part, psychophysiologists distinguish a long-term memory from a short-term memory, which stores information only for several dozen seconds, both of which are tributaries in the register of perception of a sensorial memory which stores information for only 2 to 3 tenths of a second. There's no reason to stop halfway and not support this sensorial memory upon a neuro-biological memory, molecular memory, etc. At the end of this "descent" towards increasingly constraining orders, how will we go up towards the "surface" of the memories in a "free state"? A scientistic refusal to admit that the most deterritorialized existents such as faciality, refrains, ideational processes, and abstract machines are as "in contact" with reality as *visibly* material processes, leads to the construction of systems of linear and dualistic causality, without any foundation, going from the chemical *towards* life, from matter *towards* spirit, etc. It is incontestable that components of refrains and faciality have "something to do" with the brain. (They can even be localized approximately alongside other, mainly visual and tactile components of memory, in the left anterior part of the temporal lobe, in "opposition" to the components of discursive memory intervening in language, which are "localized" towards the right side of the same lobe.[53] In fact, nothing authorizes postulating the existence of stronger interactions in a direction going from molar memories towards molecular memories rather than in the opposite direction!)

Biological assemblages depend on psychological and social assemblages as much as the latter depend on the former. Thus there is nothing "antiscientific" in putting forth the hypothesis that hyper-deterritorialized components concerning imagination, faciality, music, etc. are not only able to modify the social field, but also bodies, metabolisms, and cerebral connections! It is also good that a number of ethological researchers are oriented in this way, thus demonstrating that this science is perhaps about to abandon its childhood illnesses (taxonomism, reflexologism, behaviorism, neo-vitalism, etc.).

We are constantly brought back to the same interrogation: what holds the assemblages and their heterogeneous components together? A transcendent hierarchy of spatio-temporal forms, a support of physicochemical effects, or the contingent construction of certain components that "take on" specialized functions of transcoding and deterritorialization (what we have called "components of passage" or "diagrammatic components")? Behind our interrogation on refrains there is the question of the synchronization of biological rhythms which, before leading to the constitution of a new science—chrono-biology—has given rise to innumerable metaphysical developments. For example, Ludwig Klages, one of the founders of graphology, tried to establish an opposition between a vital rhythm in contrast with more cultural cadences. He considered that humans were only able to assemble elementary rhythms in free spatial and temporal cadences. He wrote: "Life is expressed in rhythm: Spirit, on the other hand, through means of metric cadences, forces life's rhythmic impulse to yield to the law which is proper to it."[54] But chronobi-ology, rather than seeking to "attach" trans-rhythmicity upon spirit and culture, endeavored, on the contrary, to derive it from a com-position of basic molecular rhythms. Thus it currently considers that circadian rhythms[55] would result from the generalized cou-pling—with an inhibiting effect—of what A. Reinberg calls a *population of molecular oscillators*.[56] It is significant that we find here such a problematics of "molecular packs," the same type we evoked in connection with "neuron populations" upon which memory would be based.

This "logic of packs" should in theory help us disentangle ourselves from formal categories like Life, Spirit, and Matter. But will it for all that enable us to advance on a problem like what Klages posed in connection with the articulation between vital rhythms and the most complex "cadences"? The fact that heterogeneous assemblages are "traversed" by the same type of molecular elements—for example, infra-biological molecular rhythms—indicates to us the existence of systems of interaction that function according to the machinic lines specific to different components. But here we continue to leave the "basic," the least differentiated, in order to "reascend" toward complex compositions. We will hardly be enlightened about what enables a qualitative differentiation to appear or a mutant assemblage that has the characteristic of selecting on its own the components and matters of expression compatible with its machinic choices. Components of passages cannot be simple effects of transition, simple statistical reversals bearing upon molecular populations. They are the bearers of diagrammatic keys concealed by the abstract consistency of machinic nuclei. It is through these components of passage that possible worlds and real worlds clash and proliferate.

To illustrate these types of problems, let us borrow one last example from bird ethology. W.H. Thorpe managed, during his study on the finch's refrain, to distinguish in its internal organization two types of rhythmic and melodic levels: that which relates to the basic vocal material (sub-song) and that which relates to a certain "end" of its structure, which makes it possible to differentiate the song into three stanzas and articulate them in a given order (true-song).[57] This distinction is far from redividing that of Klages between vital elementary rhythms and socialized cadences. Here the basic material is indeed already extremely elaborate on a "musical" plane and it is impossible, moreover, to distinguish in it what would arise from a social programming. Raised in isolation, young finches spontaneously find the number and the length of the syllables of the basic stanzas; in addition they have a sort of "recipe" for learning, or more precisely, as Thorpe relates it, for *selecting the melodies* they have to imitate. (If they are given several song recordings to choose from during their sensitive period, they will retain those which most resemble the typical song of their species by the quality of the tone and the form of the stanzas.) On the other hand, certain elements of organization, like the three basic stanzas' order of presentation, only pertain to a social apprenticeship. Let us announce moreover that a part is also left to improvisation and competition, since, as Thorpe notices, the details of the final phrase with their ornaments are apparently not learned, but "worked out" with other members of the group ("worked out by competitive singing"). Here the diagrammatic expression of the encodings thus finds its way only through a constant entanglement involving heredity, apprenticeship, experimentation, and improvisation. And we can see, starting from this example, that what "passes" from one assemblage to another are not simply basic materials or universal designs but highly differentiated forms, deterritorialized keys opening and closing again a territory or a species onto a particular machinic politics.

6

Reference Points for a Schizoanalysis

Molar and Molecular Existential Micropolitics

The unconscious is constituted by machinic propositions that no semiological or logico-scientific propositions can ever grasp in an exhaustive fashion. Moreover, borrowings from the discourse of the sciences, used in an attempt to define it, are often facilities that cannot guard a theory against the risk of reproducing reductionist references. Form, structure, signifier, and system[1] never cease shifting with one another in the attempt to arbitrate the ancient Manichean struggle opposing a pure subject and a pure, amorphous matter which, in addition, has become imaginary compared with contemporary scientific research. Concepts must be folded onto realities, not the other way around. Certain distinctions that seem relevant in a given context can function elsewhere as concepts that binarize the assemblages while arborifying the problems. In particular, this may be the case with the distinction that I myself advanced faciality—that of signifying faciality traits. There is also a "mechanical," molecular faciality—that of ethology—and a molecular faciality that transmutes the coordinates of perception and desire (akin to between the molar levels and the molecular levels which risks, despite all the warnings, drifting towards an opposition of the *large-small, passive-active* type... It may be advisable to better specify that there is a passive, molar faciality—that of the *imago* and

49

psychoanalytic identification—and an active, molar faciality which Proust describes to us with the transformations and reduction of Albertine's face, insofar as her face draws closer to the Narrator's during the scene of the first kiss). Some micro-refrains, for example on the prosodic order,[2] exist that are almost imperceptible to the ear, and there are also molecular stylistic cells that no less than "control" works in their totality, indeed even entire periods of the productive life of a poet or musician. (Example: Vinteuil's little phrase.) There is a molar virtuosity that applies itself so as to normalize a work in its technical details as well as in its conception as a whole… These diverse "politics of style" are in addition demarcated from one another, enter into rivalry, and spy upon one another from the corner of their eye: in fact, they participate in the same musical or poetic phylum.

Molar structures and molecular machinisms constantly interact. They are "piloted" either beginning with visible, stratified assemblages or beginning with "invisible powers" (*puissances*) proceeding from matters of expression which are unable to be circumscribed in well delimited substances from the point of view of explicit conceptual and spatio-temporal coordinates. In fact, all the intermediate combinations between situations dominated by statistical series and self-regulated assemblages are conceivable and, inside the same assemblage, can be confronted with antagonistic machinic options.[3]

Concrete assemblages, at least their machinic nuclei, are thus far from simply being the seat of external interactions which they passively undergo. They return to themselves on the side of abstract machinisms and the plane of consistency, and they send out beyond themselves on the side of the concrete machinic phylum that encompasses them. In other words, they neither draw their *local machinic consistency* from a macrophysical formalism nor from microphysical probabilist effects which would make them emerge, as if by magic, out of randomness.[4]

Scientific milieus generally only approach this question of organizing centers, the "self-managed" assemblages of life, thought, and the socius with much caution, even repugnance. Today we still await a full fledged return of the most reductionist theories in this domain. This is particularly the case with research being done on the systems developed in the continuation of Von Bertalanffy's works.[5] The mathematical analysis of systems as such certainly presents an undeniable interest, but this utilization seems contestable because in fact the framework of these theories reveals itself to be incapable of preserving the concrete richness of its object, in particular the attachments to micro-social assemblages.[6] The basic postulate of systemic research consists in admitting that the components of a given system must necessarily be sub-systems of the *same category* as the set to which they belong. Under these conditions, the hierarchical ordination of components stems from a "reinforcement of their defining relations" which is founded on a principle of complexity rising to the degree as ones passes from part to whole. Nevertheless, a multitude of examples encountered with this principle could illustrate the fact that the "most differentiated" can perfectly have recourse to a systemic subset, remain in waiting and in reserve, and become "functional" only under certain circumstances (chromosomal systems are "banks of the possible" which can only become productive under particular conditions of release). Can we say of such a subset that, in reality, it was not one and that it would be the richest system from the point of view of its defining relations, that from the start it constituted the key, the veritable whole, of the basic system? But the question at such a formal level loses all interest. What counts here is preserving the multiplicity and heterogeneity of all possible entries, all catastrophies, and all emergences of new points of metabolic crystallization.[7]

We can only be suspended indefinitely between Form and Chance insofar as we do not accept the idea that molecular populations as well as homeostatic forms, subjects and objects, times, spaces, substances, statements are all traversed by the same machinic optional matter, whose one side is turned toward the possible and the other toward the actualization of mutant realities. That which confers upon an assemblage the possibility of being totalizing-detotalizing—in order to borrow Sartrian terminology—can originate from a molecular choice, from an insignificant line of flight. The living nucleus of an individual, group, thought, or theory can be perfectly heterogeneous to the structure that seems to completely account for its operation. It is neither starting from phenomenological totalization, nor from symbolic structure, nor from the systemic set that real machinic life will be able to be understood.

In order not to crush and reduce the material and semiotic asperities to the same continuity, which would basically be undifferentiated[8] from a cosmic pulp, the economy of molecular choices relative to flows and codes must be able to account for the specific processes of the catalysis of assemblages. But how do we reconcile our propositions concerning:

1. The generalized interference among components, the fact that they constitute a rhizome traversing the ensemble of strata and assemblages;

2. This emergence of active machinic nuclei crystallizing around singularity points (historical, cosmic, etc.). Is there not a contradiction between this generalized crossing of components and the speciation of assemblages? The role imparted to components of passage, such as faciality and refrains, precisely consists in holding the terms of this contradiction together. It is at the heart of the "material" and "possibilist" texture of components that quanta of deterritorialization are negotiated that either enter into "normal" metabolic processes of flows and strata or into processes of mutation and crystallization of new assemblages. We thus find ourselves facing two states of relation:

Actualized flows and codes

Abstract machinic propositions

In the first, the economy of the possible is encysted in stabilized strata and assemblages; in the second on the contrary, its metabolism has become predominant. The redefinition of the levels of molar/molecular consistency in terms of an economy of machinic choice allows us to try to discern more precisely this insistence of machinic nuclei whose vocation is essentially creative, negentropic, etc. When strata and assemblages exist without machinic nuclei and function around stabilized redundancies or black hole effects, I will say that they arise from a *molar existential politics*. When assemblages or inter-assemblage systems interact with machinic nuclei—which are not necessarily centered on an assemblage—I will speak of *molecular existential politics*. The molar is "visible" repetition in systems of fixed coordinates. The molecular "makes the difference" for the machinic plane of consistency of possibles. It returns to the micropolitical play of the components of passage constitutive of machinic nuclei, opting for such or such evolutionary line, delimiting the processes of speciation and stratification, fixing the kinds of singularity points, freeing new quanta of possible, launching new assemblages and arranging their specific universe... It is at this level that it appears legitimate to me to maintain the molar/molecular articulation. It has less to do with a systemic inter-component than with the metabolism proper to machinic nuclei. We are witnessing a threshold phenomenon concerning the abstract consistency of the possible. Beyond a certain intensity, a certain acceleration, a certain threshold of consistency, machinic deterritorialization crosses the network of actualized flows, codes, and stratifications. What does not signify is abolished. It is crystallized in another universe which traverses all visible universes in time and space. A matter of the possible subverts and uproots the old coordinates while launching new machinic propositions. Here the essential point is to refuse any absolute break between the economy of the possible and material economy. Historical and cosmic singularities can only be preserved on this condition. Stratified law and the singular never cease interacting. The intercrossing between material assemblages, assemblages of biological encoding, assemblages of semiotic enunciation, and real or possible machinic assemblages is such that, outside local situations and on a precarious basis, it no longer makes it possible to found a transcendent system of law that would "cover" all laws and singularities.

Here we return to a problem similar to what we encountered when it was a question of rebinding the pragmatic transformations and generations onto a sort of molecular point under the same title of "optional matter." This generation/transformation relation seems in my view at present to be a particular case of the molar/molecular relation. The difference is that we no longer come to the politics of machinic choices from the point of view of assemblages of enunciation marked in one way or another by human components, but from the point of view of the things themselves, so to speak. Metaphysics or metasemiotics, it matters little what name it is given, but I see no reason to refuse the existence of the equivalent of a subjectivity or a proto-subjectivity in living and material assemblages. This molecular economy of choices is not reducible to a microphyiscs of passive elementary entities. Freud botched his brilliant intuition concerning the existence of an unconscious subjectivity by seeking to found it on thermodynamic analogies in a way that radically opposes a sphere of differentiated order and a primary sphere of undifferentiated energetic matter.[9] For the machinic unconscious, consciousness and inhibition are just figurative cases. Inhibition can be the source of disorder and the dream the source of order. And this can happen on a scale larger, as we have already said, than that which is played out by molecular options. On the contrary, some stratifications can be catalyzed on a microphysical level. On the other hand, a molar centering—through redundancy and/or black hole effect—can be installed on a molecular machinics which it holds back but which could resurface. Let me add to this that a rhizomatic molecular assemblage can be the vehicle for "molar plates" without consequently being condemned to fall into a politics of generalized stratification.

Molar and molecular consistencies install themselves in relation to one another without any discontinuity. Their fundamental dissymmetry does not bear upon their means or objects, but their ends. Molar politics is the degree zero of molecular politics; it leads to rigidity or to the black hole. But is there thus not a risk beginning from a proto-enunciation, from a proto-politics at the level of the living and the inanimate? Under the guise of making the observer and the observed communicate—to the point of compromising this distinction itself—and proposing a model of the machinic unconscious which encompasses the most diverse components, am I not about to predict a generalized invasion of the scientific field by "micropolitics" and the "subjective?" Rather than projecting "spirit" onto visible entities in the manner of traditional idealism, am I not simply miniaturizing it in order to attempt to introduce it even at the level of atomic nuclei? To this I will respond that the question is not one of knowing "if spirit clarifies matter," but on the contrary to seek to understand the operation of human subjectivity via the light of the machinisms of molecular choices, such as we can see them at work on all stages of the cosmos. The subjectivity in question here has nothing to do with a speech that inhabits the world, with a transcendental and symbolic formalism that would animate it for all time. Neither archetypal, nor structural, nor systemic, the unconscious such as I conceive it arises from a machinic creationism. This is why it is radically atheistic.[10]

What can we say about its freedom? Can there still be a question of freedom in universes which do not recognize deliberating subjects? What would a machinic freedom be? Everything here is a question of degree, of imperceptible threshold crossings. Some modes of discursivity, deliberation, and choice exist that do not rest on a signifying discourse between listeners and speakers. Some machinic redundancies, codings, signal-systems, and semiotics exist that are not founded on chains of phonemes, graphemes, mathemes, etc. In other words, the implementation of complex encodings can borrow from means very different than that of the individuated and conscious enunciation. Does not a genetic knowledge exist, and even a machinic consciousness, for example in the case of the enslavement of a driver to his car? Are not the blades of grass, refrains, and faces for birds but also for the passions, for human intelligence, instruments of knowledge and, on the same basis, pragmatic operators which can be, in a machine, spoken words, written words, figures, plans, equations, or informational memories? The signification of the world and the meaning of desire, as soon as we claim to seize them outside the dominant redundancies, require that we broaden the range of our semiotic recourses. A thousand machinic propositions constantly work upon each individual, under and over their speaking heads.[11] If we have stressed faciality and the refrain in the components of passage of human desire, it is because in some way they are specialized in "misconstruing" the other components, either by short-circuiting their rhizomatic connections, or by recentralizing them around black hole effects, by echoing them in relation to one another. But we have seen that these basic components of inter-individual communication were equally essential to the modes of capitalistic subjectification. It is on these components that a certain abstract perception of time and space rests and consequently a certain type of relation to the body, to work, to the socius, etc.

Through these components, the intensities of desire (the values of desire) are emptied of their substance, and the asperities of the world are reduced and arranged in accordance with the dominant norms and redundancies (coupling: use value—exchange value).[12] Thus it is absurd to claim to reduce unconscious subjectivity to a simple play of speech and symbol in the field of language.[13]

All types of human and/or non-human, collective or individuated, territorialized or deterritorialized subjectification and conscientialization coexist within biological, economic, and machinic processes... And, to be sure, each time it is not a question of the same subjectivity, of the same super-subject, of the same consciential authority which would miraculously transport messages, make decisions, and determine laws. Moreover, neither is it a question of a multitude of standard micro-subjects, localized in the brain like minuscule messengers. Components of subjectification and conscientialization result from heterogeneous modes of semiotization and never arise from a pure and universal signifying substance vis-à-vis a pure and universal matter of content. The serial production and massive exportation of the white, conscious, male adult subject has always correlated with the disciplining of intensive multiplicities which essentially escape from all centralization, from all signifying arborescence.

To finish with the dictatorship of the Cogito as an obligated reference for assemblages of enunciation and to accept that material assemblages, biological assemblages, social assemblages, etc. are capable of "machining" their own kind and creating heterogeneous complex universes: such are the conditions that will allow us to broach this question of molecular packs populating the unconscious with a minimum of theoretical assurance. An infinite amount of creative assemblages without the intervention of a supreme Creator, an infinite amount of components, indexes, lines of deterritorialization, abstract propositional machinisms: these are the objects of a new type of analysis of the unconscious. The most complex combinations are capable of emerging at the level which is believed to be that of "brute matters" or "primary matters." The libido, for example, is not in any way an undifferentiated, asocial and apolitical flux. On the contrary, the most summary, least differentiated components can generate the most elaborate, most conscious assemblages in appearance. Schizoanalysis must be ready for anything! It is not at all a question of preaching a universal free will but of enlarging our comprehension of objective constraints. We have seen that a hormonal flow can "stimulate" an unexpected competence in the refrain's matter just like a flow of DNA can transform a process of memorization or enlarge circadian rhythms: the seemingly most ridiculous, the most "unnatural" crossings and marriages are always of the order of the possible. Our astonishment in this domain arises from a lack of imagination or from a theoretical dogmatism. Everything is possible on condition that the enacted connections are compatible with a set of machinic propositions. It is not a question of universal laws, because the "assembling" of these propositions is situated and dated beginning with the assemblages and points of subjectification, because it is inseparable from machinic choices deploying the lines of a relatively irreversible machinic phylum that precisely defines the conditions of crossing "thresholds of reality."[14]

The question of freedom and the subject is posed through a completely new perspective starting from the moment when the combinatory of choices does not simply bear upon molecular populations whose forms, rhythms, energetic intensities, and affects would be reducible to universal mathemes, but instead is attached to all types of singularity points (infra- or extra-assemblage, micro- or macroscopic, topographical or functional...). Therefore, it is no longer conceivable to make of subjectivity a homogenous entity breaking with the cosmos. The nucleus converters of an assemblage are infinitely diversified and complexified according to the formulas of abstract machinisms or concrete phyla, sometimes by associating the most archaic stratifications with the most deterritorialized propositions.[15]

The subject and the machine are inseparable from one another. A degree of subjectivity enters into every material assemblage. And reciprocally, a degree of machinic enslavement enters into every subjective assemblage. The sole means of escaping from the absurdities and mistakes of contemporary idealism thus seems in our view to be to confer a machinic status onto subjectivity and to accept without reticence the existence of a proto-subjectivity, of an economy of choices, of a negentropic passion at every stage of the cosmos—and therefore, from the point zero of the expansion of the universe up to the blossoming of the most deterritorialized machinisms, such as those of poetry, music, sciences—in order to remain, for lack of something better, within terrestrial activities...

As soon as we refuse to accord human subjectivity an exceptional existential status and we accept that other instances besides living consciousness and sensibility can "attach" their essence on the side of actualized flows and codes as well as on the side of a machinics of the possible the question of the constitution of social, spiritual, affective assemblages and that of material and energetic stratifications can be posed in new terms: that it is a question there of phenomenally distinct worlds does not imply, in effect, that they are essentially separated from one another, that they do not participate in the same phyla, in the same machinic plane of consistency. There is "subjectivity" as soon as it is assembled from machines and singularity points. But any concrete grasping of a subject in act is only possible by abandoning trans-historical essences or phenomenological analyses oriented simply around molar ensembles. Being-in-itself or being-for-itself are only relatively equivalent to being-for-praxis, being-for-assemblage. Molecular subjectivity, the living, free, creative part of machinic nuclei, and the economy of the possible at its point of abundant growth on the real: such are the ultimate instances of the unconscious.

Norms and Stages

Abstract machines of the unconscious have nothing to do with the so-called "stages" which are supposed to punctuate, for example, the "development" of the child. The passage from one age of life to another does not depend upon the programmings constructed by psychologists and psychoanalysts; it is tied to the original reassemblages of different modes of encoding and semiotization whose nature and sequence cannot be determined *a priori*. The "stages" in question are not automatic: the child, as an individuated organic totality, only constitutes one intersection among the multiple material, biological, socio-economic and semiotic components which traverse it. For example, in the life of an adolescent the intrusion of the biological components of puberty is inseparable from the microsocial context within which they appear; they release a series of *machinic indexes* which have been shown, in addition, to liberate a new abstract machine that will be manifested in the most diverse registers: redirection of perceptive codes, folding of the self and/or poetic, cosmic, social externalization, etc. But this release mechanism in reality has nothing unilateral about it because other "external" semiotic components could accelerate, inhibit or reorient the effects of the biological and semiotic components of puberty. Under these conditions, where do the interactions of the social and the biological begin and end? Certainly not with a delimitation of the individual considered as an organic totality or sub-set of the familial group. The question here is posed in the same terms as ethology. Successively, all the machines of the socius are held suspect by such phenomena and, reciprocally, all of biology, at the most molecular level, is concerned with the interactions of the social field. On the plane of the individual, we thus should not separate manifestations of puberty, considered in their familial, organic, and educational context, from subversions which, on a larger social plane, put the collective economy of desire back into question. How do we come to misunderstand that the entire society is constantly traversed in its most innerfolds by these phenomena of the biological coming-of-age which, generation after generation, tirelessly cleans up after adolescence and infancy? It is true that the flights of desire they convey are systematically taken hold of by encodings of the family, the school, medicine, sports, the army, and all the regimentations and laws which are supposed to govern the "normal" behavior of the individual. But it nevertheless comes back to the fact that they manage to crystallize the largest scale of collective desiring-machines (from neighborhood gangs up to Woodstock, or May '68, etc.). And that this was nothing but scattered machinic indexes, first being a quick, powerless deterritorialization, then becoming an abstract machine capable of catalyzing new semiotic assemblages of desire in the social field.

Let us evoke, starting from some other examples, the relative positions and functions of machinic indexes, of the abstract machines and semiotic assemblages with which schizoanalysis will be confronted. In the first place, let us consider the embryonic writing that manifests in the draft of a child around three or four years of age. Here we can only speak of the index of a writing. Nothing is played out, nothing is crystallized, everything is still possible. But taken on by the school machine this index undergoes a radical reworking. The draft loses its polyvocality. There is a disjunction between, on the one hand, the draft—impoverished, imitative—and, on the other, a writing entirely shaped by adult expression and tyrannized by an anxiety to conform with the dominant norms. How does the assemblage of the semiotics of the school thus succeed in bearing power down on the intensities of the child's desire? I have previously evoked the insufficiency of explanations that amount to considering the repressive action of power agencies on the machinic indexes "of" the child. What would be advisable to grasp here is why, in one case, such a repression will accomplish its goals and why, in another, it fails. Let me repeat that it seems impossible not to return to the hypothesis of abstract machinisms. If there is no crystallization of an abstract machine that "conveys" repression, the assemblage of power will also lack its effect, subjects will become maladapted, caricaturesque, psychotic, or mentally incapacitated, etc., everything the overseers of the social order account as a deficiency; whereas it would be easy to see that, under non-repressive conditions, these same children never stop augmenting their "pre-school" semiotic creativity. Therefore, passing to the stage of "normal work" in the classroom, the acquisition of an average competence in matters of recitation, writing, arithmetic, etc. does not depend on a mechanical stimulus of sensory-motor schemata interiorized during the course of the various "stages" in the development of language. The stages in question here are not of the psychogenetic order, but the repressivo-genetic; and instead of considering a "latency period" coming to consummate the child's life as a destiny due to the "decline of the Oedipus complex," it would undoubtedly be more advisable to study concrete social constellations and their particular technologies of semiotic subjection, insofar as they conform to the child's enclosure in the school and the family at the decisive moment of the child's "entrance into life" (here we could speak of a "barracks-school" complex, to borrow Fernand Oury's expression).[16]

Abstract machines, generated by the so-called psychogenetic "stages" are not assimilable to general schemata at the level of perception, memory, logical integration, or the structure of behavior... In fact, they crystallize from heteroclitic compositions, they involve "regressive fixations" and archaic modes of territorialization in ultra-deterritorialized semiotic components. An enuretic child, for example, hits upon an abstract formula—a body without organs—where, in a similar repressive formula, a postural semiotics involved in a withdrawal of the self will be associated with an affective semiotics turned towards a dependence on one's social circle along with educational and therapeutic sado-masochistic machines, ranging from special beds to behaviorist techniques of "positive reinforcement" or to the tyrannical interpretations of the psychoanalytic apparatus. But the abstract machine of "making peepee in bed"[17] no less preserves the singularity of the mute dances that always remain more or less irreducible to the discursive-repressive analyses of therapists of all colors! The child's good will toward the latter in the same proportion will nevertheless be greater because it will not penetrate the impermeability of the semiotic components of its symptoms in relation to those generated by the readaptive procedures. Even if the child plays the game of repression, even if she explicitly invests it, the singularity traits carried by abstract machines will enable her to possibly escape from it. Besides, repression does not seek to completely submerge the child as an organic totality, but to graft the child onto the constitutive elements of her modes of semiotization. Thus, there is no pure and simple application of the repressive set on the set of desiring machines, but processes of mediation due to the biases of abstract machines traversing the socius and the individual. If an enuretic child demonstrates the inability to carry out "multiple division" in school as a secondary symptom, this does not presuppose a general inhibition of her logical competence—on the contrary, it can be seen that she is often capable of handling more difficult abstract problems—but only that she "organizes" a repressive *jouissance* within the framework of a rhizome: [school-teachers-parents-grading system-repressive-prohibited notation-traits of facialty bearing upon masturbation, etc.]. Her refusal of a certain type of logical discursivity demonstrates her desire to "globalize" the assemblage in question. Thus, she arranges a sort of extra-corporeal erogenous zone, territorialized on a particular "buttress;" the question of "doing division" then becomes a machinic point, the index of a potential line of flight. Under different circumstances, the same child could also "opt" for other symptoms, for example becoming mute, having anxiety attacks associated with shouting at the reading of a problem... In fact, the machines of power associated with re-education, the family, and the school ... only become effective to the degree that they succeed in attaching themselves to such bio-psycho-social zones which do not have to take on the form of neuroses related to etiquette (example: adaptive and recuperative therapeutics that consists in repressing and normalizing the child's modes of semiotization territorializing its libido on a zone of stammering without which its pragmatic field would be reorganized in a way that would open it to new horizons and new realities).[18]

Therefore, due to the bias of abstract machines, the libido never ceases to circulate between the instances of social repression and those of individual semiotization. But there is nothing necessary or automatic about this circulation; in order to be possible, two conditions must be met: 1) "individual" desire must crystallize its indexes and its machinic points on an abstract machine; 2) certain elements of the repressive socius must be able to be connectable with this abstract machine. An abstract unconscious machinism deploys the possibility of a different assemblage of the world from the void. For example, developing beyond childhood, an adolescent will instantly realize all the benefits and dangers held by the new assemblages of enunciation in which she is engaged and to which she is simultaneously judge and jury. Also, let me repeat that it constitutes a fundamentally metastable instance between the intensities of desire and the dominant semiological stratifications. However, unlike the machinic indexes which do nothing but anticipate their crystallization, assemblages sub-sist in the state of virtuality, even when they do not consolidate the means of their manifestations. Whereas indexes and symptoms can scatter and allow the return of old stratifications full force at any moment, in all places and circumstances abstract machines will continue to threaten them with a possible revolutionary upheaval. Due to a sort of immediate semiotic contamination, the most deterritorialized abstract machinisms are transmitted from one system to another. But while capitalistic abstractions are implanted in a durable way when passing from the "adult" world to childhood or from the "civilized" world to the "primitives" and barbarians, it seems that this no longer happens with precarious indexes or fragile lines of flight in the opposite direction. At this level however, nothing is definitively played out: everything depends on the constitution of collective assemblages of enunciation; a new assemblage can become locked in a closed system of semiologization—in a dualistic signifier-signified substance—or it can release diagrammatic reactions in chains or machinic flights of desire which overcome the "wall of significations" and carry out direct connections between the points of deterritorialization of sign machines and those of material and social ensembles. Abstract unconscious machines "materialize," if you will, a triple possibility:

—either their own dissociation and the return to the "anarchy" of machinic indexes (the so-called primary process);

—or a stratification relatively deterritorialized via "petrification" under the form of abstraction and the generation of significative semiological redundancies (normal or neurotic adaptation to dominant realities);

—or an active destratification through the effects of diagrammatization and the circulation of asignifying signs-particles (molecular revolution, schizoanalysis…).

An unconscious abstract machine, unlike a Freudian "complex," thus does not belong to *one* stage among others: it can participate in several stages at once under one modality or another: at the level of indexes where it represents the potentiality of a machinic integration to a "superior" degree—which will or will not be recuperated by a stratum—and at the level of strata, where it represents the potentiality of a destratifying diagrammatization. Pure quanta of potential deter-ritorialization, abstract machines are everywhere and nowhere, *before* and *after* the crystallization of the opposition between machine and structure, representation and referent, object and subject. They can also gauge the threat of a reifying totalization of multiplicities which open up the possibility of a deterritorializing multiplication of stratifications. Their existence "*before*" the appearance of an autonomous semiotic machine distributing the content and expression of signs on separated planes or things and representations prevents us from considering them as simple structural invariants of transcendental stratifications or abstractions. Although for abstract machines the strata are simply the provisional residues of processes of deterritorialization, being nothing by themselves from a substantial point of view, in order to be manifested, the former are continuously constrained to be stratified and destratified, without however remaining in a powerless face-to-face of the matter-form type. There is thus a fundamental dissymmetry between a self-enclosed formalism, the strata which become "installed" in existence, and active, open formalization which is "driven" by abstract machines at the level of machinic indexes and diagrammatism, simultaneously marking the creative and irreversible nature of processes of deterritorializaiton. Under these conditions, a homeostatic equilibrium of strata will never be guaranteed: they are threatened on the "outside" by the work of the inter-stratic deterritorialization of abstract machinisms which can result in redistributions, and the creation of new strata: and, on the "inside" by the metabolism of the lines of flight which crisscross them in all parts.

The unconscious possible, before its manifestation in semiotic structures or social and material stratifications, does not exist as a pure logical matter; it no longer sets off from nothing, it is organized under the form of quanta of freedom in a sort of valence system whose differentiation and complexity gives no precedence to the chains of organic chemistry or genetic encodings.[19] The metabolism of the possible does not simply arise from a "logical matter." It employs differentiated matters of expression according to their degree of deterritorialization. The plane of consistency, which deploys the infinite set of machinic potentialities, constitutes a sort of sensible plate of the reference, selection, and articulation of the active points of deterritorialization within the unconscious strata. There is no possible in general, but only the possible beginning from a process of deterritorialization which must not be confused with a global and undifferentiated annihilation. Thus, there exists a sort of matter of unconscious deterritorialization, a matter of the possible, which constitutes the essence of politics, yet a transhuman, transsexual, transcosmic politics. The process of deterritorialization always frees the remainders, either under the form of stratifications—spatio-temporalized, energeticized, substantified—or under the form of residual possibilities of lines of flight and the generation of new connections. Deterritorialization never stops midway, it is what is different from a nothingness which could be represented as self-enclosed and could support relations of powerlessness and mirror effects with the stratified real. Therefore, the system of abstract machines constitutes an active limit, a productive limit beyond the most deterritorialized strata and on this side of nothingness as the end of every process. Abstract machines are not an affair of psychological instances; before depending on sciences of culture, ideologies, or teachings, they arise from a *politics of desire* "before" objects and subjects have been specified. Let me repeat, there is no question here of a freedom intrinsically tied to the human condition, of a freedom of the "for-itself" in radical opposition with a stratified "in itself" unconnected with anything but its own powerlessness. In passing from one assemblage to another, a certain quantum of deterritorializing connection is gained or lost; deterritorialization can not be assimilated to a necessary causality, it can be vectorized either on the side of a stratification or on the side of an open "possibilization." Thus, it is only in terms of the "resources" of certain quanta of possible marked by social repression that we will be able to understand, for example, the so-called "latency" period described by Freudians. According to them, it will become manifested between the ages of six and eight by an "infantile" amnesia which would result from a repression bearing upon the child's entire oedipal and pre-oedipal past. But, Freud tells us, every memory is not expunged for all that: "vague incomprehensible memories" remain.[20] Incomprehensible for whom? For the white, civilized and normal adult! In fact, it is not fading memory that is in question, but the fact that the child's modes of semiotization, sensations, feelings, and sexual impulses receive a formidable effacement. Why invoke an intrinsic mechanism of repression in the development of the child's drives—which will then be related to an "originary repression" and, in the last case, to the universal antagonism between Eros and Thanatos—if this is only to mask the appearance of repressive social assemblages? Why is the child's semiotic *politics* inverted, why does it take part in repression? Why the creators of deterritorialization who disrupt previous territorialities instead of opening the process to a vaster semiotic creativity, vectorizing it on the abstractions of the dominant system? As soon as we try to renounce the schematic responses of psychogenetic determinism, the questions themselves return and proliferate. According to which particularity does a child, in the context of the repressive powers of the family and the school in a given society, resist or succumb to the "temptation" of an investment of repression? In the case of the "latency period," what sort of educational abstract machine, on the very concrete terrain of current systems, are connected to the child's abstract machines? In what way do the semiotics set in play, for example, by nurseries continue the action of the effacement of the parents' "educational" interventions? (In fact, we now believe that it is in the nursery that the division between a time of "work" and a time of "recreation" is set in place.)[21] In school, how does the apprenticeship of a writing detached from any real use sterilize the ulterior possibilities of a creative diagrammatism? How do the semiotics of space and time in the school (division between school days and vacation time, division between the space of the classroom, the teacher's space, the space of recreation, the street, etc.), how do the semiotics of discipline (sitting in rows, grades, competition, punishment, etc.) support crushing, sometimes definitively, the semiotics of the "pre-school" child? And how do they generate the semiotic conditions of the factory, office and barracks? In fact, the machine of obligatory learning does not primarily have the goal of transmitting information, knowledge or a "culture," but of transforming the child's semiotic coordinates from top to bottom. Under these conditions, we can consider that the real function of the "latency period" is a modern equivalent of the initiation camps which, in primitive societies, fabricated entire "persons" separately, i.e. adult males essentially in line with the norms of the group.[22] But here, instead of lasting fifteen hours, the initiation camp lasts fifteen years, and its objective is to enslave the individual, down to the most intimate constitution of their nervous fibers, to the capitalistic systems of production. Infantile amnesia, correlative to the "latency period," thus marks the extinction of various semiotics which are not subjected to the signifying semiologies of the dominant powers. And if neurotics, like "pre-oedipal" children, escape from its obscurity, this is precisely because these powers' systems of circumscription have failed to get a hold over them for one reason or another. Hence "pre-capitalistic" intensities continue to work on them, bombard them, and oppose them to "normal" values and significations. The role of memory—either natural, that of the adult who remembers childhood with nostalgia; or artificial, that of psychoanalytic anamnesis—consists in duplicating the first erasure of the individual's intensities and reconstructing a childhood according to the norms.

Trees and Tracings, Maps and Rhizomes

Schizoanalysis as a pragmatics of the machinic unconscious must endeavor to avoid two types of pitfalls:

1) an analysis centered on the person, on lived experience or the body, on the regulation of behavior, on the "development" of the psyche … basically the type of practices current in the United States;[23]

2) an analysis effectively centered on a verbal material, based on a transferential micropolitics of black holes and on the semiological interpretations of affects and behaviors; what I shall call: a systematic "paradigmatization" of all enunciatory contents and strategies beginning from abstract or structural references. An isolated individual, a therapist, a group, an institution, or a vast social ensemble can constitute an analytic assemblage—an analyzer[24]—which is moreover not simply reduced to a totalization of individuals, but also involves other "non-human" flows (non-human sexuality, economic flows, material flows, etc...).

Before proceeding in detail into the productions of statements and modes of semiotization, schizoanalysis will have to determine the principal micropolitical lines of the assemblages of enunciation and power formations, even at the *most abstract* level. In other words, for each case and each situation, it will have to construct *a map of the unconscious*—with its strata, its lines of deterritorialization, its black holes—open to perspectives of experimentation (and in opposition to the infinite *tracing* of oedipal triangulations which do nothing but set in resonance every current impasse and all the signifying modes of subjection in the cumulative effect of the black holes constituting transference (interminable analysis)). The pragmatic articulation of the strata of encoding are so blocked that they always unlock a minimum of possibilities of "tracing" and transformation due to the bias of abstract machines traversing the various modes of territorialization. Different types of consistency—biological, ethological, semiological, sociological, etc...—do not depend upon a structural or generative superstratum; they are worked on from the "inside" by a network of molecular machinic connections. Machinic consistency is not totalizing but deterritorializing. It ensures the always possible conjunction of the most different systems of stratification, and this is why it constitutes, if you will, the basic material beginning from which a transformational praxis could be established. Thus the modes of semiotization of an analytic pragmatics will not rely on trees, but on rhizomes (or lattices). There will be no *a priori* reason for a pragmatic chain to commence at a point S to be derived afterwards by successive dichotomies. Any point whatsoever on the rhizome will be able to be connected to any other point. In other words, each trait will not necessarily return to a linguistic trait. A linguistic trait will be able to be connected to the chain of a non-linguistic semiology or to an assemblage which is social, biological, etc... Segmentary stratifications will be correlated with the lines of flight of deterritorialization. Thus by definition, a rhizome will not be formalized on the basis of a logical or mathematical metalanguage. It will not be indebted to any psychoanalytic topic or any structuralized model. It will be able to allow semiotic chains of all kinds to connect and conjoin very different practices relevant, for example, to the arts, sciences, social struggles, etc... As a process of machinic diagrammatization, it will not be reducible to a system of representation, but it will imply the implementation of various collective assemblages of enunciation. The construction of a schizoanalytic rhizome will not aim at the description of a state of fact, the return to equilibrium of intersubjective relations, or the exploration of the mysteries of an unconscious lurking in the obscure recesses of memory. On the contrary, it will be completely oriented toward an *experimentation* in touch with the real. It will not "decipher" an already constituted, self-enclosed unconscious, *it will construct it* and will compete in the connection of fields, in the unblocking of stratified, cancerous, or empty bodies without organs, and in their maximum opening on the machinic plane of consistency. It will be brought to generate various modes of coding and semiotics, for example, on the level of the biological, sensitive, perceptive, thought via images, categorial thought, gestural and verbal semiotics, political and social fields, formalized writings, arts, music, refrains... Unlike psychoanalysis, which always seeks to make each statement and libidinal production fall back on a structure that overcodes them, schizoanalysis will attempt to circumscribe their repetitive elements in what we will call systems of tracings capable of being articulated in a map of the unconscious.

Tracings constitute some of the essential elements of diagrammatic semiotization. They do not have the function of harnessing redundancies of resonance, of representing stratified realities, but of directly jumpstarting mutational signs-particles. Within tracings, figures of expression are treated as the primary matters of an experimentation bearing upon abstract machines. Maps themselves are like laboratories where experimentations on tracings are set in interaction. Thus, here the map is opposed to the structure; it can open itself in all its dimensions; it can also be ripped apart; it can be adapted to all kinds of assemblies. A pragmatic map can be started by an isolated individual or a group, it can be painted on a wall, it can be conceived as a work of art, it can be conducted as a political action or as a mediation. For a type of performance, a particular assemblage of enunciation, or a redundant tracing being given, what is important is determining whether or not it modifies the unconscious map of a local pragmatic competence. These maps of competence do not depend on a larger competence in an absolute way. Such a map, which will serve as a reference point for a collective praxis (for example, that of an anti-psychiatric community or a small group), will have no value for a different social ensemble (for example: for the whole of psychiatry in France, or the entirety of political movements). The differential relations between *tracings of performance* and *maps of competence* are played out at the level of the various types of segmentarity of encoding. The relative "competence" of a pragmatics in relation to another depends on whether or not it employs a subtler segmentarity, more machinic, more molecular, and more deterritorialized than that of the second, which is thus found to take on a "performative" position. It is only with signifying semiologies that a hierarchical relation of double segmentarity installs itself between maps and tracings, determining a narrow margin for the possibilities of semiotic innovation. Only the appearance of a deterritorializing line of flight (example: the diagrammatic use of signs of a linguistic origin in domains that are aesthetic, scientific, etc...) will then be able to disrupt the stratifications of such an equilibrium. We have seen that at the level of semiologically pastified [passéfié], spatialized, or substantified strata, the balances and relations of force can no longer manifest themselves except from a relative deterritorialization, by setting at least two systems of segmentarity in correspondence (example: molar segmentarity of the morphemes in the first linguistic articulation and the molecular segmentarity of the figures of expression in the second articulation), whereas at the level of machinic mutations, the strata are dismantled or reorganized by diagrammatic processes generating a quantified deterritorialization via systems of signs-particles. Diagrammatic lines of deterritorialization never "definitively" transcend segmentary stratifications. Due to their interactions with stratified systems, fuzzy vectors of a non-realizable possible can result in the existing context, not to mention veritable machinic mutations.[25] No universal cartography exists. No more than an abstract set of all abstract machines would exist, for we cannot hope to trace a general map from the totality of pragmatic maps. No logical or topological category, no axiomatic can subsume all the different types of machinic consistency. Because abstract machines are non-decomposable on an intentional plane, they cannot be inserted into an extensional class. Since no abstract machine can rise above history or be the "subject" of history and because machinic multiplicities traverse the strata of different "provisionally dominant" realities on a diachronic and synchronic plane at the same time, it cannot be said of the general movement of their line of deterritorialization that it demonstrates a universal and homogenous tendency, for it is interrupted at every level by reterritorializations upon which microcosmic generations of deterritorialization are grafted once again. The cartography of abstract machinisms makes history by dismantling dominant realities and significations: they constitute the navel, the point of emergence and creationism of the machinic phylum.

Here again we find the problematic of the alternative between subject-groups/subjugated groups, which can never be taken as an absolute opposition. The relations of alienation between fields of competence always suppose a certain margin which falls upon pragmatics to locate and exploit: in other words, within *any situation whatsoever, a diagrammatic politics can always be "calculated,"* which refuses any idea of fatalism, whichever name it may take on: divine, historical, economic, structural, hereditary, or syntagmatic, a politics which thus implies, in the first place, an active refusal of any conception of the unconscious as a genetic stage or structural destiny. A group requires a continual localization of the investments of desire capable of thwarting bureaucratic reifications, leaderships, etc. "Working on" the group's map would consist in proceeding to the new uses and transformations of the group's body without organs. One could only do his or her part in such a pragmatics: it can do nothing but challenge every status of hegemony for linguistics, psychoanalysis, social psychology, and the entirety of the human, social, juridical, economic sciences, etc... Studying the unconscious, for example in the case of Little Hans, would consist

THE RHIZOME OF LITTLE HANS' PHOBIC ENCIRCLING

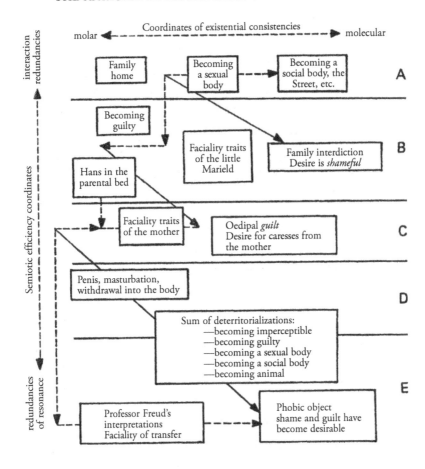

The phobic assemblage is constituted through a series of ordeals which successively take place

    A) on the family territory,

    B) on the territory of the parental bed,

    C) with the mother's faciality

    D) with the object of phallic power

    E) on the machinic territoriality of the unconscious fantasy.

There is a conjunction between the deterritorialization of the two consistency types: the phobia here follows a schizo vector.

in establishing, by taking account of the entirety of his semiotic productions, on which tree or rhizome type his libido has been brought to invest. At such a moment, how the neighbors' branch is trimmed, following which maneuvers the oedipal tree is reduced, what role professor Freud's branch and his activity of deterritorialization have played, why the libido has been constrained to find shelter in the semiotization of a becoming-horse, etc… Thus, phobia would no longer be considered as a psychopathological *result*, but as the libidinal pragmatics of a child who has not been able to find other micropolitical solutions so as to escape from these familialist and psychoanalytic transformations.

Schizoanalysis and Molecular Revolution

"Do it" could be watchword of a micropolitical schizoanalysis. The Chomskyans' axiom of grammaticality (S) is not only no longer accepted as self-evident, but also becomes the object of a kind of militant opposition. We refuse considering that semiotic assemblages of all kinds must necessarily be organized in phrases compatible with the system of dominant significations. A schizoanalytic "watchword" thus will not seek to interpret or reorganize significations and compose with them; it will postulate that, beyond their system of redundancy, it is always possible to transform the semiotic assemblage which corresponds with them. Here there is a primary begging of the question, an incontrovertible micropolitical axiom: the refusal of legitimating the signifying power demonstrated by the "evidences" of dominant "grammaticalities." The appreciation of a "degree of grammaticality" has become a political matter. Rather than remaining prisoner to the redundancy of signifying tracings, we will endeavor to fabricate a new map of competence and new asignifying diagrammatic coordinates. This is what the Leninists did during their break with the social-democrats when they decided with a certain arbitrariness that beginning from the constitution of a new type of party a split would be created between the proletarian avant-garde and the masses, which would bring about a radical transformation of their attitude of passivity, their spontaneism, and their "economist" tendency. The fact that this Leninist "transformation" has ultimately fallen into the field of redundancy of Stalinist bureacratism shows that, in this domain, the systems of maps and tracings can always be inverted, because no structural foundation or theoretical legitimation would definitively guarantee the maintenance of a revolutionary "competence."[26] In any case, the Leninists have made a new matter of expression and a new map of the political unconscious emerge in relation to which all productions of statements, including those of bourgeois movements, will have been produced by the Marxists of the Marxist First International which will literally "invent" a new type of deterritorialized working class, anticipating the sociological transformations industrial societies would come to experience.

A micropolitical schizoanalysis will never accept as established fact systems of redundance that seem in appearance to merely lead to deadlocks; it is forced to make processes of diagrammatization, "analyzers," and collective assemblages of enunciation emerge which will abolish the individuated modes of subjectification and beginning from which the previous micropolitical relations will be recorded and redefined. Yet it would not simply be a question of organizational, programmatic, or theoretical instruments, but fundamentally of the mutations in social pragmatics.

The task of such a pragmatics will thus consist in developing connections between transformational systems capable of erasing the effects of signifying generations and in discernabilizing micropolitical orientations which concern all semiotic systems heading toward "molecular revolutions." Diagrammatic transformations are capable of bringing their effects into any semiotic register: it is a question of symbolic semiologies (for example, with the effects of mimetism, transitivism, etc.), of signifying semiologies (with systems of expression based on a limited range of discrete elements: phonemes, graphemes, distinctive traits, etc.) or even "natural" modes of encoding. In each situation, the schizoanalytic objective will consist in disengaging the nature of the crystallizations of power which function around a dominant transformational component: the map of black holes, semiotic branchings and lines of flight (example: in Asiatic empires, the installation of a despotic signifying writing, or in paranoia, the emergence of a systematized signifying délire). The reversal of a signifying component and the appearance of a new diagrammatic component will reduce the effects of signifiance or individuation and will bring the enunciation to be nothing more than one element among other machinic assemblages (example: the emancipation of a writing machine from its signifying function in work that is poetic, musical, mathematical, etc.). Pragmatic transformations will synchronically assemble their compositions according to diverse political strategies; but they will also diachronically organize their mutations on a machinic rhizome. Although their evolution globally goes in the direction of a growing deterritorialization, punctuated by reterritorializations which are always more brutal on artificial stratifications, we cannot truly extract the general laws which concern them. This is quite fortunate! Pragmatic assemblages are machinic; they do not depend on universal laws properly speaking; they are subject to historical mutations. Therefore, we will speak of a "romantic complex," of a "popular front complex," of a "Resistance complex," and a "Leninist complex" which have maintained their effects outside their original historical localization, without which they could not be given the character of universality which psychoanalysts attribute to the Oedipus complex or Maoists to the complex of "revisionism." Pragmatic reference points do not arise from universals; they can always be reevaluated. For example, let us consider the fact that the most territorialized segmentarities have a "tendency" to take control of the most molar segmentarities. In fact, here there is a sort of law. But it only remains valid within the framework of a given period, until the moment when a revolutionary situation, disrupting the maps of competence, will reveal the existence of another machinism which was about to corrode a previous equilibrium in a subterranean way. A differentiation of the coefficients of deterritorialization should nevertheless make it possible to vectorize political sequences—for example, a "line" of schizophrenia against a paranoia "line"—in the struggle against bureaucratic transformations. But we will never be able to deduce, as some have thought to be able to consider beginning from *Anti-Oedipus*, that here it is a question of a new Manichean alternative. Every orientation remains provisional. In a pragmatic system, all types of entrances are always possible on the side of the performances of tracings as well as the competences of maps. In the first case, we will accept the deadlocked, repetitive nature of libidinal investments, we will even support ourselves on them in order to guarantee the minimum territorialization of a body without organs beginning from which other transformational operations will be possible (example: the positive side of regionalist struggles). In another case, we will directly support ourselves on a line of flight capable of exploding the strata and generating new semiotic connections. To schematize and return to another terminology, we will say that generative pragmatics will specifically occupy itself with cancerous and empty bodies without organs, whereas transformational pragmatics will occupy itself with full bodies without organs connected to the machinic plane of consistency. But what primarily unites these two types is that the sole fact of introducing a mode of semiotization which particularly concerns them, of memorizing potentialities, of arising from tracings and writing maps, will already begin from diagrammatic effects; the sole fact of deciding to write its dreams, for example,

RHIZOME OF THE LENINIST DIVIDE
AND THE BEGETTING OF STALINISM

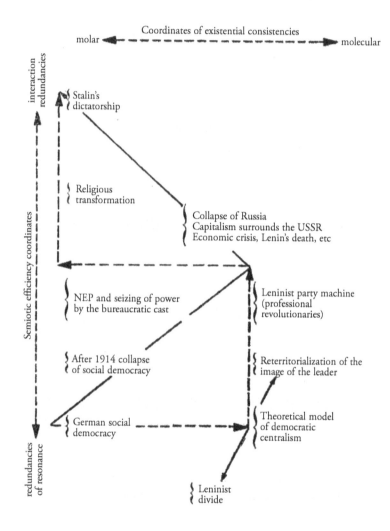

(There is a conjunction between the reterritorializations of the two components: paranoid vector)

rather than passively interpreting them, the single fact of designing them or miming them will be able to transform the map of the unconscious. One of the formidable traps of psychoanalysis resides in the fact that it succeeds in relying on the minimum transformation which represents the displacement of discourse outside the habitual conditions of enunciation: the psychoanalyst's entire "mission" is reduced at present to "restraining" the diagrammatic effects of this transformation and returning the patient's discourse to new grids of signifying redundancies.

A schizoanalytic pragmatics of collective assemblages of enunciation will constantly oscillate between these two types of semiotic micropolitics by elaborating a sort of technology of the reevaluation of the dominant significations. Under these conditions, the signifying discourse itself will be able to transform into a "war machine" with, to be sure, the constant threat of the reestablishment of a system of the redundancy of resonance. (In fact, let us note that from the point of view of a transformational pragmatics, there is no fundamental difference between a war machine and a linguistic diagrammatic machine since both take part in the same rhizome.) Let us add that the appreciation of the transformations of the consistency of semiotic efficiency developed within a pragmatic field is not an unimportant objective; in fact, there is no question of proposing a politics of novelty for novelty's sake, for example a mimetic conversion to madness under the pretext of pitting a schizophrenic line against a paranoid line. The maps/tracings pragmatic assemblages essentially intervene at the level of the traits of matters of expression. In the last resort, these are what determine the regime of the coefficients of deterritorialization, rhythms, inductions, viscosities, boomerang effects, etc. compatible with the fabrication of a body without organs. Thus, reference does not depend here on theoretical analyses or affective transferences but a composition of systems of intensity. In summation, the redundancy of the traits of a matter of expression takes on the relays of formalized traits of the substance of expression. The construction of a tree of the generative type will thus not be independent from that of a rhizome of the transformational type. At the heart of a generative tree, a new rhizome can branch out, and what will perhaps even be the most general case, a microscopic element of the tree, a radicle, will begin the production of a new type of local competence, whereas one of the different semiotic components (perceptive, sensitive, thought via images, speech, socius, writing), overcoded in a generative tree, will furthermore be able to blossom. An intensive trait will set to work on its own, a hallucinatory perception, a synesthesia, a perverse mutation, or a phantasmagoria will detach itself and, in one stroke, the hegemony of the signifier will be reassessed.[27] Generative trees constructed according to the Chomskyan syntagmatic model which McCawley, Sadock, Dieter Wunderlich, etc. are forced to adapt to linguistic pragmatics (cf. *Langages*, June, 1972) would thus be able to open themselves and develop in all directions. A performative statement, for example, a promise or an order, can change the *bearing* of a situation—this has nothing to do with its signification—according to the appearance of a new transformation. It is obvious that an oath does not at all have the same bearing when it is stated in the context of a transformation of conjugal, religious, or police "power." Saying "I swear" before a judge or in a dramatic scene does not have the same function, nor does it engage with the same type of character or even the same type of intersubjectivity. Therefore, the question is not simply knowing if a pragmatic transformation intervenes on different levels: semantic, syntactic, phonological, prosodic, etc., but one of studying *how* it intervenes on a micropolitical plane. And when we do not notice its incidence, this is because the analysis has not been fully carried out! This is exactly the opposite attitude of the linguists who seek to minimize the role of pragmatic components and only accept taking account of them when they are no longer able to avoid them. Here we will no longer interrogate syntax and semantics in order to detect if they harbor pragmatic elements; we will interrogate the pragmatic semiotic compositions of assemblages of enunciation so as to slow down the paralyzing effects of the significative redundancies there. When Boukharine avows his guilt in his trial, he knows perfectly well that he lies from the perspective of the "real" context, and yet he speaks the truth from the perspective of the militant personage to whom he intends to remain faithful until death. This ambiguity is already perceptible in the reading of official accounts, and there is all the space for thinking that a syntactic, phonological analysis, etc., of the discourse which he has effectively given would make it possible to extract the effects of transformation from an oral expression: "the trial of Moscow," and the international success that this formula has long known (it would obviously be absurd to envision that we can typify, once and for all, such transformations of power tied to the school, the tribunal, the party, and the family insofar as they modify, for example, the signification of a performative or seek to extract it from "universals").

We generally consider the acts of citizenship to be the crowning achievement of a series that begins with an engagement with familial values. Thus modes of mental organization are staged which begin at the most primitive levels, like that of oral fixations, up to the most ethereal levels of sublimation. But, in reality, things do not happen this way: all "stages" can engage simultaneously and can return to a point of the system so as to make it explode. Let me repeat: no genetic finality or general competence of a dominant adult language will ever constitute a totalizing reference for particular performances. The objective of a schizoanalytic pragmatics is to determine where a coincidence between the maps and certain disjunctions will be utilized, what the range of a signifying power takeover on a given system will be, or what kind of power formations will branch out over the signifying S organizing and overcoding a body of statements and propositions. A repressive proposition, for example, does not operate in the same way according to whether it is assembled by a molar military enunciation or a microfascist molecular enunciation. Each situational rhizome will correspond with dialects, indeed particular idiolects. And in the case where the latter will be crisscrossed by a language or a general grammaticality, it will always be a question of a dominant instance of overcoding like *la francophonie* in relation to the vernacular languages of old French colonies, which are today progressively captured by new power formations.

Two Schizoanalyses

One of the essential tasks of schizoanalysis will then consist in discernbilizing these mutational components, vehicles of semiotic asperities, of deterritorializing points-signs able to traverse the stratifications of an assemblage, somewhat like the "tunnel effects" described by physicists.[28] Unlike psychoanalysis, first of all such a mode of the unconscious will not be content to attach affects from the "outside" through the technique of transference. The analyst will no longer take shelter behind a claim to neutrality so as to hide himself from the other, without, for all that, never being engaged by the conversations in his office. The analytic process—individual or collective—will be implicated by its object even in its fundamental nucleus (as a process, it is the status of the object and the subject which will thus be constantly reevaluated). Due to its risks and dangers, an analytic pragmatics will have to make micropolitical choices by opting, for example, for the acceleration or deceleration of an internal mutation of assemblages for the facilitation or prevention of an inter-assemblage transition... Instead of indefinitely tracing the same complexes or the same universal "mathemes," a schizoanalytic cartography will explore and experiment with an unconscious in action. It will not simply be dedicated to identifying diachronic results—symptoms, neuroses, sublimations, etc.—but, beyond the manifested equilibrium states or subjective catastrophes, it will be applied to illuminate the least apparent situational potentialities according to the synchronic axes actually traversing (or capable of traversing) the assemblages in consideration. In addition, these two analytic series will constantly be cross-checked against the same types of interrogations each time: why this assemblage instead of another? Why this enclosure, this consolidation? What does this black hole effect contain? Does it indicate the release of a general effect of inhibition, or, on the contrary, a reconversion of the assemblage's metabolism into non-arborescent lines of flight? What benefit is there in disrupting such a homeostatic inter-assemblage equilibrium? Is there a grave threat of external repression that will attempt to block all the inter-assemblage systems (of the "eat-work-sleep daily grind variety")? On the contrary, do credible developments of rhizomatic openings exist? These intra- and inter-assemblage questions will only be omitted at this degree of generality. So as to address them from an angle which would not itself simply be a trap returning to social or psychological abstractions, it will be necessary to more thoroughly grasp the points of singularity, points of non-sense, and semiological asperities which phenomenologically appear to be the most irreducible.

According to their different capacities for "extracting" machinic singularity traits, we will be able to distinguish between several types of schizoanalytic practices. When a schizoanalytic assemblage[29] will take as its *object* a preexisting assemblage or will set out to create new ones, we will be able to attach its functionality to the generative pragmatics or the transformational pragmatics we previously mentioned. If we advance this distinction, despite its slightly artificial character (because in fact the two types of pragmatics are fundamentally indissociable), it is simply to underline the fact that a schizoanalytic intervention is not necessarily "extremist," that it has nothing to do with "savage" interpretations, and that even, in a sense, it will frequently require much more prudence than psychoanalysis with its trenchant interpretations and its often unmasterable transferences. It is not up to schizoanalysis to force or slow down events. It never loses sight of the fact that compromises, retreats, advances, breaks and revolutions arise from processes concerning which it is not at all a question of pretending to control or overcode them, but simply to semiotically and machinically assist them.

1) Generative Schizoanalysis

The role of components of passage will here be circumscribed only within the development of weak interactions between assemblages, with, if possible, a view of dismantling or unraveling their alienating mechanisms, their oppressive stratifications and redundancies, their black hole effects, indeed even warding off or deferring the potentials for catastrophe which they present. In fact, in the best case it will be a question of exploiting the indexes and lines of flight able to develop ulterior re-assemblages. In this first direction, schizoanalytic micropolitics will therefore not lead to a systematic deterritorialization of assemblages: on the contrary, it will accommodate long durations of reterritorializing stagnations of "regression," the establishment of neo-archaisms, etc...—delaying the proper time of machinic processes which will finalize the necessary destratifications.

Here schizoanalytic assemblages of enunciation always remain more or less alienated in capitalistic power formations and enslaved to their micro-mega-machinisms (public facilities network, the media, etc...): the components of passage implicated in such processes will never be affected by a univocal signification. Thus, at this level of "interpretation," it will always remain relative to the "point of view" of the assemblages of enunciation in consideration and to the optional matters which they concretely select.[30] "No watchwords, only passwords" could be the slogan of a schizoanalysis whose assemblages will primarily be situated beyond every dialectics of transference, Freudian interpretation, and, in a general way, any position of representation. Its objective will be simply the illumination of *new machinic sense* in situations where everything seemed played out in advance. (Asignifying sense to which a singularity point is attached to make it stand out.) Thus let me repeat that it will be brought to systematically refuse any constraining reference to socio-historical systems of causality or genetic stages determining the future. Its programs of experimentation will have nothing to do with archetypal or symbolic phantasms; on the contrary, their attachment to present realities will contribute to continuously re-elucidating the significations and determinisms congealed in the past.

2) Transformational Schizoanalysis

Here it will no longer be a question of simple internal changes, of continuous generations, but of radical modifications of the mechanisms inherent in the nuclei of assemblages, and thus of the creation of new assemblages. Components of passage will now engage in strong interactions, charges of deterritorialization, and mutant abstract machines. Whereas in the first perspective it was a question of molar relations of subjection and alienation, here molecular vectors of machinic enslavement will be employed.

The intervention modes of components of passage could be subdivided according to their *point of departure* beginning with:

—already constituted assemblages and inter-assemblage relations;

—or molecular populations, matters of expression "in the nascent state."

But such a distinction would remain unfruitful if it were not previously related to the micropolitics of choices that underlies even the constitution of the components of passage. Actually, it does not matter that these molecular populations and these matters of expression are extracted from "old assemblages" or even united for the occasion! (An innovative novice music can give birth to an archaic music; on the contrary, a conformist music can emerge from novel technical processes.) What counts here is the establishment of a *molecular politics* resulting in the development of new machinic nuclei. From then on the accent must be placed, not on the molar characterization of the *"generations"* of the assemblage (formalist, structuralist, systematic...)[31] but on the analyses of specific *transformation* processes proper to each component of passage. How do they modify the previous "uses" of molecular populations and matters of expression? How do they molecularize the politics of all components?

We will be particularly concerned with locating the different types of "assembling" that enable a component to *pass* to the rank of component of passage.[32] In this regard, three essential functions could be distinguished:

—*discernibilization* of components: (example: the methods of semiotic magnification, "colorization," and crossing in Proust, or those of acceleration, deceleration, thickening, and deformation of spatio-temporal coordinates in Kafka).

—*proliferation*: a component begins to work on its own and detaches itself, if need be, from the assemblage within which it was stratified. (Example: a project which was marginal at first, "Well, if I return to the dance"—imposes itself in relation to other projects, drags a cluster of components along with it, and ends by reassembling all the perspectives of an individual.)

—*diagrammatization*: a component releases a mutational machinism capable of traversing heterogeneous domains from the perspective of their matters of expression. (Interactions which are somatic, psychic, ethological, social, economic, artistic, etc.)

All of these processes constitute so many modalities of a similar process of *"controlled" deterritorialization*. Each time it is a question of liberating quanta of machinic possibles and assembling active nuclei [noyaux] beginning from singularity points—which may or may not be semiotically and subjectively formed. It is through this "internalization," this "infiltration," [noyautage] this "engineering" [machinisation] of deterritorialization that various levels of reality can take part in a *capture of consistency*. Realities only exist via their metabolization beginning from such assemblages. But the latter's ability to subvert traditional realities and articulate, express, and semiotize them in new ways rests on the fact that they can release components *traversing* petrified stratifications. And this power of crossing itself implies that these components are overactive because they are endowed with a surplus of deterritorialization in relation to "cooled down" components. Thus an assemblage only succeeds in crossing certain thresholds of reality due to putting diagrammatic components into operation—this operation is understood in a very broad sense, and thus takes us outside of the framework of systems of solely semiotic signalization.

At this point, we can reassess our problem concerning the various departure situations for a schizoanalytic process (either the extraction of components from existing assemblages or the creation *ex nihilo* of new components). In fact, at every stage of such a process the question of degrees of existential consistency and the semiotic efficiency of inter-intra-assemblage transformation will never stop being posed. From the most fantastic possible to the most irreversible materializations, everything in between is possible! It is still advisable to appreciate their relativity.[33] Fundamentally, this constitution *ex nihilo* of new assemblages does not conceal any mystery. It proceeds through successive passages of the capture of reality, of the capture of the consistency of one complex of possibles with another; consistency conserves its double nature: on the one hand, it is the consistency of the possible at its most abstract level, and on the other, the consistency of an assemblage as the manifestation and interaction of heterogeneous components. Machinic incarnation is thus not automatically synonymous with reterritorialization. It is also the "most deterritorialized" that will perhaps release a supplementary degree of reality from the moment it will be attached to a constellation of singularity points. Even when it will be made to construct an entire transformational trajectory (a diagrammatic cartography) in order to access and modify the nuclei of assemblages, it is always at the most immediate level of matters of expression that schizoanalysis will apprehend the abstract machines traversing different consistencies of the real. A pragmatics of assemblages does not presuppose a phenomenology of essences or a phenomenology of existents, but instead a machinic phenomenology taking account of every entity escaping the subject's immediate consciousness to the extent that it presents a definitive degree of machinic consistency ("purely" theoretical consistency, experiential consistency, aesthetic, fantastical, etc...). By renouncing stages and universals, transcendental ideas, structures, archetypes, key signifiers, and other "mathemes," it thus does not set off from nothing or run blindly against the wall of the visible and the actual. By selecting at its "convenience" vectors carrying abstraction and reality within the entire range of the possible, it continuously constructs its own support system. With it, the most abstract machinisms will be able to fall "within hand's reach" as soon as it will have been able to deterritorialize and "engineer" [machiniser] the hands of the body, the spirit, and the socius in an adequate way.

Schizoanalysis in Three Dimensions

We do not envision schizoanalysis as a technique or a science resting on laws and axioms, still less as a body of professions requiring initiatory training. In particular assemblages, it only achieves existence on the condition that a certain type of mutational process has *already* begun in the social field and the machinic field. The relative reference points for a new practice of analysis reassembled here are thus in no way proposed in the basic principles of schizoanalysis. Here there is no question of "cures" or anything like that. These reflections are the result of an experience, and they remain inseparable from a personal trajectory in the determined social, political, and cultural domains.

Thus, I have come to consider that every idea of a social object, every intra-psychic entity must be substituted for a much more inclusive but less reductive notion: that of assemblage. A social fact, a fact of behavior, a psychic fact, before being able to be defined on the material, subjective, semiotic, economic plane ... must be grasped at the level of the machinic territoriality which is proper to it. In paraphrasing a famous phrase, we will proclaim: "assemblages are not things." And, which particularly concerns those interested in the human and social sciences, it seems important to us to remember that, thanks to some guidelines, we will always have to rediscover here, if we wish to resist distorting them, three essential dimensions:[34]

—the first, relative to *components of passage*,[35] insofar as they take on the role of facilitating the crystallization of machinic nuclei and allow them to thrive by "nourishing" them with the quanta of possible that they draw from their own matters of expression;

—the second, relative to the instances that specify the assemblages as *assemblages of enunciation* (or semiotization), namely all the means of expression, representation, communication, and indeed subjectification or conscientialization which grant them a particular capacity of recognition, a "sensibility" with regard to intra-extra assemblage relations;

—the third, relative to *machinic nuclei* that simultaneously detach assemblages from the rest of the world and reconnect them to the entire "mechanosphere." Every living being, every process of enunciation, every psychic instance, and every social formation is necessarily connected (machinically enslaved) to a crossroads-point between, on the one hand, its particular position on the objective phylum of concrete machines and, on the other, the attachment of its formula of existence on the plane of consistency of abstract machines. It falls upon the machinic nuclei to integrate these two types of connection in such a way that the most abstract machines succeed in discovering the means of their manifestation and the most material machines for their metabolization and, eventually, their semiotization.

As soon as we are dealing with the "living," the "subject," consciousness, or the unconscious, the imaginary or the symbolic which will be claimed to operate in a direction of opening, disalienation, or liberation, we will thus have to preoccupy ourselves with never losing sight of the course of things at hand, which concerns the assemblages considered as well as their assemblage "analyzers":

—*singularity points*, contingencies irreducible to serial generations; anything that makes real history never coincides with the play of structures, for example faciality traits, refrains, corporeality, landscapity, and territory escaping from the systems of dominant redundancy;

—a surface of enunciation, a body of reference, yet a body without organs, a body which is not shut in on itself, not totalitarian, "me-ish," ["moïque"] and which we will classify in the register of *machinic territorialities*;

—machinic nuclei articulating heterogeneous components ordered from the most territorialized to the most deterritorialized, from the most abstract to the most semiotically efficient, and organizing them between them in such a way that they develop an "internal milieu" and a "foreign policy."[36] Let us add to this that between these three poles, three types of relations form:

—relations of *subjection* (molar alienation) between singularity points and machinic nuclei: the incarnation and materialization of machinisms (abstract to various degrees) leads to rendering them irreducible to the systematic modes of generation (alienation here becomes synonymous with belonging to history, which does not signify in any way that we must identify history with capitalistic alienation);

—relations of molecular *enslavement* between machinic nuclei and machinic territorialities. Diagrammatic "representation" (or proto-subjectivity, or the machinic unconscious) no longer carves out individuals from alienated and stratified relations and structures. On the contrary, it develops supplementary degrees of freedom within the phylum of concrete machines and never stops enriching, and propagating the plane of consistency of abstract possibles;

—and finally relations of *desire*, like mutant deterritorializing flows or components of passage, capable of distancing the two preceding sides of incarnation and machinic creativity while modifying the effective interactions between: the abstract machines of the plane of consistency, the concrete machinisms of the machinic phylum, and the machinic territorialities of expression. (Diagrammatic angle.)

Hence the following schema:

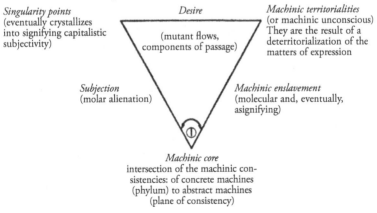

Singularity points
(eventually crystallizes into signifying capitalistic subjectivity)

Desire
(mutant flows, components of passage)

Machinic territorialities
(or machinic unconscious)
They are the result of a deterritorialization of the matters of expression

Subjection
(molar alienation)

Machinic enslavement
(molecular and, eventually, asignifying)

Machinic core
intersection of the machinic consistencies: of concrete machines (phylum) to abstract machines (plane of consistency)

Eight "Principles"

Is schizoanalysis a new cult of the machine? Perhaps, but surely not within the framework of capitalistic social relations! The monstrous development of machinisms of all types, in all domains, and what seems now to have to lead the human species to an unavoidable catastrophe, could also become the royal road to its liberation. In that case, is it still the old Marxist dream? Yes, up to a certain point. Because instead of taking history as being essentially ballasted by productive and economic machines, I think that, on the contrary, these are the machines, all the machines, which function in the manner of real history insofar as they constantly remain open to singularity traits and creative initiatives. Today how do we contest that a single generalized revolution will not be able to simply improve the mode of life on Earth in a sensible way, but may even save the entire human species from its destruction? It is a question of confronting both the immense coercive material means and the micropolitical means of disciplining thoughts and affects, of *militarizing* human relations. When we turn towards the West, the East, or the South, the question remains the same: how do we organize society otherwise? Will repression always remain a basic given for every social organization? But nothing in all this is unavoidable, other social assemblages, other machinic connections are conceivable! On this point, it matters little if we seem to stumble through Marxism: there is nothing good to gain from a return to first natures.[37] There is no more general solution than the slightest catharsis on the smallest scale! Nothing can be resolved except through the establishment of highly differentiated assemblages. Yet it must be clear that revolutionary machines that change the course of the world can only come to light or take on a consistency effectively allowing them to pass to the act based on a double condition:

1) that they aim towards the destruction of relations of capitalistic exploitation and the end of the division of society into classes, castes, races, etc...

2) that they establish themselves by breaking with all values founded on a certain micropolitics of muscle, the phallus, territorialized power, etc...

We have now returned to the question of schizoanalysis. It is not a matter of viewing it from a new psychological recipe, but from a micropolitical practice which will only take its direction from a gigantic rhizome of molecular revolutions proliferating from a multitude of mutant becomings: becoming-woman, becoming-child, becoming-elderly, becoming-animal, becoming-plant, becoming-cosmos, becoming-invisible...—as so many ways of inventing, of "machining" new sensibilities, new intelligences of existence, a new gentleness.

At this point, if I had to give in conclusion several recommendations of good sense, several simple rules for the direction of the analysis of the machinic unconscious, I would propose the following aphorisms, which furthermore could be fully applied to other domains, beginning with that of "great politics:"

1.—"*Don't hold back*." In other words, don't lay it on too thick or too thin. Remain right at the limit, adjacent to the becoming in process, and give way as much as possible. (Thus there is no question here of cures which would carry on for years, indeed dozens of years, like in the current mode of psychoanalysis!)

2.—"*When something has happened, this proves that something has happened*." This is a fundamental tautology that marks an essential difference with psychoanalysis whose basic principle expects that: "*when nothing happens, this proves that something happens in reality, something in the unconscious*." This is a principle that allows the psychoanalyst to justify his or her politics of silence and unlimited expectations. In truth, it is not often when *something really* happens in the assemblages of desire. It is also advisable to guard all their contours in such events and all their vitality in the components of passage which are their manifestation. Psychoanalysts would like us to believe that they are in constant contact with the unconscious, that they arrange a privileged connection which ties them to it, a sort of red telephone, like that of Carter and Brezhnev! The dreams of the unconscious know how to be understood by themselves. Unconscious desire, assemblages which are not expressed by the dominant systems of semiotization, manifest themselves through other means *which do not deceive*. No need here for spokespersons or interpreters. Such mystifications claim that the unconscious works in secret, that it is up to a certain type of detective to decipher its messages and above all to affirm that it is always alive, latent, and repressed, even though it be visibly dulled down, exhausted, or dead, and even though its last chance for existence would reside in its reconstruction, sometimes by starting with almost nothing at all… What a relief, albeit somewhat cowardly, to meet someone who deems you, against all appearances, to have an inexhaustible unconscious wealth while everything around you—society, family, your own resignation—appears to have conspired to empty you of all desire, of all hope of changing your life! A service like that is priceless, and one understands very well why psychoanalysts are paid so much![38]

3.—"*The best position for accessing the hiding place of the unconscious does not necessarily consist in remaining seated behind a couch.*"

4.—"*The unconscious drenches those who approach it.*" We will know that "something happens" when the schizoanalytic assemblage illuminates an "optional matter": it then becomes impossible to remain neutral because this optional matter drags everyone who encounters it in its wake.

5.—"*Important things never happen where we expect.*" Another formulation of the same principle: "The doors for entrance and exit are not the same." Or still: "the matters of components initiating a change are not generally of the same nature as those of the components which effectuate this change." (Example: speech will be converted into the somatic, or the somatic into the economic, or into the ecological, whereas the ecological will be converted into speech or into socio-historical events, etc., etc...) The fruitfulness of a schizoanalytic process will be measured by the variety and the degree of heterogeneity of these sorts of rhizomatic transferences, of the kind that no species of signifying semiology, no universal hermeneutics or political programming will be able to claim to translate them any longer, set them in equivalence, or remote control them so as to finally extract a common element easily exploitable by capitalistic systems. A signifier does not decidedly represent schizoanalytic subjectivity for another signifier! As long as components do not succeed in organizing their own machinic nuclei and their own assemblages of enunciation, they remain recalcitrant in the face of the dominant signifiers' claim to interpret them. And, afterwards, it is these components that ingest the signifying component. (It must be repeated that this is not at all synonymous with a systematic primacy of non-verbal components "before the time of machines.")

6.—Because in passing it has been a question of transference, I think that it will be most advisable to distinguish in all circumstances:

—transferences through subjective *resonance*, personological identification, the echoes of black holes;

—the machinic transferences (*transference-machines*) which proceed on below the signifier and global persons through asignifying diagrammatic interactions and which produce new assemblages rather than indefinitely representing and tracing old stratifications.

7.—"*Nothing is ever given.*" No stage or complex is ever crossed or ever surpassed. Everything always remains on the plane, available to all the re-usages but also to all the downfalls. A black hole can conceal another. No object can be affected by a fixed identity; no situation is guaranteed. Everything is an affair of consistency, assemblage and reassemblage. The circulation on the marketplace of a symbolic consistency guaranteed cent for cent ("how did you get over your castration complex?") is a dishonest and dangerous operation. Above all on the part of the people who claim to have achieved it themselves during the course of a so-called instructional analysis!

8.—Last, but in fact, first principle: "*any principle idea must be held suspect*." Theoretical elaboration is so much the more necessary and must be ever more audacious to the degree that the schizoanalytic assemblage will have taken stock of its essentially precarious nature.

7

Annex: The Molecular Transition of Signs

MACHINIC GENEALOGY OF ICONS, INDEXES, CODES, SIGN SYSTEMS, LANGUAGES AND DIAGRAMMTIC SEMIOTICS

Passing from codes to sign systems and then to languages, linguists have the impression of crossing successive degrees in the order of the creative capacity of semiotic concatenations. And nevertheless there is no reason to grant any title of nobility to productions which depend on language rather than to those concerning other systems of encoding or signs! For example, genetic codes throughout the history of life or iconic artistic systems throughout the history of humanity have been at least as rich, if one wishes to call them that, as linguistic systems of the literary phylum or the scientific phylum. In fact, the "machinic creativity" of a system and its belonging to a machinic and historical phylum does not concern systems of signs and codes as such, but assemblages that articulate these systems via abstract machines. (The assemblage itself conceived as the manifestation of the more functionalist side, abstract machinisms being the more constructivist side.) Thus there is not on one side the small blocks of a semiological construction and, on the other, an amorphous mass of the possible. The possible is a matter as differentiated as the most material matters. An unconscious redefined, as I attempt here, as an operator of this optional matter of the possible will thus have to be able to accommodate the introduction of the most diversified components of encoding and semiotization on an equal footing so as to be able to offer an optimal grasp upon the multiple universes of machinic creativity. But we will be able to advance in this way only on condition of better understanding what traverses these components, what happens—what passes—between their basic semiotic elements (signs, signals, symbols, icons, indexes, signs-particles, etc.). In the sense I bestow upon them, categories of form, information, and message are way too general, way too inclusive and removed from concrete realities to answer for this purpose. This is what will lead me to reconsider their customary usage and articulate them in a new type of "genesis" of encoding entities and semiotic entities.

Iconic Components[1]

A visual form (but also a physico-chemical signal, a rhythm, a refrain…) is detached from an assemblage A by an assemblage X. Assemblage A remains passive. It is indifferent to the fact that f has been detached by X, Y, Z… The extraction of f does not aim at a particular series of assemblages. Element f does not belong to a specified potential interlocutor. Moreover, it is also unable to belong to A, i.e. it has nothing but a virtual existence. (For example, when an animal face is semiotized in a cloud.) The following cases of indices are approximated to the degree that a relation crisscrossing machinic consistency is established between A and f and to the degree that this relation passes from a virtual possible to a real possible. Abstract machinisms relative to this type of icon are essentially accountable for this degree of consistency.

Figure 1: abstract machinism of iconic consistency

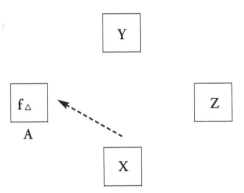

Indexical Components (or Components of Indexation)

The preceding relation between X and the sub-set f of A has become real; f effectively belongs to A (it is no longer a projection, a phantasm, or a minimally consistent virtuality). When a component of indexation is integrated into a semiological assemblage of designation, f will be converted into a morpheme of the referent.[2] At this stage we will only be able to say that there was an emission of a *messenger entity*. This emission is effectuated upon any azimuth: in other words, there is still no specification of a particular type of assemblage designated for f.

Here, abstract machinisms must answer for the fact that the degree of consistency of the relation of passage remains fixed at its maximum point: that of real actualization.

Figure 2: abstract machinism of indexical consistency

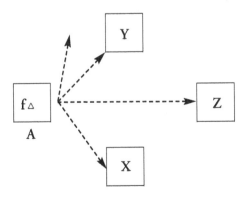

Components of Encoding

The recipients of f are specified: a series R of assemblages M, N, O... is characterized by the fact that each of its elements is "equipped" with the same components receptive of f; assemblages that do not have this equipment cannot receive f. The passage of the messenger entity from one assemblage to another has become transitive. We shall call it: *machinic redundancy*.[3] These redundancies can be incarnated in a line divided into chains so as to discursively convey information, or into two-dimensional images maintaining well determined figure/ground relations, or into three- and four-dimensional systems of molding, catalysis, field induction etc...

The abstract machinism initially "charged" by this type of redundancy thus establishes itself "astride" A and the assemblages of series R. It has to respond from:

—the definition of the relations internal to the component (from its machinic "biology"), i.e. from the division of the messenger entity, the information it retains, what it puts aside, the standard deviations it tolerates, the threshold of consistency before which it disappears, its matters of expression, etc...

—the definition of series R (M, N, O...) external to the component (from its machinic "ethology"), i.e. what differentiates it from other types of assemblages, from the nature of the redundancies that it implements (machinic redundancy or redundancy of resonance), from the nature of other assemblages, lines of flight, black holes, the catastrophes to which it is potentially referred and from the type of trajectory, the channels of transmission and possibly from the mediating systems from which these redundancies borrow, from the characteristics of serial times of encoding relative to the "machinic inertia" of the system.[4]

Figure 3: abstract machinism of machinic redundancies

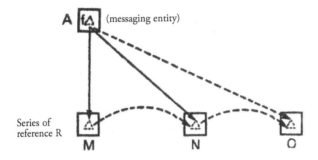

(The dotted lines mark the potential character of messenger entities in a series of reference and enables the assemblages covered by machinic redundancy to be virtual.)

Components of Semiotization

Unlike the preceding case, assemblage *A* belongs to the series of reference; relation *f* of *A* to *M* has become reflexive. *A* is thus able to return to its own entity messenger. Redundancy can return to itself. There is no longer a basic transmitting assemblage, no longer an irreversible direction for the trajectory of the redundancies of the messenger entities which we shall call here: *semiotic redundancies.* The determination of the trajectories of these redundancies is no longer coded in an intrinsic way by particular basic assemblages. It belongs to the entire series. The set of semiotic redundancies constitutes a subset messenger *E* from series *R*. We shall call this subset *E* a *component of passage.*[5] This component itself can belong to a series of assemblages different from *R*. We shall note that the fact that all assemblages have to refer to the same component of semiotization develops a relation of linear succession between them.[6] (Components of passage can still be laid out in a rhizome, but the basic components must be aligned.) In the case of the components of expression of semiological assemblages founded on the discretization and digitilization[7] of messenger entities (constituted by a battery of signs and asignifying signals or figures) we wind up with the formation of *syntagmatic chains* of designation (or the "en-signment" of the morphemes of the referent).

The abstract machinisms of components of semiotization will have to resolve three types of problems:

—those relating, as in the preceding case, to basic intra-component relations,

—those relating to the interactions between basic components and components of passage, particularly the reflexive character of semiotic redundancies and the proto-linear character which is conferred externally onto the series of basic components,

—those relating to the autonomization of the sign system internal to the component of passage (system of redundancy to the second degree or semiotic system properly speaking).

Figure 4: abstract machinism relative to semiotic redundancies

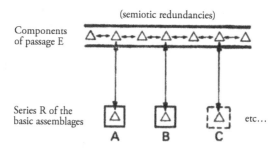

Components of Subjectification

Components of semiotization were characterized by the existence of an assemblage-substrate having "delegated," to some extent, part of their function of semiotization to a specialized component (component of passage or reference). The deterritorialization of these components of passage and their differentiation into two content-expression poles will radically alter the system of redundancies. The abstract machinisms of components of subjectification will have to account for seven types of redundancies:

—Three types of redundancies result from the reconversion of those of the preceding case (which correspond to the summits of the semiological triangle).[8]

I) *redundancies of morphemes of the referent*:

II) *asignifying redundancies* of expression (corresponding to Hjelmslev's figures of expression):[9]

III) *iconic redundancies* of represented contents (corresponding to the Saussurian signified) more or less deterritorialized and "mentalized" visual or auditory images, relational schemata (what C.S. Peirce calls icons of relation, diagrams), more or less abstract modes of categorization, etc.

—Three types of inter-redundancy redundancies, redundancies to the second degree, are developed beginning from the preceding three (which correspond to the three sides of the semiological triangle).

IV) redundancies of *designation* between the first and second;[10]

V) redundancies of *representation* between the first and the third;

VI) redundancies of *signification* between the second and the third.

—And finally, a redundancy to the third degree (corresponding to the center of the semiological triangle).

VII) subjective redundancies which constitute the key to the assemblages of subjectification to the extent that they are established from the last three types of redundancies.

Figure 5: seven semiological redundancies

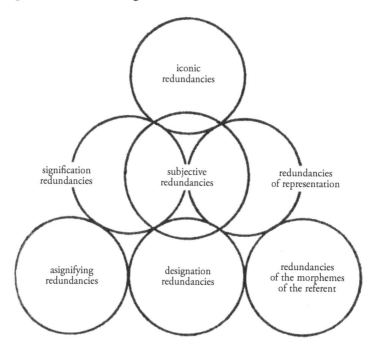

The passage from figure 4, relative to components of semiotization, to figure 5, relative to semiological redundancies, can be decomposed according to the two following phases:

First phase: bipolarization of semiotic components between deterritorialized elements of expression and reterritorialized elements of content.

Figure 6: bipolarization of semiotic components

deterritorialized expression   deterritorialized content

Second phase:

—opening of the semiotic component;

—constitution of an angle of signifiance whose intersection point moves over the axis of redundancies of signification between the most asignifying point of expression and the most signifying iconic object of heights. This point of intersection defines the quality of the feeling of signification which presides in a given operation of subjectification. (This is an objectifying subjectification where the subject is treated like a signifier; that is to say a fusional subjectivity, together with a pure iconic otherness, where the subject itself is treated as an empty icon, as the paradigm of all paradigms);

—the staging of a space of representation between redundancies of the referent and iconic redundancies is located:

1) at a certain distance from the absolute mental point of reference previously evoked, thus determining particular qualities and the reterritorializing degree of the icon of reference (God, empty soul, etc.),[11]

2) at a certain distance from a point, as mythical in the same respect as the preceding one of pure materiality is irreducible to any process of deterritorialization;

—finally, the interior sweep of the semiological triangle across the two sides of the angle of signifiance: the lower side approaches or moves away from the ideal axis of nominalist designations; the higher side approaches or moves away from the ideal axis of a pure and ineffable divine signification.

Abstract machinisms corresponding to the interactions and resonances existing between the seven systems of redundancy lead to the standard definition of four types of semiological consistency relating to:

—the material reality of the referent,

—the reality of representation and concepts,

—the reality of sign systems,

—the reality of individuated subjects.[12]

Figure 7: opening of the angle of signifiance

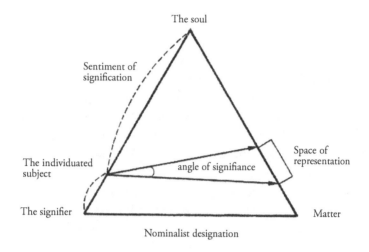

Nominalist designation

According to varied combinations and degrees, these diverse consistencies coexist within each semiological assemblage. The reality of intensive flows, intrinsic codes, layers, black holes and abstract machinisms is thus "negotiated" and "output" through what I would call the modes of dominant reality. Each of these reality-occurrences[13] depends on an "adjustment," on a modulation of consistency which concerns the inter-assemblage relations. Every type of society, but also every social subset at the time of every sequence of social life imposes its semiological formulas. (At such an hour on the playground, material, semiotic, mental, and subjective realities must correspond to what has been enacted by the Minister of education.) Signifying semiologies rest on four basic paralogisms relative to the reality of *brute Matter*,[14] to the reality of *the living Soul*, to the reality of the *signifying Verb*, and to the reality of the *individuated Subject*. One finds them in all circumstances and in the most various forms, not only within explicit codes (in religious, moral, political orders, etc...), but more especially throughout models of the social formations of the unconscious. The components of ideological denotation, signifying mediation, contextualization, and subjectification based on "dominant realities" are tightly gripped by institutions-agencies of power and the media, which are like so many operators of a "grammar"[15] of the unconscious.

Within each particular assemblage, the accent will be placed upon such and such type of redundancy, but no hierarchy, no priority of right could be established between the seven semiological redundancies. This explains why the production of sense could not depend in a univocal way on a system of syntagmatic and phonological double articulation or a system of generation and grammatical transformation. The categorial base of languages only seemingly concerns the elementary formulas of production. As sophisticated as it is imagined, the operation of a language is irreducible to a grammar. It always concerns social assemblages, constellations of singularity point traversed by *irreducibly* complex[16] abstract machinisms. The capitalistic passage of speech and territorialized semiologies under the control of scriptural components involved a miniaturization and a syntactic systemization of the relations of substitutability of segments of discourse which has not at all simplified, mechanized or universalized languages. The mechanisms of the "receptivity" of the morphemes of the referent are differentiated and particularized[17] to the same degree to which social relations and relations of production are complexified.

At the subjective level, this "modelization" of sense appears throughout what René Thom called "feelings of signification." They would result, according to him, from phenomena of "acute resonance"[18] between the concepts evoked by words and the real properties of objects in the outside world.[19] The point of view adopted here leads, on the contrary, to refusing the phenomena of significative resonance any grasp on reality and to ascribe it merely to diagrammatic, asignifying, and asubjective interactions of a meta-semiological nature. In the world of representation, which is always "faked" by the relations of social forces, signifying subjectification constantly moves between two limit feelings:

—a fusional feeling of appropriation which envelops conforming significations, promotes objectal, individual, egoistic identities, systematically reduces "everything excessive," crushes semiotic asperities, makes all values and desires equivalent, puts every local memory into a central memory...

—a feeling of "cartographic" hyperlucidity which presides on the contrary, over the location of transversal itineraries, thwarts micropolitical black holes inherent to personological, oedipal deixis (it, I, you, he, we, me, the other, thou...), facilitates the extraction of proliferating singularities, the rise of minor languages, the promotion of a politics of active memory loss, the liberation of creative memory which Proust calls involuntary memory...

Consciential Components

The components of subjectification are drawn in two opposite directions:

—towards the "exterior" on the side of morphemes of the referent, traits of matters of expression, diagrammatic icons which "inhabit" the representation,

—towards the "interior" on the side of a sort of maelstrom or semiotic black hole.

This black hole effect is produced by the node of resonance that emerges when a point of recentering is constituted between semiological redundancies. It tends to attract and isolate redundancies of every nature from their substrate, emptying them of their contents. It constitutes a point of *semiological powerlessness* in the same way that it constitutes a point of *machinic superpower*, because beginning from this, diagrammatic signs-particles will be emitted which we will see at work in the following assemblage.

Consciential components thus appear in reaction, in counterpoint, to subjective components. Their abstract machinism tends to confer a machinic autonomy onto the redundancies of resonance, to make them follow their own politics.

It is advisable to specify here how redundancies of interaction are distinguished from redundancies of resonance:

—redundancies of interaction, whatever their degree of deterritorialization and their degree of existential consistency (degree of reality or virtuality), only cease taking support from redundancies relatively more territorialized than themselves. For example, subjective redundancies take support from redundancies of signification, representation, denotation and these last on those of the sign-machines, the referent, and the iconic and conceptual world. The relation of deterritorializations thus always goes in the direction of reterritorialization here;

—redundancies of resonance, on the contrary, tend to be emptied of their substance; their own movement leads them to lose all support from stratifications, flows and codes. Their abstract machinism no longer has a function of attaching them to systems of redundancies of the first, second, or third degree; it propels them toward hyper-deterritorialized redundancies of infinite power and nullified efficiency.

As the "inverse" of redundancies of resonance, consciential redundancies have a function of determining subjectivity at the point where it is the least discernible, at the point where it escapes all reference, all relations of the figure-ground, subject-object type, etc. Their exploit consists in reterritorializing a black hole resting... on nothing. Consciential components turn nothingness around itself and, by doing this, exacerbate the process of subjectification which starts to spin around itself. Not content with having lost any object, any support, subjectivity proceeds to discover what it has lost until remembering it never had anything.

The paradox it makes us support, in connection with these nuclei of pure self-destruction, holds so that at the same time:

—they run up against a wall of absolute deterritorialization from which they seem to never be able to escape;

—they develop the richest "foreign policy" possible by irrigating the semiotic productions of all the other assemblages. This wall is insuperable for all the semiotics productions captive to spatio-temporal and substantial coordinates of significance, but it is infinitely porous to sign-particles which are used as a vector in abstract machines. It is through this wall, and only through it, that we will be able to "escape from language."

Two basically divergent micropolitics emerge with the entry of consciential components (all the intermediate combinations are obviously found within concrete assemblages):

—the first leads so that all systems of machinic redundancies "are doubled" by systems of resonance. A veil, a fuzzy resonance is woven over all the machinic singularities. By taking support from a particular type[20] of semiological redundancy, a "world of replacement," a world of simulacra is reconstituted, for better or worse. (The four paralogisms of significance are then promoted to the rank of ontological foundation);

—the second, that we shall examine in more detail in connection with diagrammatic assemblages leads so that absolute deterritorialization is, to some extent, "output" into relative deterritorialization, into quanta of deterritorialization, into matter of the possible, equipped with a power of trans-semiotic crossing which radically overturns the prior givens of the strata of encoding and semiological assemblages. (Consequently, redundancies of resonance tend to be transformed into redundancies of interaction of a new type.)

Figures 8 and 9 illustrate respectively:

—the abstract machinism of semiotic involution leading to the appearance of a subjective black hole effect at the heart of the semiological triangle. It also allows us to locate several concepts which structuralist psychoanalysis proposed in its attempt to ward off the subjective black hole which it cultivates, in addition, to great "profit" (politics of transference, silence, neutralization of all content, interpretative overcoding of every semiotic asperity, etc.);

Figure 8: abstract machinism of the involution of the semiological triangle

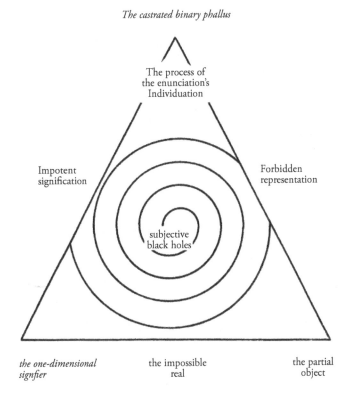

The castrated binary phallus

The process of
the enunciation's
Individuation

Impotent
signification

Forbidden
representation

subjective
black holes

*the one-dimensional
signfier*

the impossible
real

the partial
object

Figure 9: seven consciential reterritorializations of subjectification corresponding to the seven redundancies of the semiological triangle

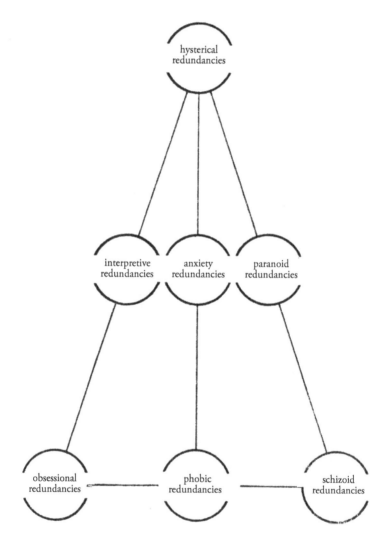

—the abstract machinism presiding over the general invasion of the seven semiological redundancies, starting from a particular type of *consciential resonance*. The resonant node is conferred onto one or several circles which not only take control of the component of con-scientialization, but also every other component. To indicate each of the "bastions" of resonance constituted, I have borrowed a series of labels from psychiatry. It is not a question of re-gilding the blazon-ry of traditional nosographic entities, but only of evoking several clinical syndromes to which these deterritorializing investments can lead when they are pushed to the limit. It goes without saying that other ways of considering semiological components within the framework of schizoanalytic monographs relating to concrete assemblages would also legitimately lead to other cartographies of the setting in resonance of systems of redundancies.

Diagrammatic Components[21]

With consciential components, a new type of binary machinism is established on the "brink" of the subjective black hole. The "edge" of this machine exerts its effects according to two antagonistic modalities:

—it yields broad sections of resonances that submerge all the semiotic components and deploy a molar world of simulacra whose tiniest recesses are haunted by the passion of abolition secreted by the subjective black hole;[22]

—it diffuses a dust of diagrammatic signs-particles that conta-minates, but this time on a molecular level, these same components in order to inflect their operation in the direction of an optimiza-tion of their machinic potentialities.

Strictly speaking, these signs-particles are no longer semiotic entities, since they arise as much from the singularity traits of the referent and the abstract machines "detached" from the plane of consistency as from sign machines. In a sense, they return us to the starting point of this machinic genealogy when we dealt with icons, indexes, and intrinsic codes within which they had not been differentiated from specialized components charged with enacting a syntax and a "foreign policy." But they are infinitely deterritorialized and deterritorializing. Being able "to stick" to every abstract space of machinic potentiality, they are the support of a molecular mode of an almost unlimited semiotization. The abstract machinisms conveyed by icons, intrinsic indices, and codes remain encysted in the stratifications and assemblages depending on pre-established frames of reference. Those carried by signs-particles primarily concern a possible quantification in the "nascent state" which confers on them a specific power of destratification, deformation, desemiologization, and desubjectification with regard to the existing assemblages. This results in the fact that the figures of expression engaged in a diagrammatic process are no longer referred to signifying representations. The relation that they maintain with such representations when they are surrounded by them is never essential. Thus the systems of logical, topological, algebraic algorithm, the processes of recording, memory storage, and data processing used by mathematicians, sciences, technology, harmonic and polyphonic music, etc., do not have an aim to *denote* or *fill* in the morphemes of a fully constituted referent, but to produce them through their own machinics.

Unlike representative systems of formalization which are bipolarized on a content-expression couple, diagrammatic systems are established directly at the intersection of the most deterritorialized formalism and the most stratified and territorialized traits of matter, morphemes, and singularity points. The relation of semiological extraction: form-substance-matter is thus profoundly overturned:

—semiological subjection (the signifier-signified biface) is disaggregated,

—form and matter establish a new type of circular connection due to the bias of signs-particles,

—the loops of the "capture of form" (of formalization) tend to be miniaturized and to indefinitely accelerate their cycle,[23] (fig. 10)

—a system of "elementary" quanta of deterritorialization which can be assimilated to infinitesimal black holes, substituted for ancient modes, more massive or more globalizing modes, for coding and morphemization.

Figure 10: diagrammatic cycle of deterritorialization

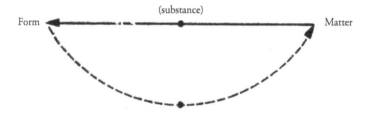

The abstract machinisms of signs-particles characteristic of the diagrammatic function have to respond to the articulation of three movements of deterritorialization:

—that which affects semiological sign-machines and generates the systems of figures of expression entirely polarized on the abstract machinisms of the assemblages "treated" by this function;

—that which affects the mental icons, the objects from up high, the conceptual and generative systems of asignifying diagrammatic figures, of icons of relation able to implement new connections;

—that which affects the morphemes of the referent and generates "new realities" (particulate, chemical, biological, social, aesthetic, etc.).

The cyclic movement of the conjunction of these three vectors (cycle of the diagrammatic function), tends to render indistinct, to fuse the final transformations of these three morphemic, semiotic, and iconic orders. Signs-particles are constituted to the degree that the signifying economy's residues of molar resonance are emptied of their substance. The deterritorialization, miniaturization, acceleration, and proliferation of signs-particles operate a centrifugal emptying of the semiological triangle (fig. 11) (symmetrical to the centrifugal emptying of the subjective black hole).

The micropolitical play of consciential components is established between two possible ways of treating the deterritorialization of the black hole: either the molar system of redundancies or the molecular machinisms of micro black holes. Here we find Hjelmselv's intuition relating to the congruence of the form of expression and the form of content. But this congruence, which glossematicians hardly extend upon, returns to the signs-particles of the employment of traits of matters of expression, singularities of contents, and abstract machinisms through their motionless but infinitely rapid crossing. It is thus nothing mechanical, it is not "given," it is always "returning" throughout this micropolitics which could be termed ontological.

In Hjelmslev's system, sense remained entirely dependent upon form.[24] It is only by postulating the existence of a universe of abstract machines beyond all formalism that we can understand how sense manages to release itself from the linearity of modes of encoding, from formal syntactic constraints and from the arbitrariness of relations of linguistic signification. Operative machinic sense is by no means an "amorphous mass"—according to Hjelmslev's expression—waiting upon an external formalism that would come to animate it. Machinic sense, a sort of short-circuit between abstract machines encysted in reality and abstract machines detached from the plane of consistency, is manifested across a spatial, temporal, substantial, multidimensional, and deictic rhizome in the midst of which it operates every possible transmigration, every

Figure 11: centrifugal emptying of the semiological triangle

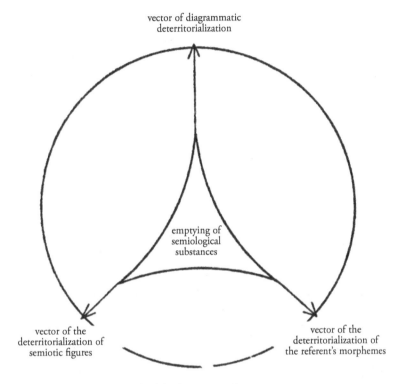

vector of diagrammatic
deterritorialization

emptying of
semiological
substances

vector of the
deterritorialization of
semiotic figures

vector of the
deterritorialization of
the referent's morphemes

Cycle of the diagrammatic function

transmutation (and not only translations through resonance). Signs-particles work on the same reality: through the enactment of systems of magnification, acceleration, deceleration, and all kinds of discernibilization, they "deter" the "mineralized" abstract machinisms, they open up new fields for machinisms which remained in the state of pure potentiality.

Signs-particles associate the smallest degree of actual consistency with the greatest degree of potential consistency, insofar as they represent an intermediate link between, on the one hand, abstract machinisms and, on the other, asignifying semiotic figures, the morphemes of the referent, and the most deterritorialized representations. While conveying themselves on the tangent of abstract machinisms, while miniaturizing the ensemble of semiotic vectors, while emptying them of their semiological substance, they tend to escape even from the system of redundancies. One can thus draw out a sort of division of labor between:

—abstract machines which exist absolutely independent of systems of redundancy;

—abstract machinic subsets of signs-particles which "inhabit" each element of redundancy without themselves being redundant and which deploy coordinates of redundancy (coordinates of space, time, substance, subjectification, etc.);

—concrete machinic subsets relative to figures of expression, relational icons, singularity traits of the morphemes of the referent, to diagrammatic operators of faciality, refrain, etc., which parasitize, phagocytize, and guide the territorialized redundancies and which are themselves swept along by the flow of the most heterogeneous redundancies.

In the last analysis, the consistency of an assemblage depends upon the degree of diagrammatism of its components. An assemblage is inconsistent when it is emptied of its quanta of possibles, when the signs-particles desert it to emigrate towards other assemblages, when the abstract machinisms that specify them become sclerotic, degenerate into abstraction, and become encysted in stratifications and structures, when finally it subsides in a black hole of resonance or falls to the threat of pure and simple disintegration (catastrophe of consistency). On the contrary, it takes on consistency when a deterritorialized machinic metabolism opens it up to new connections, differentiates and complexifies what I defined earlier as its "machinic nucleus," when it extracts singularity points from its internal texture in order to make them pass to the rank of singularity traits and machinic redundancies, and thus reveals in reality the quanta of possibles that it possesses with regard to the plane of consistency of abstract machinisms.

This genealogy of semiotic components develops according to three phases:

—the first is characterized by a differentiation of the morphogenesis of machinic redundancies and a specialization of components (icons, indexes, codes, and semiotic components);

—the second by a neutralization of the preceding systems with the deployment of redundancies of resonance (subjectification and signifying conscientialization);

—the third by a miniaturization and proliferation of deterritorialized machinisms (signs-particles and abstract machines) with diagrammatic components.

These three phases are not the expression of a dialectical movement of exhaustion, insofar as they are all worked on by the same kinds of abstract machinisms.

Let us also note that the degeneration of the semiological triangle not only affects the components of designation, representation, and signification, but also those of subjectification. On this subject, let us emphasize that diagrammatic desubjectification is not necessarily synonymous with a collapse of components of conscientialization; quite the contrary. A subjectivity exists independent of the consciousness that Freudianism proposed to explore, but there also exists a consciousness independent of individuated subjectivity which should be one of the essential resources of every schizoanalysis. This machinic consciousness could manifest itself as a component in assemblages of enunciation "mixing" social, technical, and data processing machines with human subjectivity, but can also manifest itself in purely machinic assemblages, for example, in completely automated and computerized systems. Thus, beyond the traditional unconscious of "normal-neurotic" interiority and the passages to the limit of sub-jectification towards "psychotic" redundancies, the field of the machinic unconscious will be opened, a hyper-conscious diagrammatic unconscious no longer maintaining anything but a distant relationship with the significations of dominant semiologies.

RECAPITULATION CONCERNING COMPONENTS OF PASSAGE

A certain number of observations relative to the components of passage implied in various types of assemblages have been gathered here.

Components of Passage in General and the Economy of the Possible in Nonhuman Machinic Assemblages

• A component is differentiated from flows and strata insofar as it belongs to an assemblage. A component of passage in particular even works upon the constitution of the assemblage: either because it belongs to its machinic nucleus, or because it potentially calls upon the constitution or the destination of a machinic nucleus.

• Components of passage are not detached from other components in the manner of a Gestalt: bearers of a possibilist machinism, they traverse the set of an assemblage's components (internal and external).

• They are what guarantees the machinic consistency of an assemblage or what modulates the passage of different thresholds of sufficient consistency: the passage from an imaginary possible to a mathematical possible, from a theoretical possible to a technical possible, economic possible etc., passage from semiotics to reality, passage across thresholds of durability, etc. The local increase in machinic consistency is not comparable to a reduction in entropy. Nothing exists that is equivalent to a general principle of decline in machinic consistency. Furthermore, this consistency is not quantifiable on the basis of a general standard; the possible cannot be circum-scribed in a dimension or a defined set in a univocal way, but only through assemblages of proliferating and fuzzy subsets.[25]

• The abstract machinic possible can be "output" according to various modalities and various supports:

—the modalities occur:

• via a catastrophic mode: the abolition of an assemblage: absolute deterritorialization;

• via a black hole mode: relative deterritorialization: system of totalization; homogenization through resonance...;

• via a quantum mode of deterritorialization: transmission of forms, structures, systems, metabolisms (through molding, catalysis, crystals of code, informatic sequences, diagrammatic processes...);

• more generally by the association of the preceding modalities.

—the supports concern matters of expression deterriotari-alized to differing degrees:

• for support, the hyper-deterritorialized possible of signs-particles has a trans-cosmic, trans-semiotic plane of consistency and abstract machines that escape all spatio-temporal and substantial coordinates;

• for support, the possible of concrete machinic proposi-tions has a semiotic plane of consistency traversing all possible substances of expression (equivalent to the two Hjelmslevian levels of form of content and form of expression);

• for support, the possible of material flows and strata has intrinsic codings encysted in their matters of expression (pertinent traits of matters of expression);[26]

• for support, the evental possible has singularity points irreducible to any coordinates. On the contrary, evental possibles attach themselves to "coordinating" assemblages. An essential affin-ity exists between the possible of the most abstract machines and that of the most singular points, due to the fact that they are both located upon the tangent of an "absolute impossible," a sort of seat of radical creationism; the singular is consequently deployed as law, and the general is singularized as concrete manifestation;

• for support, the possible of assemblages, inter-assemblage relations, and their components has machinic nuclei within which an optional matter and a politics of subjectified choices are discernibilized (proto-subjectivity and proto-alterity). What are negotiated on this level are the crossings of threshold among the preceding possibles.

Generally, the analysis of the machinic unconscious, defined as the machinic ecology of assemblages, will thus amount to shedding light upon the components of passages as they are likely to intervene in the articulation of the various modalities and the various supports previously evoked.

Components of Passage and the Economy of Choices in Assemblages of Semiotization

• This type of assemblage is founded upon a compromise between:

—generative molar structures constructed from systems of resonances centered on the effects of micro-black holes,

—and transformational machines bringing into play asignifying diagrammatic semiotics.

• Here, components of passage must be specified in relation with this system of triple articulation between:

—assemblages of enunciation territorializing all intensive multiplicities by fixing them on an individuated, conscious, deliberating subject. To some extent, they clog the effects of the black hole;

—assemblages of asignifying expression tending to make the quanta of possibles carried by the various matters of expression proliferate;

—assemblages of content tending, on the contrary, to delimit the range of diagrammatic processes, to fix their paradigmatic frameworks which will constitute so many signified matters for power formations, so that the forms extracted from the matters of expression by components of passage will all concern a socially homogenized, signifying substance.

By again taking up the preceding description of the machinic genealogy of signs, we can schematize in the following way the two fundamental types of components of passage of the assemblages of semiotization:

There are three elements of departure:

—substantial ensembles (content and/or expression) represented here by squares (level of existential consistency);

—forms (content and/or expression) represented here by points (level of semiotic efficiency);

—matters of expression (support and motor of the extraction of the forms of substances, or of the substantification of forms) represented here by arrows.

A signifying component of passage generates formal loops, subjective redundancies, by passing from one matter of expression to another:

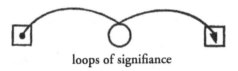

loops of signifiance

(The loop corresponds to Hjelmslev's substance of expression; it can be instituted as the means of expression of a generative molar process [black hole or stratum].)

An asignifying component of passage does not generate such loops but directly unites the movements of formal extraction on the plane of consistency.

the plane of abstract machinic consistency

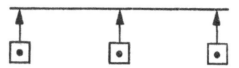

the mode of concrete semiotic efficiency

Diagrammatism goes "over the heads" of subjective and signifying loops; it makes the figures of expression work directly (phonemes, graphemes, mathemes, informatemes) with abstract and concrete machinisms and the singularity points of the "referent."

Components of Passage and Capitalistic Subjectification

• This type of assemblage is founded on a double movement:

—of the deterritorialization of the flows, strata and assemblages which generate a global super-machinism integrating every "originary" human activity (productive and nonproductive);

—a reterritorialization on artificial objects, on machinic assemblages controlled by the dominant powers, on every mode of subjectification.

• Under these conditions, components of passage can be divided into two types of categories:

—components of integration: for example, those converting subjectivity into labor power (understood in a very broad sense), those populating the unconscious of affects, representations, and designs for the ensemble of systems. The operators of this social unconscious are power apparatuses, community facilities, the media, public transportation, etc.;

—components allowing the economy of individual and/or collective desire to escape as little as possible with this generalized integration: lines of flight, indexes of every nature.

In fact, on a real terrain, such a division of components is not directly operative: the same components, for example technico-scientific or artistic components, can simultaneously exploit several registers of possibilist deterritorialization and stratifying reterritorialization. For example, the signifying economy tends to be directly controlled by the asignifying economy of Capital considered as an integral of power formations, while the abstract components of Capital are made to reterritorialize on neo-archaisms.[27]

• The distinctive criteria making it possible to detect components of "molecular revolution" or schizoanalysis are to be located in the same movement of the deterritorialization and artificialization of the processes. Diagrammatic representation, the map, tends to exceed the demarcations between realities, territories, and the machinic economy of possibles.[28]

• The politics of Capital consists in directing a reterritorialization of the social formations and assemblages caught in the deterritorializing machinic turmoil. Liberation from capitalistic constraints happens, not through a politics of return to archaic territorialities, but through the crossing of an additional degree of deterritorialization. The program of assemblages of machinic desire consists in founding human life and social life not on a permanent dependence of closed and abstract structures, but according to their own movement.

• A schizoanalytic perspective seeks to determine, within a component of passage (a new social tendency, a machinic mutation, a technical miniaturization—for example, the radio libre (free-radio) phenomenon in the early 1980s), the machinic nuclei which release diagrammatic processes from the appropriation of the models of redundancies and images, and which correspond to the optimal conditions allowing a possibilist machinics to create new realities and new modes of subjectification and sociality.

II

———————

REFRAINS OF LOST TIME

1

Swann's Love as Semiotic Collapse

In Search of Lost Time is a prodigious rhizomatic map. It is not a question of psychoanalyzing or schizoanalyzing it. It is a schizoanalytic monograph as such. Proust, Joyce, Kafka, Beckett… are veritable specialists of hyper-deterritorialized mental objects, and everyone could learn a lesson from them! This does not mean that it is prohibited to index and scientifically attempt to exploit the material they have collected. But the radical separation of the literary field and the scientific field, which seems to be an axiom of Western culture, has the effect of stupefying people's minds. Literary critics do not take into account the fact that such a work like this constitutes a scientific exploration in the same category as the work of Freud or Newton. And scientists are not generally disposed to the means that make it possible to confront the type of problematic which is developed there. And then it must even be said that they don't have the minds for that! For example, soon it will have been half a century since Von Weizäecker recommended that the systematic study of "perceptive overlapping" should be developed—sensorial hyperesthesia, synesthesia, synopsy, metamorphoses, etc. But, to my knowledge, apart from several pages Merleau-Ponty has dedicated to these questions[1] and several neurological and physio-pathological works on hallucinogenic intoxications—forgiving their extreme dryness as reading material—it is still to the "works" of Henri Michaux and to the American writers of the "beat generation" that it is advisable to turn to today if we wish to access a minimum amount of information on these questions, so essential for apprehending the diversity of the modes of subjectification and semiotization. As an indication, but very summarily, very schematically, and to support ourselves on Sherrington's old classification, for lack of something better, we could, for example, "situate" the respective "specialties" of Kafka and Proust in relation to one another. Both are interested in the mutations of perceptive components, in the phenomena of the magnification, displacement, overlapping, acceleration, or deceleration, etc… of sensorial coordinates. But their research is centered:

—for Kafka, on proprioceptive components, such as those of posture, balance, muscular tone, blood pressure, etc., which lead to dilations and contractions of time and space (taking account of the very singular way in which he "drugged" himself through insomnia and anorexia);

—and for Proust, on exteroceptive components (tango-receptor, thermo-receptor, algo-receptor, photo-receptor, stibio-receptor, gusto-receptor and phono-receptor) and secondarily interoceptive components, particularly respiratory.[2]

Without explicitly embarking upon a theory of incorporeals and abstract machines, Proust will never stop insisting on the fact that the "musical effect," and more generally that of works of art, does not arise from the imaginary, but from reality: "this music seemed to me something more true than all known books. Sometimes I thought that the reason was that the things we feel in life are not experienced in the form of ideas, and so their translation into literature, an intellectual process, may give an account of them, explain them, analyze them, but cannot recreate them as music does, its sounds seeming to take on the inflections of our being, to reproduce that extreme and *internal point* of sensation which is the thing that causes us the specific ecstasy we feel from time to time and which, when we say 'What a beautiful day! What beautiful sunshine!', is not conveyed at all to our neighbor, in whom the same sun and the same weather set off quite different vibrations (III, p. 374–375/V, 346). The whole of the *Recherche* focuses on the existential consistency of such unclassifiable realities. Sometimes Proust assimilates them to material entities, and he compares the work of a musician like Vinteuil to that of a Lavoisier or an Ampère (I, 351/I, 364), sometimes he leans towards a "realism of ideas": "Swann had regarded musical motifs as actual ideas, of another world, of another order, ideas veiled in shadows, unknown, impenetrable to the intelligence, but not for all that less perfectly distinct from one another, unequal among themselves in value and significance" (I, 349/I, 362). At certain moments, he attempted to analyze the matter of expression of "Vinteuil's little phrase" in terms which evoke what will be, five years later, the distinctive oppositions of the phonologists of the Prague Circle:[3] "he had realized that it was to the closeness of the intervals between the five notes that composed it, and to the constant repetition of two of them, that was due this impression of a frigid and withdrawn sweetness"; but, as though he were conscious of the "reductionist" abuses to which the future structuralist interpretations would give rise, he immediately proceeds and adds that "in reality he knew that he was reasoning this way not about the phrase itself but about simple values substituted, for the convenience of his intelligence, for the mysterious entity he had perceived…" (I, 349/I, 362). Without really giving himself up to one theory instead of another, Proust constantly revolves around the same difficulty: he cannot accept the vague, fuzzy, evanescent nature of the sensations that assail him. It should be remembered that the inaugural event of his work has been this horse-drawn promenade in Combray, during which he has managed to go "*to the end of his impression*"[4] for the first time (at that time it was a matter of expressing with words this "something analogous to a jolly *phrase*" which received the relative displacements of the steeples of Martinville and Vieuxvicq (I, 180–181/I, 184–185). Of this reality "in the nascent state," he can affirm but one thing: it does not simply arise from a discursive analysis such as human language can sustain. On the contrary, this is what we will have to address in order to enrich language, to ripen it, and generate a new discursivity in direct contact with what I call the economy of desire. "The suppression of human speech," (Proust always writes a propos of "Vinteuil's little phrase") "far from letting fantasy reign there, as one might have believed, had eliminated it; never had spoken language been such an inflexible necessity, never had it known such pertinent questions, such irrefutable answers" (I, 351/I, 364). And years after the redaction of *A Love of Swann*, Proust will return in *The Prisoner* to this question which he seems to have never stopped pursuing: "Musicologists could take those phrases and find their analogues, their *antecedents*, in the works of other great musicians, but only for secondary reasons, outward resemblances, analogies discovered through ingenious reasoning rather than felt through direct impression. The impression conveyed by these phrases of Vinteuil's was different from any other, as if, in spite of the conclusions which science seems to be reaching, *individuals did exist*" (III, 255–256/V, 234). A science of the individual is what Proust's thought has hit upon, influenced as he was by the scientistic conception of matter reigning then, including in the scientific milieus. Be that as it may, his religion is at least constructed on one point: one cannot consider human subjectivity as something empty and undifferentiated that would be filled and animated from the outside.[5] His entire analysis leads him towards the possession of trans-subjective and trans-objective abstract machinisms, concerning which he will furnish us with a rigorous description and, this goes without saying, supreme elegance: "Even when he was not thinking of the little phrase, it existed latent in his mind in the same way as certain other notions without equivalents, like the notion of light, of sound, of perspective, of physical pleasure, which are the rich possessions that diversify and ornament the realms of our inner life" (I, 350/I, 363). And when, in the course of a paragraph, Vinteuil's little phrase emits its own opinions (I, 348–349/I, 361–362), it is momentarily substituted for three accredited interlocutors from this "region" of the *Recherche*— Swann, the Narrator and Proust himself as a real scriptor—it is under its most asubjective, asignifying face that for a brief moment the collective assemblage of its enunciation is revealed.

Nothing predisposed Swann to fall in love with Odette. Familiar with refined salons but keeping himself from attachments which would be too exclusive, he assumed a principle of balancing his relationships with the women of high society by courting escorts "with healthy, plump and rosy bodies" (I, 195/I, 203). That Odette had been at the moment of their encounter, an "demimondaine"—which he was not aware of or rather unconsciously refused to acknowledge—thus does not constitute in itself an obstacle to his having had a simple "adventure" with her. But her type of beauty does not "appeal" to him. It was Odette who was first passionately in love with him—she will confess this much later to the Narrator—moreover without any result for a long time. Her first success will consist in making him attend a reception at Madame Verdurin's, her protector and her only real support in the "world." At that time salons functioned as "initiation camps" for the tribes of high society. Swann goes to Madame Verdurin's salon a little like an ethnologist who establishes contact with an unknown ethnic group. The people of the Verdurin salon were in effect well lower in status than he. And nevertheless it is this slightly vulgar and sometimes rather ridiculous bourgeois salon which has become "the semiotic converter" and even the infernal machine that was to shake up his entire existence.[6]

The Verdurin collective assemblage employs two components of passage:

—a refrain: "Vinteuil's little phrase."

—a constellation of faciality traits resulting from the mixture of two faces: that of Odette and Zipporah, a biblical figure extracted from a Botticelli fresco.

During the whole period of "Swann's love," these two components have a sort of parallel:

—either they disrupt the organization of other semiotic components and develop "liberating" transformations in Swann's life;

—or they open up obsessive and repressive reterritorializations. (But it is above all this second perspective which will prevail.)

During the period of "the Narrator's love," six times longer in the novel's organization, they will generally lead in diverging directions:

—faciality traits, after being differentiated and diagrammatized to the extreme, in reaction bring about a massive reterritorialization of the Narrator's passion for Albertine and will end up losing all their effectiveness;

—for its part, the refrain never ceases to go beyond itself, transversalize itself, and it will lead the Narrator to carry out a veritable and durable micropolitical mutation.

Thus, we consider that the part of the novel dedicated to Swann arises from what I have called, in the preceding essay, generative schizoanalysis (that of weak molar interactions, of stratified objects and relations) and that the remainder of this work constitutes a transformational schizoanalytic revision of this primary nucleus, of this passionate "first attempt" which has led Swann to the brink of madness ("I'm turning into a real neurotic" (I, 317/I, 328)).

We will only be able to grasp the nature of the "denouement" of Time regained, i.e. the release of the *Recherche* as an analytic process of the machinic unconscious, after having followed the coming and goings throughout the work in which the components of refrains and the components of faciality take part in. "Vinteuil's little phrase" previously appeared in the Odette-Zipporah complex. It crystallizes the new assemblage in the pure state before any facialitary incarnation when Swann, several months before meeting Odette, listens to Vinteuil's music for the first time. His immediate love for this deterritorialized musical sequence lets Swann hope for the "possibility of a sort of rejuvenation" (I, 210/I, 218).[7] But the appearance of a neurotic black hole centered on Odette's faciality comes to dash all his hopes. Not only will he no longer master the refrain component, but in addition he will lose control over the facialitary components he possessed until then. In fact, the machinic mutation which is the vehicle of Vinteuil's little phrase completely catches him off guard. He himself is not a musician, and even though he is abreast of the revolutionary transformations occurring in the music of his era, he does not really experience them "from the inside." Until then, his position was completely different in relation to iconic components. He is considered one of the most important art critics in aristocratic salons; in particular, he follows the first developments of modern art with an impressive competence. And generally, a new face is not something that would distract him for long; he has even adopted an extremely particular procedure to "seize" it or give it a supplementary attraction which consists in associating it with a painting he is very familiar with. Proust explains to us that this is Swann's way of dispelling "his remorse for having confined his life to worldly relationships" (I, 223/I, 231). In thus slipping the frivolous world into art, he believes that he exorcizes it. However, it could be thought that this procedure also has the goal of guarding him against the impassioned rages which would lead him to *effectively* escape from his world, and not simply by exploring the Verdurin salon or chasing after young maids. By "aestheticizing" his encounters, he is always brought to "recuperate" and neutralize all the semiotic asperities, machinic indexes, lines of flight, and desire drives of an iconic order. This time, however, his procedure will not have functioned. Why has this happened?

What is the origin of this devastating power of Odette's face? What endows the constellation of faciality features inherent in it with the capacity of triggering such a semiotic collapse? For Swann, is it not a question of a "regressive identification" with a maternal figure? Of the consequence of a deficiency of a symbolic paternal pole which would prohibit him from properly "assuming" his "castration"? To reconstitute a reassuring psychogenesis it would suffice to let oneself go, be it but for an instant, to the usual psychoanalytic fantasies. After all, has not this Zipporah, whose face is superimposed on Odette's, been given to Moses by his father, Jethro the priest, as a token of his return to the God of Abraham? And hasn't this Sistine chapel fresco been conceived as a counterpoint between the life of Jesus and the life of Moses? Doesn't this indicate to us that we are here on a double register: that of Swann's archaic fixation on an *imaginary* equivalent of the bad incestuous mother-whore-girl and that of an essentially *symbolic* Christian inscription of an originary absence of the paternal function? Moreover, isn't it after his marriage with Odette, and from a sublimation of his incestuous passion, that Swann will ultimately be brought to assume his Jewish condition during the Dreyfus affair? Consequently, what good is it to wonder about the singularity of *this* face, the matter of expression of *this* musical phrase, the assemblage of *this* salon, the circumstances of *this* political conversion… With little authority and lots of bluff, one may be able to force all these details back into the framework of traditional psychoanalytic interpretations. Why reevaluate this type of explication which seems to present no problems for anyone today? I am certainly not claiming to substitute one reading grid for another, one which would guarantee the "right answer." It is the very principle of interpretation that I intend to dispute. The analysis of the unconscious must follow—at its own risk—all the lines of the rhizome constituting an assemblage, whatever be the matters of expression of its components and the black hole effects they release, and the breaks or chain reactions such a process may involve... In Swann's case, for example, we will not say that identification is nothing! It will simply be considered a particular procedure functioning in the framework of particular assemblages beginning from particular components and matters of expression.[8] Considered in isolation, it is of no interest; it would not give rise to any *a priori* interpretations or return to any "matheme" or any universal "imago." Schizoanalysis will pose a completely different question: for example, is such a behavior, habit, or ritual called upon to take on a diagrammatic role? And how is this known, if not through a patient exploration not only of the "classified ways," but also all the trails, all the impassable paths, indeed of what seem to be obvious impasses. General principles will be of no use for us when it will be a matter of determining whether such a component of passage will or will not be able to continue functioning outside a given pragmatic field. For example, we should question why the face-portrait identification technique so important for Swann's love is no longer found in the loves of the Narrator; whereas, on the other hand, Vinteuil's little phrase, after a long eclipse, will here have an essential place and even play a decisive role in the novel's "resolution." We shall prove that this difference does not pertain to the intrinsic qualities of the iconic component or refrain component, but only to the fact that the latter is the only one that begins to make the writing machine "proliferate." Thus, here music will not have been a sublimated "stopgap" opening up a symbolic derivation of the libido, but an essential tool in the launching of a machine catalyzing new semiotic components, liberating new potentialities of deterritorialization and involving, in return, a shaking up of the ego, which makes pathological formations appear which insert themselves effortlessly within certain sociological "inertias" of the era.

We must not lose sight of the fact that the little phrase will never be completely self-identical, that it will never lead to the same politics within the various assemblages where we will rediscover it and that, from one field to the next, it will be brought to prioritize and exploit the different aspects of its matters of expression. Thus, it will be impossible to assign it a single essential quality, a single structural function, as will almost always be the case—but only for contingent reasons—with the iconic components of faciality. It is a whole register of machinic traits and asignifying signs-particles that will be discernibilized here, enacted according to the different field consistencies and the different semiotic efficiency modes of the enunciation assemblages. As *an asignifying machinic index* at the time of the "presentiment" of a new love a year before meeting Odette, the little phrase will become a sort of *ethological indicator*[9] of Swann's entry into Verdurin's territory. Reduced to the state of an obsessive catchphrase, the anchoring point of a black hole in formation, i.e. the point of engulfing everything meaningful in life as well as the most ordinary significations, it will also announce itself as the swansong of Swann's passion for Odette, it will even contribute to dismantling certain neurotic aspects without transforming for all that into a diagrammatic component of passage which would develop a radical renewal of his existence. In effect, Swann will never completely recover from this amorous crisis. Something will definitively remain broken. The Narrator and the baron Charlus, confronted in turn by the same type of black hole of passion, the same type of neurotic jealousy, will also have these crises when facing similar initiation ordeals (equally entailing the intrusion of a hyper-deterritorialized musical component into their life). But they will choose radically opposed paths.

The baron Charlus will get stuck in his jealous passion for A MUSICIAN to the point of complete degeneration; whereas the Narrator will use his love and his knowledge of MUSIC in order to dismantle a mechanism of passion against which he rebels, and submit himself to a profound revolution which will enable him to give himself body and soul to his work. Like a composite hero of the Greek world and the Old Testament, the Narrator will only be able to overcome the obstacles blocking his way on condition *that he himself lead the people who are the most precious to him to sacrifice*: his grandmother, his mother, Albertine. In order to reach a type of *becoming-woman*, which constitutes the essential workings of his creation, he will have to destroy everything that would rejoin him to the world of women. The double death of Odette—with all its artifice—cannot, in my view, be explained otherwise. All things considered, the key to the amorous enigma of the assemblage: Swann-Charlus-the Narrator has nothing to do with the drama of Oedipus; but rather, pertains to an overarching discovery concerning the destiny of Orpheus, which is to say that he and no one else has cast Eurydice into Hell and that he only uses his musical powers in order to resurrect her so as to be able to renew his sacrifice, thus demonstrating, for all to see, that he is finally done with this kind of passion which has paralyzed him for so long.[10]

I now intend to study the "little phrase's" different assemblages of enunciation that distinguish the *Recherche*. I will concisely describe the circumstances, the context that characterizes them, and also the various matters of expression which they set to work. Concerning each of them, I will attempt to extract what appear in my view to be the most significant micropolitical results. (There exists, for example, a dominant component, a component of passage, a rhizomatic opening, an effect of arborescence, black hole effects, etc.)[11]

2

Nine Assemblages for a Refrain

First Assemblage: a salon, the previous year: the proto-phrase or the system of "fac-simile."

We are given few specifications about the conditions under which Swann listens to one of Vinteuil's musical pieces for the first time, a year before meeting Odette. We know that he was barely familiar with contemporary music; he shows a certain difficulty in grasping the nature of the little phrase and in discerning its effects.

The sonata is played on violin and piano. Proust specifically enumerates the different phases of Swann's semiotization of the "little phrase":

—in the beginning, he only perceives "the material quality of sounds secreted by instruments" (I, 208/I, 216);

—afterwards he comes to better grasp the bulk that constitutes the part of the piano which is "multiform, undivided, smooth, and colliding like the purple tumult of the waves when the moonlight charms them and lowers their pitch by half a tone" (I, 208/I, 216);

—an evanescent musical form begins to appear, but he is incapable of determining its contours or even if it is a melodic phrase or a harmony;

—he ends by clearly distinguishing "one phrase rising for a few moments above the waves of sound" (I, 209/I, 217);

—but this form, which is extracted from the ensemble, remains fragile. So as to capture it, memory must rely on a system of "fac-similes" (I, 209/I, 217) allowing him to have access to a summary mental transcription of its scope, of its symmetrical groupings, its writing, its expressive value. This primary diagrammatic compo-nent, which remains essentially mnemotechnical, can be characterized in the following way:

1. It is deterritorializing. The "little phrase" is the vehicle of abstract machinisms whose effects will first of all be felt in the reg-ister of perception. Swann, who is not a musician, yields to impressions which are "without extension, entirely original, irre-ducible to any other order of impressions." Proust insists on the fact that "an impression of this kind is, for an instant, so to speak, *sine materia*" (I, 209/I, 216).

2. It is constituted from asignifying redundancies interacting with other components, combining with them on the most deterri-torialized level. (The notes that we hear tend "depending on their loudness and their quantity, to spread out before our eyes over sur-faces of varying dimensions, to trace arabesques, to give us sensations of breadth, tenuousness, stability, whimsy" (I, 209/I, 216–217).

3. It announces the possibility of a rhizomatic opening. The little phrase's effect upon Swann is not simply aesthetic. He discovers in it "the presence of one of those invisible realities in which he had ceased to believe" (I, 211/I, 219), and he feels the desire and almost the force of "dedicating his life" to them. By virtue of the little phrase, he could be cured of the moral dryness from which he suffers. An entire conformism, a whole micropolitics of conformity to the dominant realities, is thus threatened by his irruption. In counterpoint, one senses the struggle Proust himself led against his too perfect adaptation to worldly models and above all to the aes-thetic models of his era. (His long progression as a critic which allowed him to free himself from Ruskin's theories and rid himself of a certain idolatry of the "exemplary model.")[1]

With this first assemblage of enunciation the potentiality of a diagrammatic charge has been revealed. But this still does not mean that it will be effectively enacted. It's as though we possessed the reactive forces capable of propelling a supersonic airplane but still not what we call its units (the wings, fuselage, stabilizers, etc.). The assemblage is simply the vehicle of a *machinic index*. Furthermore, this first diagrammatic charge will be immediately dissolved: for several months the little phrase will no longer be a concern. (Swann ignores it so he will be able to rediscover it one day.) The fact that this first assemblage comes to a sudden halt is not due to an accident internal to the process of semiotization (as would have been the case with the appearance of a semiotic collapse or an arborescent formation which would have paralyzed its whole production). It results from the assemblage's *lack of consistency* itself. The syncretism between contents and expression remain fragile—"impressions" of all kinds which flutter around music are not truly attached to its perceptive texture. Fac-similes retain a formal nature (of the mnemotechnical order). Under these conditions, the abstract machinism carried by Vinteuil's little phrase is forced to remain in waiting, as in a stem cell or embryonic protophrase stage. There has been no black hole effect here, but simply the default shutdown of existential consistency. The diagrammatic's switch has tripped. And yet a charge of deterritorialization and an abstract machine have been put in flow; they indicate a line of flight through which Swann's entire life could be transformed. Through fragments, successive approximations or multiple recoveries, this abstract machinism will never stop traversing and driving the process of the *Recherche*. The little phrase will end up revealing itself for what it is: one of the essential motors of the Proustian machine. But in Swann's memory, at the end of this first assemblage only a vague nostalgia will subsist of it. It will remain for him like the memory of a fugitive love, of an "unknown passer-by" (I, 210/I, 218).

Proust has given us a confirmation that this breakdown of the diagrammatic effect is even extrinsic to the process and depends on an "insufficient" wiring of the assemblage, when he notes that Swann will not manage, after this first hearing, to obtain specifications about this musical piece, since its performers have departed upon a long voyage immediately after the concert. It is only within the framework of the second assemblage that he will become aware of its composer's *proper name*, i.e. of an essential component of the little phrase's diagrammatism.[2]

Second Assemblage: Madame Verdurin's home: the incubation of the refrain and the beginnings of Swann's love.

For Swann, accepting to return to the Verdurins' home already constituted a notable departure from his refined habits, frequenting only their salon, and renouncing for several years to attend the most aristocratic receptions, marks a radical break in his existence. We will find Vinteuil's little phrase inscribed upon both sides of this break. On one side it is "attached" to Swann meeting Odette, and, on the other, it reappears after several years when Swann begins to liberate himself from his passion and attends a large aristocratic reception for the first time.

We have already evoked the fact that the Swann "before Odette" was attracted to grisettes. He generally maintains a fairly tight compartmentalization between his high society life and his working class associations. However, a sort of perversion of the aesthetic order sometimes began to make these two domains overlap. He brings himself, for example, to involve a "young maid" in an exhibition of impressionist paintings about whom she "understood nothing," or to invite a "little worker girl" to a variety theater peep box to watch a decadent play.[3] Assuredly, there was nothing there that would "unclass" him: the possibility of such deviations from the codes of the upper castes is itself one of the essential secret clauses of these castes. Real bad taste, that which is advisable to avoid at all costs, is precisely what he could expect to encounter in a salon like that of the Verdurins, where the pretentious of the *nouveaux riches*, pedantic professors and doctors, bohemians and demimondaines were brought toegether. Swann only went there because of his attraction to Odette. But he discovers there a world much different from what he imagined: the faults and ridiculousness in fact mask the good heartedness of these men and women,[4] among whom certain are veritable scholars and artists called on to play a primary role in the aesthetic revolution of "modern art." From this point of view, the Verdurins' "little gang" fully knows what it is up to. It shows extreme contempt for everyone gravitating around Saint-Germain Faubourg (a contempt which surely conceals jealousy). The aristocrats are ranked in the "tedious" category, who are unable to understand anything whatsoever about true beauty. The Verdurins' judgment does not stem from very elaborate aesthetic theories, and in a sense, their dilettantism even has something quite superficial about it. But the fact is: as a *collective assemblage*, their Salon will "select" some of the greatest artists and writers of their era. The ridicule, tics, and pettiness of each character matter very little in and of themselves. Madame Verdurin's outbursts, her facial neuralgia, her feigned dread waiting for the pieces that she loves, all this matters very little. The collective assemblage is "connected" to the machinic mutations that overtake it on all sides, while Swann's encounter with a woman who formerly went by the nickname of "Miss Sacripan" (I, 849; I, 860/II, 429; II, 440) will not have acquired such a devastating intensity to the extent that she will be inserted there as a "revealer."[5]

It is thus in this framework that Swann comes to rediscover the "little phrase" and the name of its creator will be revealed to him. Vinteuil's work takes on an important place in the liturgy of Madame Verdurin's salon. Here we do not ignore that it is a question of a music which has already made a strong impression in an "advanced school." However, the interest shown for it conceals a conventional nature. Hardly anyone but Madame Verdurin and the painter Elstir[6] have a sincere attachment to this music. The latter—one of the four great creators of the *Recherche*, alongside Vinteuil, Bergotte, and the Narrator himself—seems to be the only one fully aware of the value of Vinteuil's work. For example, he will talk to Swann about the Sonata in F# that it is a "a truly great machine" [une très grande machine]"[7] (I, 212/I, 220). But he does not specify his judgment in any other way.

We could be tempted to attribute the reserved or distracted attitude of the other members of the little gang to the incompetence or absence of taste. But then how do we explain the importance that the reference to Vinteuil has taken on in this salon? Merely due to an allegiance to Madame Verdurin? Before becoming the "national anthem" of Swann's love, everything leaves one to believe that the little phrase already functioned like a sort of unconscious cornerstone of the collective assemblage, in spite of the degree of stupidity or snobbery of the people composing it.[8] A completely different hypothesis can also be given: no one is indifferent to Vinteuil's music, but everyone fears it, and everyone manifests their reaction in their own way. Madame Verdurin's mannerisms and flirtatiousness, her protesting to the idea that she would be tortured by another hearing of the Sonata,[9] her histrionics and her somatic troubles may contain a grain of truth: Vinteuil's music may *effectively contain a danger*, a sort of malediction and by no means should it be approached without precaution. The "collective resistance" towards it manifested by the members of the salon would be nothing but the translation of the apprehension of its diagrammatic nature by the group, and it would be organized according to two modalities:

—for the majority of the "little gang," it would only feel like an *attenuated diagrammatics*, i.e. a musical machine which has had some sort of effects, and which perhaps always has them, but which cannot have them here and now. This group is "immunized" against these types of things and one of its spokespersons declares that it is pointless to "seek the little beast" in this music, as Swann seems to want to do;

—for Swann, for Madame Verdurin, for the Narrator and, to a lesser degree, for Elstir, it is a question of a "*delayed diagrammatism*" (paraphrasing the psychopharmacologists). The danger is not immediate, but everything can be expected from its ulterior effects.

Various indications that appear to confirm the existence of such a "collective resistance" should allow us to better grasp the nature of the stakes that it conceals.

1. The music which is interpreted in the second assemblage is nothing but an *extract* from the Sonata. Madame Verdurin's pianist is content with playing the andante part and, moreover, he deliberately skips the entire central part of this movement where the first appearance of the little phrase is developed and which connects it to its second appearance (I, 351/I, 364). This extract, this abbreviation, this "anthology piece" does not make it possible to grasp the music's movement in its entirety, and such a selection certainly diminishes its power. However, how do we explain that it does not destroy the specific level of the refrain? In order to destroy or over-activate the refrain's abstract machinism, the assemblage of enunciation would have to cross a supplementary degree of deterritorialization. Let us say that the little phrase here has gained in "definition"—in the televisual sense of the term—but it has lost in extension, it doesn't "carry" as far as the first assemblage, its effects have been circumscribed, its profile has been made ordinary.

2. The *enunciatory assemblage* remains fuzzy. No doubt the young pianist, constantly escorted by his aunt, is presented to us as a familiar character of the salon, but we will still have to wait

sixteen-hundred pages before knowing his name.[10] Thus, we can not hope for any semiotic proliferation or any development of the novelistic content along this direction. This "reserve" relative to the enunciatory agent seems to correspond for Swann to a foreclosure of a masculine homosexual component.[11] In fact, when the refrain, much later in the Septet, will have its interpretation entrusted to the character of Morel, we will witness a true blossoming of its matter of expression and, through the Charlus-Morel pair, a whole new expanse of Proust's neurotic jealousy in the *Recherche* is opened up for exploration.

3. The "erasure" of the violinist and the masculine homosexual component also seems to have curbed the entry of a *feminine homosexual component*. In the first assemblage, the violin carried a feminine presence (which is compared to a passer-by "introducing the image of a new sort of beauty…") (I, 210/I, 218). With the interpretation of the little phrase on violin—although anonymous—during the concert in the house of the Princess de Saint-Euverte, we will leave the domain of *metaphor* for that of a much more compelling lure: "There are tones in the violin—if we cannot see the instrument and cannot relate what we hear to our image of it, which changes the sound of it—so similar to those of certain contralto voices that we have the illusion that a singer has been added to the concert" (I, 347/I, 360).

However, the fact that in the second assemblage the little phrase is only entrusted to the piano does not make this feminine presence which inhabits it completely disappear. Going out on a high note held for two measures and "taken as a sonorous riddle in order to hide the mystery of its *incubation*," it seems to have acquired even a certain consistency. Swann rediscovers this feminine presence with the certainty that he will never lose it again, and he keeps it as proof of… the reflection of its smile.[12] This development of the constitution of an *abstract feminine faciality* will play an essential role in the evolution of Swann's love. Sometimes we will see it incarnated in Botticelli's Zipporah; sometimes it will be reassuring or, in the worst moments of his amorous disappointments, it will become his secret confidante. Sometimes it will lead him to the brink of an irremediable neurotic alienation, but nevertheless this is what will make him keep an ultimate distance vis-à-vis Odette and will keep him from doing away with her image. It plays according to its own rules at the heart of passion according to interests which fully exceed the "case" of Swann. At this stage, there is no point in establishing a clear-cut distinction between the refrain and deterritorialized faciality. In fact, it is the same abstract presence which will express itself through both. The refrain smiles, whereas the smile of the abstract passer-by dances to the rhythm of the refrain. The "incubation" of the little phrase still has not come to its end. We are no longer in the stage of the "fac-simile" or the index, i.e. a disempowered representation, but we are still not at the establishment of a machinic assemblage in direct contact with realities which are psychological, material, social, aesthetic... An abstract machine has begun to take on consistency and crystallize multiple and heterogeneous potentialities. It is fixated on Vinteuil's name; it opens up towards a "school of advanced music;" it animates the face of Botticelli's Zipporah; it is carrying various homosexual valences... *But its consistency always remains insufficient* for confronting head-on resistances of all kinds which mobilize against it and whose target, let us underline this fact, is not simply the existence of masculine and feminine homosexual components, but much more fundamentally the *libidinal machinism of a becoming-woman* which traverses the entire *Recherche* and is one of the most significant illustrations given to us in the first chapter of the novel with what I will call "*the primitive scene of Montjouvain*": the Narrator, still very young, witnesses the amorous frolicking of Madamoiselle Vinteuil with her friend and the ritual profanations directed at the portrait of her recently deceased father.

It is via a double mechanism of isolation and misunderstanding, that Swann in a way *distances* himself[13] from this profanation scene around which the Narrator's destiny has been built up:

1. It does not directly concern him and the Narrator will only begin elucidating it again a very long time after after his death (generation gap).

2. He does not make the connection between the name of the Sonata's composer and the Vinteuil who was his neighbor in Combray, this somewhat pitiable old piano teacher, this former village organist, who lived close to the sea of Montjouvain (I, 160/I, 163). It only crosses his mind "that they could be related."

On Swann's side, the becoming-woman will thus remain blocked in every way:

—the semiotization of the little phrase is still insufficient, the machinic crystal is not refined or purified enough;

—the enunciatory assemblage remains fuzzy, it does not allow Swann to "attach" a masculine or feminine homosexual component;

—the matter of expression "lacks" the becoming-woman which remains fixated, encysted in a provisionally unproductive sadistic-voyeuristic scene. From then on, it is no longer surprising that Swann's love "falls back" on Odette's faciality, despite the fact that the latter inspires a sort of repulsion in him.[14]

Odette's face crystallizes an image which is opposed to what he loves, and thus it assumes a function of distantiation in relation to the aesthetic and micropolitical revolution which is the vehicle of the little phrase's becoming-woman. Paradoxically, it is up to Odette to be the primary organizer of the resistance to Swann's love, at least in its most deterritorialized aspects. Regardless of the sufferings she puts him through, she remains faithful to the secret mission which seems imparted to her: bring him back to reason, protect him from this crazy love which subjects him to the "unknown" of the little phrase—her most formidable rival.[15] Furthermore, Elstir made a sort of warning to Swann: Vinteuil was probably threatened by mental illness and one could see signs of this *in certain passages of the Sonata*: "Swann did not find this comment absurd, but it bothered him; for since a work of pure music contains none of the logical relations whose alteration in language reveals madness, madness recognized in a sonata appeared to him something as mysterious as the madness of a bitch, the madness of a horse, though these can indeed be observed" (I, 214/I, 222).[16]

Third Assemblage: each night and sometimes in the countryside: the national anthem and the love potion.

Swann has remained insensible to Odette's charms insofar as he has not allowed himself to be involved in Madame Verdurin's salon.[17] Now he regularly returns there and then everything changes: day by day Odette occupies a more important place in his life. As he nevertheless continues to frequent the circles of high society and a certain "little worker girl," he only comes to the Verdurins' home late in the evening. Those faithful to the salon have also acquired the habit of reserving his seat next to Odette for him. And when he arrives, the young pianist acknowledges his entrance by playing the "little phrase," which has been quasi-officially dubbed: "the national anthem of their nascent love."

However, the role of Vinteuil's music is not limited to this formal function alone. It also acts on Swann like a love potion, so much so that one may justly ask whether Odette has not gone to the Verdurins' home simply to make him drink such a beverage! We know, because she confided in Madame Verdurin that Odette considers Swann "some sort of ideal" (I, 227/I, 236). His tastes, his habits, his luxuriousness belongs to a world very different from hers, a world which is the object of her covetousness, but which she feels will be very difficult to attain. No doubt very early she has had the presentiment that she could only attach herself to Swann on the condition of reaching him on his most sensitive and most vulnerable ground, i.e. on the ground of art (without doubt this is what will lead him to return to the Verdurin assemblage).

Swann has fallen into Odette's trap, the Verdurin salon and the "little phrase." Now he is about to undergo a sort of " entrance exam" despite himself. But he senses that he does not have the "means" for his love. He is not less gifted, less energetic than the Narrator will be, but the entire difference that separates them is based on a threshold of consistency which he does not succeed in crossing. When he again takes this question up from scratch, the Narrator is very careful not to fall into a certain type of love, amorous fascination, and contemplative dependence in relation to the "little phrase." He will manipulate it liked a parcel bomb which is best approached carefully in order to disarm it and perhaps recuperate some of its mechanisms... It is still only through pure redundancies of resonance, a sort of reverie, in the second state, that Swann apprehends the "crystal of potentiality" enclosed in the "little phrase." But it is not a question of a lure or a phantasm for all that. The affair is serious; everything could effectively start to change. The charge of potentiality of which it is the vector is objective; it suffices that it go to the root of its mode of semiotization for it to bring about a real revolution within him.[18] For the time being, the assemblage remains in a sort of supersaturated state. Will the machinic index become a *component of passage*? Will Swann be able to assume this transformation? Sometimes he comes to desire the disappearance of this embarrassing evidence: "just as the jewels given to us, or even the letters written to us by a woman we love, we resent the water of the gem and the words of the language, because they are not created exclusively from the essence of a passing love affair and a particular person" (I, 219/I, 227).

Odette has reached her goals. But perhaps beyond what she expected at the beginning of this adventure! The effects of the faciality-refrain potion have rapidly become uncontrollable. And she is not so satisfied becoming this same Zipporah, daughter of Jethro, which he has extracted from the fresco of the Sistine chapel that Botticelli has consecrated to the illustration of seven episodes of Moses' youth. On this occasion, he has elaborated a veritable secret liturgy: long contemplating a reproduction of Jethro's daughter who has posed on his worktable, he is forced to imagine that it is, in reality, a photograph of Odette (I, 225/I, 233). By pronouncing a certain ritual formula—"Florentine work"—he comes, Proust explains to us, to make Odette's image penetrate into a dream world where she was denied access until then (I, 224/I, 232). Thus, the composite Odette-Zipporah faciality is incarnated more and more painfully in a deterritorialized constellation of faciality traits, which, furthermore, will very soon become persecuting. Like the bas-relief of Jensen's "Grandiva," this face-icon of Odette-Zipporah will escape the line that was supposed to determine its trajectory and begins to live and develop on its own account. The oscillation between, on the one hand, the reterritorialization of real encounters on Odette's face, the Odette-Zipporah of the reproduction and, on the other hand, the deterritorialization of desire towards another potentiality, another music, another relation to refined society, another lifestyle, which, for example, would release Swann from his role of token hostage of racist high society, will never manage to find a point of equilibrium. Spurred on by jealousy, she accelerates matters, and the sentimental ambivalence skillfully maintained at the beginning of the relationship will collapse into a black hole of passion.

In some way, Odette finds herself dispossessed of her victory. Swann has indeed fallen in love, but essentially with the abstract feminine presence manifested by the refrain-faciality conjunction that has stolen her image. In this regard, his attitude has completely changed. He no longer takes refuge behind a so-called fear of "new friendships" in order to justify his "escapist" behaviour (I, 198/I, 206).

He publicly courts her with diligence. But always by keeping his distance. Odette is disoriented, she "had not been used to seeing men have such ways with her…" (I, 232/I, 240). The entire salon hovers around their relationship. In private Monsieur and Madame Verdurin discuss about the signification to be given to this kind of courtly love: "Anyway, if there's nothing going on, I don't think it's because the gentleman thinks she's *virtuous*," M. Verdurin said ironically. "And after all, one can't say anything, since he seems to think she's intelligent. I don't know if you heard what he was declaiming to her the other evening about Vinteuil's sonata; I love Odette with all my heart, but to construct aesthetic theories for her benefit, you'd really have to be quite an imbecile!" (I, 227–228/I, 236).

What the frequenters of the salon cannot perceive is Swann's mad love for a deterritorialized presence. The "little phrase" holds the key to another world; it could give him the means of radically changing his way of life or conceiving his relationships in a different way; it could allow him to rediscover the taste and force of dedicating himself to his true calling: art criticism… (when it penetrates him, he will feel himself transformed "into a creature strange to humanity, blind, without logical faculties, almost a fantastic unicorn, a chimerical creature perceiving the world only through hearing") (I, 237/I, 246).

Odette will actively endeavor to neutralize this invisible rival; she will employ everything to reterritorialize it, appropriate it, to make it her friend, her confidante, her servant, in short to utilize her diagrammatic power to her exclusive benefit. For example, she will promise Swann to always listen to it in his presence: "'Why would you need the rest?' she said to him. 'This is *our* piece'…" (I, 219/I, 227). The mutations that Vinteuil's refrain has undergone in the course of the previous assemblage being insufficient, it seems that now Odette makes it her talisman, she "carries" it like a jewel in her corsage: but all this proof will do nothing but reinforce its power, purify its specific chemical reaction, and concentrate its machinic impact.

From then on, everything is decided for Swann: the little phrase will turn itself against him and lead him to the brink of madness. Having lacked any connections with the heterogeneous components of the external real, it will devote itself to digging a subjective black hole within which all its energy will be engulfed. His love will turn into hatred, without him succeeding in freeing himself from Odette for all that. He will find himself suspended in the void, reality forcing him to flee from the inside. He will attach himself like a drowning man to the last shreds of his relationship with Odette.

The process of fragilization, of the loss of substance, of the loss of the assemblage's consistency will nevertheless still take several months during which things will sometimes seem to sort themselves out. During this period, a provisional compromise between faciality and the little phrase is established on the following bases:

—the abstract feminine presence "negotiates" its reterritorialization, it is incarnated in an icon adjacent to Odette (Boticelli's Zipporah),

—in counterpart, Odette provisionally accepts that Swann handle their relationship in his own way, and that it remain within the framework of a courtly love.

Fourth Assemblage: on Odette's out of tune piano: the "anesthetic same old tune" and the black hole of passion.

The "courtly" compromise collapses on the occasion of a missed rendezvous with Odette. Stupefied, Swann discovers the extent of his pain; he no longer supports an "uncontrolled" absence of Odette; he realizes that he has entirely fallen under her control. A new compromise assemblage will be established so as to confront the black hole that is revealed. A certain number of degrees of freedom being sacrificed, a phase of tranquility—quite relative in any case—will, nevertheless, finally settle in.

This new assemblage implies:

—the mobilization of the sexual component in the amorous "fixation" so that it will otherwise be out of question for Swann to "amuse" himself with some little worker girl. The artificial, somewhat crude character of this intrusion of sexuality in the relationship between Swann and Odette is, in a certain way, compensated by a "courtly ritual" associating components of protection and submission, which, in a way, recalls what I previously evoked concerning the offering of the blade of grass among various bird species.[19]

—a change of position of the component of faciality: Zipporah's image loses its relay character between concrete faciality and a machinism of openess. The Odette-Zipporah identification apparatus has nothing agreeable about it; it takes on a forced, almost deranged character:

Sometimes when Odette looks at him with a sullen mien, Swann again sees a dignified face figuring in Botticelli's *Life of Moses*: "he would place her in it, he would give her neck the necessary inclination; and when he had well and truly painted her in distemper, in the fifteenth century, on the wall of the Sistine Chapel, the idea that she nevertheless remained here, by the piano, in the present moment, ready to be kissed and possessed, the idea of her materiality and her life would intoxicate him with such force that, *his eyes distracted, his jaw tensed as though to devour her, he would swoop down upon that Botticelli virgin and begin pinching her cheeks*" (I, 238/I, 247).

Odette will end up refusing to participate in such a game; she will continue to play Vinteuil's little phrase on the piano for Swann, but she will no longer want to hear anything of Botticelli.[20] Furthermore, it will no longer be a matter of concern in the *Recherche*, and thus a certain classical faciality will definitively pass out of its field. It will be up to the Narrator to connect another type of constellation of faciality traits—less global, more fragmented—in the diagrammatic refrain. In waiting for future resurrections, the refrain loses its machinic autonomy. It is reduced to the state of a tiring same old tune. Swann makes Odette play it on her out of tune piano ten times, twenty times in a row. She plays it so ungracefully. She is unable to correctly interpret such a score and she prefers much more the pieces like "La Valse des Roses" or "Pauvre Fou" by Tagliafico which constantly remains open on her music-stand: "How can you expect me to play if you hold on to me? I can't do everything at once. Now decide what you want—should I play the piano or play with you?" "From the sight of Swann's face as he listened to the phrase, one would have said he was absorbing an *anesthetic* that allowed him to breathe more deeply" (I, 237, 238/I, 236, 237).

Despite its painful nature of retraction, protection and submission, the assemblage organized around the black hole of passion still maintains some room for manoeuvre. Occasionally the little phrase ends up bringing deterritorialized objects into existence, allowing Swann to "breathe" a little:

"But as soon as he heard it, the little phrase had the power to open up within him the space it needed, the proportions of Swann's soul were changed by it; a *margin* was reserved in him for a bliss that also did not correspond to any external object, and yet, instead of being purely individual, like the enjoyment of that love, assumed for Swann a reality superior to that of concrete things" (I, 236–237/I, 245).

However, the marginal position which it will henceforth occupy in the assemblage will no longer allow him to transform it profoundly; it will simply contribute to balancing the faciality components within it which gravitate towards the impasse of the black hole. It stands in for the role of buffer component which was played by Zipporah's faciality. On one side it hollows out the assemblage, it stirs up trouble in Swann's soul; on the other, it calms and reassures him.

The situation increasingly worsens with the arrival of the Forcheville character who will embody the distance in time and space which grows little by little between Swann and Odette and reveal the refrain's incapacity, in this sort of field, to "reassemble" the modes of temporalization which are confronted there. Swann is excluded from the Verdurin salon along with Vinteuil's refrain; it has been replaced by the "Moonlight Sonata" which now serves as the indicator for the arrival of… Forcheville, Odette's new boyfriend. The "little phrase" is no longer mentioned in the long passage of the *Recherche* dedicated to the description of the most dramatic period in Swann's life, which is that of the second stage of the black hole on the edge of catastrophe, dragging Swann towards the precipice of what is generally represented as madness.

Fifth Assemblage: an unforeseen exit at the Marquise de Saint-Euverte's home: the reactivation of the refrain and the resorption of the black hole.

Swann's love was built up around the "little phrase" in Madame Verdurin's Salon; and it is the "little phrase" that will be entrusted to initiate its resolution, but in another Salon, one of the most exclusive of Saint-Germain Boulevard, that of the Marquise de Saint-Euverte. In the interim, its enunciation has only consisted of assemblages that have impoverished its matter of expression and attenuated its diagrammatic virulence. With Saint-Euverte's Salon, the "little phrase" is once again performed on piano and violin, and with the latter instrument, relaunches certain traits of expression enabling one to restore a part of the abstract feminine presence which Swann fell in love with at the time of the first assemblage. From then on, the question of becoming-woman in the *Recherche* will return in all its poignancy.

After several years lived in "immense anguish" and "formidable terror," Swann experiences a few periods of remission during which he begins looking for definitive remedies to cure this love which has become a veritable sickness.[21] The Baron Charlus, his faithful and handy ally, advises him to revisit Saint-Germain Boulevard and insists that he returns to the Marquise de Saint-Euverte's home for the last great evening of the year where people have been invited to listen to musicians whom she will afterwards use for her charity concerts (I, 322/I, 334).

How will this new assemblage, "Swann-returning-to-the-marquise-de-Saint-Euverte's-salon," manage to dismantle the semiotic components which have been neutralized themselves after such a long time in a black hole effect? Essentially through the uncovering, and discernibilization of six components among them, thanks to different processes that expose them again, laying bare their deterritorialization point (magnification, deceleration, repetition, splitting, "proliferating" new matters of expression which at times resemble the processes of "mitosis" in cellular reproduction).

The six components which we will successively examine are:

1. the subjective component of the statement corresponding to this phrase of the *Recherche*;

2. the group of environmental and iconic components (everything related to the way in which Swann lives space, architectural and iconic relations, movement of objects, individuals, etc...);

3. components of faciality;

4. musical components;

5. the transformations of "feminine presence" resulting from these modifications;

6. one of Swann's dreams which "condenses" the resolving assemblage of the black hole of passion.

1) The split of the subject of the statement: the Swann-Charlus divide

The baron Charlus, of which this is the first "operating" appearance in the *Recherche*, has only succeeded in getting Swann to reestablish this contact with social life on condition of committing himself to accompanying Odette during his absence and, implicitly, on condition of watching over her and extending his influence in order to persuade her to be more understanding, more gentle toward Swann. The subject of the statement is thus itself divided: Charlus distances himself from Swann, and with him a new homosexual component takes on consistency, acquiring a novelistic identity which develops its own trajectory in the *Recherche*.

For Swann, escaping from the black hole certainly implies the differentiation of such a semiotic component, but it is undoubtedly sufficient and perhaps necessary that it is only a question of *an attenuated component*, of a homosexuality held at arm's length. In other words, a component which is not "of passage," which does not lead to anything specific, any doing it, any creative process.

Someone is brought from *the outside* to help Swann and in the same movement "takes on for him" a homosexual component which nevertheless plays a large role in the "chemistry" (I, 304/I, 316) of his love and jealousy.[22] This movement of Charlus towards Swann is a decisive turn. Throughout the beginning of the *Recherche*, Proust opened the door to a possible heterosexual conflict between Swann and Charlus (I, 99/I, 101). The Narrator's family was then scandalized by the way in which Swann was treated by the Charlus-Odette couple.[23] But such an eventuality is definitively abandoned with the turn that Swann's love takes.[24] The relation between Charlus and Odette is neutralized, asepticized. "Between M. de Charlus and her, he knew nothing could happen…" (I, 315/I, 327).

Therefore, at this stage Charlus's homosexuality takes on the function of blocking a romantic line of flight and in no way makes it proliferate. Thanks to the intervention of a homosexual—used here as a sort of eunuch, a confidant of classical tragedies, or even a surgeon who asepticizes an "operating field"—we can put an end to Swann's love. Why is Charlus "neutralized" in a way during this "operation?" Is it merely to be able to help Swann more? If it is true, as we said before, that he distances himself from Swann so as to "resolve" his problem, how does it come about that the outcome of the novel does not focus on him? At this point, let us note that although he will achieve much more than Swann in terms of the knowledge and practice of contemporary music, this will not prevent him from "lacking" in turn the unconscious metabolism of the refrain and, for the same reason, the creative end of becoming-woman. Charlus will never be able to *beat time to the feminine* as he had been able to learn the "little phrase." Despite his elegance, he remains too crude, too clumsy, too classically homosexual. His relation to time and music will not pass through Vinteuil's refrain in its most deterritorialized aspects, but through Morel, i.e. a musician in flesh and blood, subjected to the constraints of fashionable and musical milieus. Charlus will face a jealousy problem similar to Swann's. But no one will come to help him, and his failure will lead him to an irremediable decline.[25] Charlus's homosexuality will remain masculine; it will never open itself onto a becoming-woman like Proust's which will be simultaneously masculine and feminine and which, moreover, will be constantly associated with multiple deterritorialized becomings: becoming-child, becoming-wasp, becoming-orchid, becoming-landscape…

2) The division of architectural and iconic components

This split of the subject of the statement that gives "birth" to Charlus is accompanied by a curious division of spaces with Swann's arrival at the Marquise de Saint-Euverte's town house. On the monumental staircase leading to the reception salon, Swann has the impression of simultaneously climbing towards what leads to a little dressmaker's home where Odette and Charlus have visited.[26] But this first transposition of spaces is immediately followed by a second: now it is the stairs of the Ducal Palace in Venice, the stairs of giants, which is evoked. Thus the Swann-Charlus split already announces the birth of a "new Narrator," one who will be able to undertake the masterpiece of the *Recherche*. In fact, upon the Narrator's arrival at the Guermantes hotel, the day where his vocation will be revealed to him, we will rediscover the same type of proliferation of spatial components. (Stubbing his foot against some misshapen paving-stones, certain impressions related to his trip to Venice then incite in him "the sensation [he] had once felt on the two uneven flagstones in the baptistery of St. Mark's...") (III, 867/VI, 175). But Swann will not have the resources to "liberate" himself from Odette by going on a trip to Venice! He will take this trip in the imaginary, or rather in the register of images. He rediscovers his technique of iconic identification: passing by the columns lining the stairway, picturesque evocations begin to proliferate: he envisions the figures of Mantegna, Dürer, Goya, Benvenuto Cellini, and Giotto standing before him. The "art criticism" component, after this large gathering, is no longer simply focused on the Odette-Zipporah faciality couple, as this had been the case at the beginning of his love. It attaches itself to the people present in the Marquise de Saint-Euverte's home: instead of releasing a mechanism of fascination of the black hole type, it undeceives Swann's gaze and allows him to anchor himself in external reality again.

3) The splits concerning components of faciality

It is mainly the masculine character who will undergo the effects of a deterritorializing schizz which will profoundly rearrange their faciality traits—to the point where some will seem almost on the brink of decomposition.

"But even the ugliness of these faces, though he knew it well, seemed new to him since their features—instead of being signs usable in a practical way for the identification of a certain person who had until then represented a cluster of pleasures to pursue, worries to avoid, or courtesies to pay—now remained coordinated only by aesthetic relations, within the autonomy of their lines" (I, 326/I, 338).

Unlike the preceding, this transformation of faces will therefore no longer be based on aesthetic criteria. Swann, for example, will begin to look at his two friends, the general de Froberville and the Marquise de Bréauté, as "figures in a painting" (I, 326/I, 339), but their face will immediately overflow the framework of these picturesque comparisons. There is a very particular machinism tied to the monocles which will literally make their constellation of faciality traits explode. Little by little, all the men with monocles gathering around Swann will become the victims of the same deterritorializing machinism.[27] In general de Froberville's home, the monocle has become like a monstrous wound resulting from being "struck between his eyelids like a shell splinter in his vulgar, scarred, overbearing face, in the middle of a forehead which it blinded like the Cyclops' single eye." He transforms Monsieur de Bréauté's gaze into sort of "a natural history specimen under a microscope," in Monsieur de Forestelle's home, he becomes a "superfluous cartilage... whose material was exquisite," in the home of Monsieur de Saint-Candé, he becomes a ring of Saturn, in the home of Monsieur de Palancy, he has a carp's head. (He seemed to be transporting with him "an accidental and perhaps purely symbolic fragment of the glass of his aquarium" (I, 327/I, 339–340).

The monocles, "having now been released from signifying a habit, the same for everyone" (I, 326/I, 339), have broken with the world of "attested," facialized significations and begin functioning via an asigniying mode. Until then, the deterritorialization of spaces and icons was made in *reference* to other spaces and other icons (the stairway of the little dressmaker, the clothes of the schoolteacher...). Now we can no longer be supported by pre-existing referents. These are the faciality traits which themselves produce their own reference and which, engaging in a path of creation, transfigure pre-established referents. In particular, they will attach themselves to the black hole which has taken possession of Swann's subjectivity for several years. This black hole becomes embodied in the series of monocle-faces. But far from creating the play of a phenomenon of resonance which would accentuate its devastating consequences, the production of this new series of micro black holes will, on the contrary, come to prevent the mechanism by making matters of expression proliferate. Better than a fragile anchorage in external reality through a simple trace of one icon over another, they make it possible to produce *another reality*. The molecular revolution thus begun—but which will not be brought to its end in the framework of the present assemblage—consists in reevaluating the style of the sophisticated person Swann was before his acquaintance with Odette: a person sure of himself in appearance, but compulsive, vulnerable from the moment he is exposed to desiring machinisms like the little phrase or Odette's face. That which is hollowed out before him with these micro black holes is the pseudo-consistency[28] of the fields in which he has evolved until now. The balance between empty consciential redundancies and the resonant redundancies of faciality (p. 218) is broken. The implosion of signifying subjectivity projects a high-voltage matter of expression whose asignifying particles will have been able to radically change Swann's life, but whose effect will have no other path—through a new default consistency of the "Swann assemblage"—than by "escaping from the affair," by "correcting it," by bending it to the most orthodox conjugality.

4) Appearance of a new prototype of the "little phrase"

Swann decided to turn away from everything which could remind him of the happy period of his love, and especially all of Vinteuil's music, insofar as it could stimulate representations reviving his pain.

Certain words, certain expressions, for example, have become taboo. But the little phrase, in Madame de Saint-Euverte's salon, pounces on him again and for a while disorganizes the fragile equilibrium he has attained. A pianist starts playing Lizst and Chopin as he begins to leave. He has explored his sophisticated relationships, and he dreams of only one thing: meeting up with Charlus to hear news of Odette. He's already out the door of the salon when general de Froberville calls him back to ask him if he would like to meet Madame Cambremer, a young woman Swann knew in Combray, when she was just Madamoiselle Legrandin.

This feminine presence tied to Combray's past will retain Swann. In some way, it will catch him on the fly and constrain him to rediscover the little phrase. He precipitates the danger, he would like to flee, but he cannot evade it. A violinist joins the pianist and the trap is shut: "It's the little phrase from the sonata by Vinteuil; don't listen!" (I, 345/I, 358). At first, he is overcome by grief. It is as though Odette had entered the salon and with her all the intensities of the past: the snowy curled petals of the chrysanthemum, the embossed address of the "Maison Dorée," the way her eyebrows had come together when she was eager to see him again after their first meeting, smelling the fragrance of the hairdresser's iron before going to meet with Odette, rediscovering the young worker girl, the rains that fell so often that spring, the icy chill of the moonlight... Then he lets go, calms himself and rediscovers Vinteuil's music. He did not hear this music with Odette, but its caricature. For the first time, he hears the whole movement within which the little phrase is found. Thus, he can situate it in its proper place, in its authentic environment and understand the meaning of its entrances, its exits, and its long periods of absence: "There were marvelous ideas in it which Swann had not distinguished at first hearing and that he perceived now, as if they divested themselves, in the cloakroom of his memory, of the uniform disguise of novelty" (I, 351/I, 364).

Until that moment, the iconic, spatial, facialitary components have been affected by various effects of splitting, proliferation, and overactivation. But with this irruption of the little phrase, it is instead about a new birth. It begins from scratch with the launch of a new prototype whose mission is twofold: lift Swann from the black hole, and, faithful to his first vocation, lead him down towards the paths of creation. It will attain its first objective, but will fail to reach the second.

Is there not somewhat of a contradiction in claiming that the little phrase will now work *against* the black hole, whereas previously it had been said to be working on its behalf? In fact, as I specified earlier, a unique composition of such an abstract machinism does not exist; its actions cannot be completely separated from a machinic phylum and the emergence of heterogeneous singularity traits. It is the support of the most deterritorialized machinic interactions; it has a "transversalist" function which consists in making the other components function together, giving them a consistency from the assemblage's nucleus. Whatever its function in relation to other components—and here we shall see that instead it will remain on the second level and that it will once its "mission" is "accomplished" it will itself vanish—it conserves a privileged position as the intangible, atopical, "unlocalizable" cornerstone of the assemblage. This is due to the fact that the machinic propositions which it articulates only concretize on the occasion of limit problems, of the frontier between various components, and yet, on condition that "something be made to pass" through these limits and these frontiers. The privileged character of the little phrase in the assemblage arises from its capacity to process (and deal with) matters of expressions. The abstract machinic refrain inhabits "Vinteuil's little phrase," but it also works at the core of the inter-component metabolism. Whether or not a component becomes "of passage" depends on its effectuation. Its hyper-deterritorialized nature is required for the capacity of an assemblage to establish diagrammatic maps and tracings enabling it to "pilot" its internal metabolism and its external affairs. This polymorphism ensures that it does not remain impermeable to the contingencies of history, to relations of force, to relative mutations in matters of expression. Vinteuil's refrain becomes enriched from one assemblage to the next. But, paradoxically, it becomes enriched "*in gaps*." It integrates the machinic keys that it encounters in its passage by simplifying, deterritorializing and examining them. With Swann's anxiety and mortal jealousy, it has "gained"… by losing something of its refined origins. With its future translations until Vinteuil's septet and its ultimate machinic reduction on Albertine's pianola, it will lose even its contour and identity. Its abstract machinism will only become more powerful and the "becoming-woman" which inhabits it, escaping from all systems of representation, will end up being transformed into a "becoming-creator" that can switch on the prodigious factory which the *Recherche* constitutes.

The Saint-Euverte assemblage calms Swann's love and opens a path towards resolution to the extent that it "nourishes" the refrain of new matters of expression which will "disperse" the central black hole effect. Instead of a negative deterritorialization merely directed towards self-annihilation, here we witness a positive, germinating deterritorialization developing heterogeneous qualities, unlocking unknown potentialities. Swann will certainly still remain haunted for a while by Odette's face, but from this day forth other interests will be awakened in him, which will, for example, focus on Mme de Cambremer who has been pointed out to him during this reception. Such a flooding of the black hole by matters of expression will only be possible to the extent that an abstract machinism—here that of the refrain—has created the conditions of a synchronic functioning of components, i.e. in the last analysis, of a passage of quanta of deterritorialization from one matter to another. Nothing could be further removed from the symbolic mechanism of Freudian sublimation. On the contrary, here we are at the heart of a material unconscious. In this regard, the importance of the violin's reappearance in this recovery of matters of expression should be emphasized. It does not take on a diagrammatic function as such here. We can imagine a flute or a human voice having the same function. What functions here is the *differential effect* of the matters of expression, it is the fact that we play out the differences rather than crushing them against one another, reducing them to univocal expressive schemata. The opening to the real, along with creative and perceptive affectivity, is subservient to the employment of matters of expression *in their disparity, in their heterogeneity.* What singularizes such and such a trait of a matter of expression is its nature of excess in relation to the significant redundancies; it is the fact that a difference can never be completely recuperated by any "correspondence grid." What "passes" from one component to another is not simply a "message," a measurable quantity of form or information, but an effect which escapes from the dominant significations. Rather than being folded onto themselves, matters of expression, through the bias of these irreducible singularities, develop unforeseen alliances and outline vertiginous potentialities which will perhaps vanish just as soon, or perhaps radically overthrow the "destiny" of the assemblage.

Of his own initiative, Swann never would have made the least effort to "relaunch" the "little phrase." He passively experiences the dream of the machinic nucleus with these faces which grow gaunt, these spaces which open on the schoolmaster's clothes, this musical phrase which changes timbre. Refined silhouettes of seductive women emerge from the melancholic gray: memories, projects of voyages, landscapes are means of semiotization to the search... In Swann's amorous assemblage the black hole effect was nothing but the accumulation, the echoing of all his semiotic impasses, all his inhibitions. But its removal sets in play elements that engage the

Recherche in a future which cannot be circumscribed around the character of Swann alone. The marvel of the evocation of the "little phrase" in the Marquise de Saint-Euverte's salon has a reach that surpasses the momentary revelation that it has for Swann, and goes well beyond the highs and lows he will experience after this evening.

In truth, this "machinic demonstration" of the little phrase only concerns the "Swann problem" incidentally; fundamentally, it aims to provide some essential resolving elements to the "Narrator's problem."

5) The transformations of the "feminine presence" components (abstract and concrete)

It should be recalled that in the second assemblage, the refrain's feminine component (the manner of *beating time to the feminine*) remained distinct from the sexual component whose responsibility was imparted to an anonymous "little worker girl" external to the novel. This is the black hole of lack, dependence, and jealousy which had tied together sexuality with Odette's faciality. In the framework of the Saint-Euverte assemblage, the sexual component initiates a decisive turn: Mme de Cambremer allows Swann to cross a threshold, to gradually extract himself from the black hole and, in an ulterior way, to establish a conjugal compromise with Odette. Its role as component of passage stems from the fact that it associates different functions: it "replays" the encounter of Odette, but in the framework of a very different field.

1—She does not play music, does not mutilate it, does not recuperate it as "indicative;" on the contrary, she helps it when she rushes on stage, while a pianist plays a polonaise by Chopin, to catch a wax candle falling from the piano which was about to *set fire*[29] to a lampshade. Unlike the little worker girl, she fully participates in the collective assemblage of enunciation.

2—With her we do not rediscover the opposition woman of society/woman of the people. She is both sides at the same time. She moves in an aristocratic milieu, but she is of relatively popular extraction—for the princess of Guermantes, her parents are "people of the country" (I, 334/I, 346).

3—She is not anonymous: she is attached to Combray's maternal phylum: she has a future in the *Recherche*.

4—She has something to do with contemporary music. She looks down on the music of Chopin and Liszt, so dear to her grandmother: she has the highest praise for Wagner's music...

The Wagnerian leitmotiv is undoubtedly not the vehicle of the same type of becoming-woman as Vinteuil's refrain. Proust is very ironic concerning Madame de Cambremer's musical snobbery! Be that as it may, here the little phrase rediscovers a "worthy interlocutor," acceptable by the people of the Saint-Germain suburb, relevant to Combray's past, and capable of relaunching the sophisticated seduction of Swann. As support of the little phrase's abstract feminine presence, the "little Madame Cambremer" does not impose a faciality on Swann like the Odette-Zipporah type associating images and territories via a syncretic mode with the most deterritorialized objects of desire. As we have seen, this type of faciality has been relegated to the monocled men who have very little to do with the subtlety of music. Under these conditions, the little phrase is about to regain a certain autonomy, keeping Odette at a distance. Listening to it, Swann perceives it like a "protective goddess, a confidante of his love" (I, 348/I, 361) which made him admit with "the grace of a resignation that was almost gay" that he will have to renounce his passion and that "it means nothing...."

"From that evening on, Swann understood that the feeling Odette had had for him would never revive, that his hopes of happiness would not be realized now" (I, 353/I, 366). What has benefited? The little phrase? Madame de Cambremer? Odette? Each has scored some points without any of them prevailing in a decisive way. Swann will marry Odette, yet will say that she has ruined years of his life, that she never truly pleased him, that she "was not his type" (I, 382/I, 396). With the little Madame de Cambremer, he will start a relationship about which Proust gives us only fragmentary indications, and the little phrase will hibernate in the memory of the Swann-Odette couple until the following generation, when the Narrator will pick it up again. One thing is acquired: escape from the sexual component of the black hole of faciality.[30]

One question remains at the end of this fifth assemblage: why is the sexual component the only one found to be "unblocked," why is Swann pinned down, furthermore, in a very ordinary compromise? And he seems very close to posing this question himself upon hearing Vinteuil's sonata. He becomes aware that this music constitutes a language more rigorous than human language; he compares Vinteuil to experimenters of genius, such as Lavoisier or d'Ampère... "And for the first time Swann's thoughts turned with a stab of pity and tenderness to Vinteuil, to that unknown, sublime brother who must have suffered; what must his life have been like? From the depths of what sorrows had he drawn that godlike strength, *that unlimited power to create?*" (I, 348/I, 361).

What is it that keeps Swann from committing himself to the path of experimentation and creation as the becoming-woman of the little phrase invites him? He would have the means, from the perspective of matters of expression, but the asignifying machinism that would be able to operate such a reconversion has still not been perfected.

We will have to wait for the "recomposition of the Septet," by the unfathomable couple of Mademoiselle de Vinteuil and her friend, so that the becoming-woman of creation finally has access to a sufficient "vector" and so that the promises of the refrain can be fulfilled.

6) The dream of the "young man in a fez"

The complete dissolution of the black hole centered on Odette's face will still take quite a while. This period of remission and latency is not treated in the *Recherche*: it is inscribed "in the gaps" between "a love of Swann" and the description of the Narrator's loves. Nevertheless, in the form of one of Swann's dreams, Proust gives us a sort of summary of the mechanisms which are competing here.

A motley group walks along the seashore; Dr. Cottard, Elstir, Odette, Napoleon III, the Narrator's grandfather, and a person X, the "young man wearing a fez." The waves are very menacing; they reach the group; Swann feels the freezing water splash against his cheek. Then Odette tells Swann to wipe his face. First transformation of faciality: Mme Verdurin gives Swann a surprised look, *while her face changes shape, her nose lengthens, and she grows a full moustache.* Second transformation: Odette's eyes are "about to separate from her like teardrops and fall on him..." (I, 379/I, 392). Suddenly Odette turns her wrist, looks at a little watch and says: "I have to go." Swann becomes frustrated: he would like to *hollow out Odette's eyes*, crushing her lifeless cheeks. "*After a second,*" which represents "*many hours,*" the painter explains to Swann that Napoleon III is Odette's lover and that he has left just after Odette to meet up with her. Abrupt working of the assemblage following the splitting of the principal subject of the statement: it is not Swann who feels pain upon hearing the news, but rather a "*young man in a fez*" whom he endeavors to console. He wipes his eyes, removes his fez to make him more comfortable, and explains with tenderness that Odette's attitude is perfectly justifiable: "Really, she's doing the right thing... I told her a dozen times she should do it. Why be sad about it? He above all would understand her" (I, 379/I, 393). Proust explains that Swann had talked to himself in this way and that the young man, who is not identified at first: "like certain novelists, he had divided his personality between two characters, the one having the dream, and another he saw before him wearing a fez." After several considerations about Napoleon III who is identified with Forcheville, he then compares the character generation process in the dream to that of the division of "certain lower organisms." Thus, we see the "young man in a fez" *take upon himself* and *transfer* Swann's love and his grief just like the Narrator will later in the novel. Then the dream accelerates: a series of nervous and agonizing images illustrate—and simultaneously ward off—the black hole effect: "Utter darkness descended on him in an instant, an alarm sounded, inhabitants of the place ran past, escaping from houses in flames; Swann heard the sound of the waves leaping and his heart, with the same violence, pounding with anxiety in his chest. Suddenly the palpitations of his heart redoubled in speed, he felt an inexplicable nausea; a countryman covered with burns flung at him as he passed: "Come ask Charlus where Odette ended up this evening with her friend, he used to go about with her in the old days and she tells him everything. It's them that started the fire" (I, 380/I, 394).

All the ingredients making up the remedy, the compromise, are evoked here:

—the dissolution and neutralization of the "persecuting" faciality traits of the Odette-Mme de Verdurin couple;

—the splitting of the enunciatory assemblage by the creation of a new character the "young man in a fez," prefiguring the Narrator, who "endorses" Swann's love and his grief;

—the implicit promotion, with this new character, of a masculine homosexual component;

—the compulsive and conjured scenario of the intolerable separation scene.

And it is up to, which seems self-evident, Madame de Cambremer to prevent this new fire risk! At the culmination of the dream, she emerges on the *side of the real*: Swann is awakened by his valet who announces the arrival of his hairdresser; this is in fact the day when he has made all his arrangements to meet her in Combray, desiring to associate "in his memory the charm of that young face with the charm of a countryside he had not visited in such a long time" (I, 381/I, 394).

Sixth Assemblage: Madame Swann plays the sonata for the Narrator: the refrain of transition.

Years after marrying Swann, Odette plays Vinteuil's sonata, while her husband comments on the work for the adolescent narrator. Their daughter Gilberte, whom the narrator is in love with, does not witness the scene. The Narrator only shows an intellectual interest toward this work: "and whereas Swann and his wife could make out a distinct phrase, it was as ungraspable to my perception as someone's name that you try to remember when the mind retrieves nothing but a vacuum, into which, without your assistance, an hour after you stop thinking about them, the complete set of syllables that you have been vainly groping about for suddenly leaps" (I, 530/II, 104).

Whereas for Swann, the little phrase progressively organized into a gestalt, into a "fac-simile," it seems that it must be structured for the Narrator like a morpheme within a linguistic corpus.[31] In other words, it "sticks" much less to the iconic and affective components.

The interest that Swann takes in it has also descended to the lowest level. This music has become lunar, it barely evokes more than "the Bois de Boulogne in a catatonic trance" (I, 533/II, 107) and several traces in the sky of an old fire, but of "*a colorless fire without danger.*" Landscapes and faces become discolored, dematerialized.[32] "It's swapped them for my worries and my love affairs, which have been completely forgotten" (I, 534/II, 108).

As for Odette, she instead gives the impression of exhibiting the "little phrase" as a curiosity, a decorative trifle, a defused mortar shell from the last war… Moreover, she too also evokes the heat of the old fires by linking the "frequenting" of the little phrase with that of Madame de Cambremer "who was said to have lost her heart to Charles" (I, 534/II, 108–109). But this allusion remains affectionate in regards to Swann: it seeks above all to flatter his pride. The refrain will still remain in hibernation for a long time. For two thousand pages, there will hardly be a reference to it, and we cannot help but think that Proust hesitated considerably before setting it back on track and making it re-intervene as the diagrammatic operator of the Narrator's vocation. Perhaps because he had explored its limits in "Swann's Love." Sometimes he tries to relaunch this type of formula and make it play a similar role.

Let us relate four attempts of this kind of which some are barely sketched out:

1—In *Sodom and Gomorrah*, an explicit beginning, which will not give rise to any development, of a *musical refrain* of the same type as Vinteuil's "little phrase" concerning the Narrator's loves:

"Some incantatory gesture having excited, as I was putting on my dinner jacket, the alert and frivolous self that had been mine when I used to go with Saint-Loup to dine in Riverbelle or on the evening when I thought I would be taking Mlle de Stermaria to dine on the island in the Bois, *I was unconsciously humming the same tune as then*; and it was only on becoming aware of this that, by the song, I recognized the intermittent singer, who indeed knew only that one song. The first time that I had sung it, I was beginning to be in love with Albertine, but I thought I would never get to know her. Later in Paris, it was when I had ceased loving her and a few days after having possessed her for the first time" (II, 1035/IV, 429).

2—In *The Prisoner*, there are *noises in the street and merchants' musical tunes*.[33] The Narrator seeks to free himself from his relationship with Albertine which has ended up like that of Swann and Odette, on the path of a tyrannical jealousy. During a moment of respite—a spring day "interpolated in the winter"—he lets himself go to the "series of popular melodies, elegantly arranged for various instruments, from the china-mender's horn to the chair-caner's trumpet, and including the flute of the goat's-milk seller" (III, 116/V, 102–103). This symphony in the street organizes noises, cries, calls evoking nursery rhymes in counterpoint to musical refrains ("Ah! The bigorneau, two under the bigorneau…"). Proust remarks in passing that this music of the crowd "is more language than music" (III, 117/V, 104). This does not mean, though, that we are taken back towards ordinary spoken language. On the contrary, the musical refrain opens up here, through an incredibly brilliant stylistic composition[34] to other systems of intensities; guiding it one step further across the threshold towards the constitution of a trans-semiotic refrain adapted to the necessities of the *Recherche*'s work.

3—In *The Fugitive*: the memory of Albertine—who died several months ago—is embodied in *a refrain centered on her name*.

"As for Albertine herself, she hardly existed for me as more than a name which, apart from some rare moments of respite on waking, kept inscribing itself into my brain over and over again. If I had thought aloud, I would have repeated it endlessly, and my verbiage would have been as monotonous and limited as if I had been *transformed into a bird*, like the one in the legend whose call repeats endlessly the name of the woman that he loved when he was a man" (III, 432/V, 400).

Let us note that there too it is no longer a pure and simple return to spoken language pure and simple. It is no longer a refrain of becoming-woman that the Narrator encounters here, but a becoming-bird. As we recall, when Swann resorted to a magical phrase—"Florentine work"—to embody Odette's face in that of Botticelli's Zipporah, the formula then remained distinct from the image and the "refrainization" moved in the sense of a reterritorialization of the one and the other, and the one by the other. Here things happen completely otherwise. A line of flight sketches a "being of flight."[35] For a moment, the becoming-woman of the *Recherche* is embodied in a becoming-bird and now animates Albertine's name as it used to her face.

4—In *The Fugitive*, the "Sole mio" of a gondolier.

The Narrator is about to leave Venice. He hesitates reuniting with his mother who is already on the way to the station. He has tempted to jump at this occasion to free himself from the grip she has over him. Despite herself, she puts obstacles in the way of his projects: to dedicate himself unreservedly to the "Venetian crystallization," all while waiting for the arrival, several days from now, of the baroness Putbus and her following (III, 651/V, 615). He remains fixated, all willpower dissolves as he remains fascinated by the song of a musician in a boat facing his hotel. "I will remain in Venice alone." But the refrain does not lead to the decision. At the last moment, the mechanism of fascination stops: the Narrator rushes to the station, catches his train with the doors already shut, and leaves again with his mother.

None of these various refrain formulas has resolved the Narrator's problems, and the question will have to be taken up from a different angle. Before pursuing the exploration of the "little phrase's" trajectory further, we must consider a difficulty which stems from the structure of the *Recherche*, to its nature as a palimpsest and rhizome, which results in constant superpositions and overdeterminations among characters, actions, places, etc.[36] We are constantly referred to two modes of the refrain's existential consistency:

1—*A mode of diachronic consistency.* Its various prototypes are set in orbit by successive assemblages of enunciation. In this regard, there is a fundamental difference between Swann and the Narrator.

For Swann, the refrain begins and ends its career in sophisticated salons, whereas for the Narrator, on the contrary, it is played in private by Odette, the Narrator, and Albertine. (Mme Verdurin's concert, which is attended by the Narrator, is situated in the interval of these private auditions; besides, it is no longer the Sonata which is played, but the Septet.)[37] In the first case, the refrain is received passively, massively, like something unavoidable, irrupting from the outside, overwhelming the existence of what it touches. In the second case, it is the object of a constant analysis: it is re-elaborated, mastered, and finally transformed into something else. It does not interfere with the Narrator's passion and jealousy in their most convulsive aspect. We have passed from assemblages of power—totalitarian-totalizing—to assemblages of analysis and creation.

2—*A mode of synchronic consistency.* All the forms of refrain act upon one another, but it is in its final state, that which is the vehicle of the most diagrammatic abstract machinism, which is the most "connected" to all the other components, that it attains an interactive mode of efficiency.[38] Thus, it is necessary that this final threshold be crossed so that, retroactively, the others can be crossed as well. The little fac-simile phrase, the incubated refrain, the love potion, the compulsive catchphrase, the overactive refrain, etc., are thus traversed by the same machinism, by the same machinic phylum. Things will go the same with the other machinic "concentrates," in other registers, such as the madeleine of Combray, the three steeples of Martinville, the goodnight kiss, the magic lamp, etc. Blocks of childhood, involuntary remembrances, crystals of perceptive intensity, faces, and landscapes only find their status in the *Recherche* only to the extent that they are *already engaged in the metabolic process of the refrain considered in its terminal stage.* Consequently, concerning each of them, it would be appropriate to separate what relates:

—to the abstract machinism of "refrainization,"

—to the "intractable" residue, to the moment of inertia and territorialization which singularizes it.

This type of question was already posed concerning the "double play" of the feminine presence tied to the "little phrase." But it is impossible for me to go further in this direction; indeed, a systematic approach of all the components of the *Recherche*, considered from this angle would imply a study of a completely different scope! Be that as it may, one can hypothetically accept that each of them arises from a double origin, of the kind which we could say simultaneously:

• that everything comes from Swann,[39] i.e. from the past, from childhood memories, from familial and territorial attachments (generativist schizoanalytic perspective);

• and that everything comes from the creative appeal of Vinteuil's Septet, which itself ceases being localizable through a musical refrain, and tending rather to exist via the form of a pure abstract machinism (transformational schizoanalytic perspective).[40]

Accounting for the elements that arise from this synchronic consistency constantly incites us to approach things "from the end," from the most completed, to envision, for example, Swann's love through the Narrator's vocation, and more generally the fundamental couples of the *Recherche*[41] as so many approximations of the same *becoming-woman* which coincides moreover with a *becoming-creator*. From Swann's "point of view," i.e. in a sense, from the diachronic point of view, the various components pertaining to childhood, involuntary memory, urbanity, different forms of homosexuality... can only remain separated from one another, stratified, and merely support properly codified relations amongst themselves (otherwise, semiotic blockages, black holes, and catastrophes will appear). From the "point of view" of becoming-woman-creator, i.e. from the synchronic point of view, the same components are only important to the extent that they make it possible to engender becoming-child, becoming-plants, faces, landscapes, etc. And these becomings themselves never stop intersecting to the point that the characters and places which are its manifestation change "on the spot," or rather exchange attributes with each other. *And these changes and exchanges no longer result from the nature of things or from the effect of time, but essentially arise from a re-creation of the world.*[42]

Seventh Assemblage: the Narrator plays the Sonata: "the diagrammatic leitmotiv."

"Making the most of the fact that I was still alone, and half closing the curtains so that the sun would not stop me reading the notes, I sat down at the piano, opened Vinteuil's sonata which *happened* to be lying there…" (III, 158/V, 141).

Obsessed with jealousy, the Narrator has asked Françoise to look for Albertine at Trocadéro. What he cannot stand is the idea that she can profit from this "escape" by reuniting with Mlle Vinteuil, whom he imagines to be her lover. (His conviction results from a lie told by Albertine's: to "make herself interesting," (III, 337/V, 310) she claimed to have raised by a friend of Mlle Vinteuil's). Waiting for her return, he can enjoy a moment of respite and music, "very different than that of Albertine's society," helps him plunge into his inner depths and "discover something new there."

What stands out, in this assemblage of enunciation, is the *text* of Vinteuil's Sonata as a matter of expression, barely explored until now. It is through its intermediary that the Narrator truly gains access to the "little phrase." "A measure of the Sonata hits me, a measure which I knew but however this hearing differently clarifies things I have known for a long time and where we notice what we have never seen before." This "little phrase" is what first Swann retained; he only had access to the rest of the Sonata much later. In this music, the only things that mattered to him were the synaes-thetic impressions it stimulated. And he attempted to preserve its brute, syncretic nature; he was afraid that an access which was too "discursive" or too "musicological" would weaken its particular "chemical reaction." The situation is the opposite for the Narrator. Syncretism is effaced over against a graphematic semiotization itself oriented in a trans-semiotic intention. The magic of the little phrase opens up to the outside. It no longer tends to be folded back on itself, to degenerate into a same old song; it is now assimilated into a Wagnerian leitmotiv—"I could not stop myself from mur-muring: 'Tristan'..." (III, 158/V, 142)—in other words, to a complex musical entity which "traverses" multiple melodic, har-monic, orchestral, dramatic, poetic, scenic, plastic, choreographic[43] components, without counting the territorialized refrains which it attracts to itself, such as "the half-forgotten shepherd's pipe tune" (III, 161/V, 144).[44]

The diagrammatic reorganization of the refrain at this point appears to affirm itself in two directions: the theme of the return to Combray and certain constellations of faciality traits.

1. The return to Combray

Everything the little phrase did for Swann, at the end of the fifth assemblage, was to help him extract himself from the passionate black hole, to prompt him to return to Combray, and to associate a new face with the landscapes of his childhood—which nevertheless referred to the past—that of Madame de Cambremer. It seems that it is precisely at this point that the Narrator seizes things for his own sake. Reading Vinteuil's sonata brings him back "to the old days of Combray" (III, 158/V, 141). He seems to hesitate committing him-self to the same path as Swann by associating music with jealousy: "the alternation of the sexual pleasure motif and the anxiety motif corresponded to my love for Albertine—a love from which jealousy had so long been absent that I had once been able to admit to Swann my ignorance of that feeling" (III, 158/V, 141). But he attempts it again. If he turns towards Combray, it is only from "Guermantes' way" where he believes to be waiting for a machinism which is essential to his becoming-creator. "No, approaching the sonata from another point of view, looking at it in itself as the work of a great artist, I was carried back on the wave of sound towards the old days at Combray—I do not mean Montjouvain and the Méséglise way, but our walks towards Guermantes—when I had wanted to be an artist" (III, 158/V, 141–142). Thus, it is not a question of a vague, global, syncretic, regressive return to the past founded on redundancies of resonance, but, through the generation of an asignifying scriptural component, a question of a diagrammatic undertaking which demands, in the first stage, the clearest disjunction possible between the beneficial—public, worldly, aristocratic—way of Guermantes and the troubled, fascinating way of Méséglise and above all, of Mountjouvain. However, this is still only a stage of clarification: indeed, the true work of putting the creative machine in its place will only begin the moment when the "shiftiness" of Montjouvain—where becoming-woman takes root—having been sufficiently explored, crafted, chiseled, and assimilated, will manage to communicate, to be "transversalized" with the "brilliance" of Guermantes, which, meanwhile, will itself have lost what is essential to its splendor.

2. Constellations of faciality traits

Swann "pasted" a photograph of Botticelli's Zipporah onto Odette's face, and then… he experienced ecstasy. The Narrator installs the score of Tristan over Vinteuil's sonata and compares them "as one looks at a photograph" to specify a resemblance (I, 159/I, 164).

With Swann, the face and refrain are shut off in a closed universe, accompanied by a danger of the black hole, semiotic inhibition, or catastrophe. The Narrator devotes himself to distinguishing what the refrain is in the most rigorous way—here, by the reading of the partition and the play of possible connections with the works of other composers. But the putting into effect of this scriptural component will not limit its effects to Vinteuil's music alone; it will profoundly transform the other components, particularly that of faciality. Becoming graphematic, the refrain will abandon the defensive and finally attack on all fronts.

A first attempt at this opening onto the outsides was described 1300 pages before the passage evoked here, when the Narrator referenced the use of a musical reading technique to decipher Albertine's face, whom he had just met in Balbec. "That morning, we were one of the couples who here and there punctuate the esplanade with their momentary meetings, pausing long enough to exchange a few words before separating to take up again their two diverging trajectories. I took advantage of this brief immobility to make a thorough check of the place where the beauty mark was to be found. Just as a phrase of Vinteuil that had delighted me in the sonata, and which my memory kept moving from the andante to the finale, until the day when, *with the score in hand*, I was able to find it and localize it where it belonged, in the scherzo, so the beauty mark, which I had remembered on her cheek, then on her chin, came to rest forever on her upper lip, just under her nose. In the same way, we are astonished to come upon a stanza we know by heart, but in a poem where we did not realize it belonged" (I, 877–878/II, 456–457).

As if to emphasize that the Narrator will not repeat Swann's error, including the amalgamation of the loved one's face and the liberating refrain, Proust derives the latter from the andante—where Swann had always localized it—towards the final scherzo. In some

way, the andante brings with it a "globalizing" conception of faciality, whereas the scherzo develops, with this grain of fleeting beauty,
a diagrammatic reading of disseminated or constellated faciality
traits. Furthermore, Proust will not hold on to this first transfer of
the refrain; afterwards, he will have it move from the Sonata to the
Septet, to finally make it escape from Vinteuil's music altogether.[45]

The component of faciality which remained in the dominant
position within Swann's assemblage will fall under the powers of this
new variant of the refrain. In its essence, the Narrator's love is a passage from one face to another,[46] and at each moment we never
rediscover in it the equivalent of an identifying mechanism of the
Odette-Zipporah type. In fact, it is love which has itself become a
diagrammatic refrain here, stripping away Albertine's face and mul-
tiplying her character. Albertine is "innumerable" (III, 488/V, 455),
she participates in a "collective" being (III, 596/V, 560), in a
"galaxy" (III, 561/V, 526) embodying multiple dimensions and successive approximations of the becoming-woman in which the
Narrator is involved.

The transformation of its object into a multiplicity, into a
"galaxy," does not mean that this love is lost in ambiguity, vagueness,
or amorphousness. Bypassing the black hole of passion and becoming graphematic, the refrain releases an extremely effective
component of *perceptive reading* and *creative writing*.

We previously related that one of the essential problems of the
Recherche was the depth of perception.[47] The transformation of
becoming-woman by the refrain and the refrainization of the
"Young Girls in Flower" radically modify the data. The existence of
a feminine presence associated with Vinteuil's little phrase
remained very precarious. We remember that it is very difficult for
it to somewhat manage to indicate to Swann a possible access to
creation. But it is inevitably found to be redirected by Odette's
faciality, i.e. by a component of reterritorialization ("the rest was so

often yellow, languid, sometimes marked with little red specks...")
(I, 222/I, 230). The "Young Girls" constitute a deterritorialized-deterritorializing assemblage. It does not suffice to say, as we shall, that the Narrator deciphers Albertine's faciality traits "like" a musical text, for becoming-woman, by transforming into a deterritorializing collective being, produces a matter of expression similar in all points to a musical universe. Proust will compose and orchestrate his own score on the basis of this deterritorialized matter. In other words, we have come to the point where the same type of abstract machinism henceforth traverses the world of the "Young Girls," Vinteuil's music, Elstir's painting, and Proust's phrases.

Eighth Assemblage: the "premier" of Vinteuil's Septet in Madame Verdurin's home: the group of "rhizomatic leitmotivs."

Baron Charlus has organized a chamber music concert in Madame Verdurin's home during which one of Vinteuil's posthumous works will be presented. In order to highlight Morel's talent, the young violinist he is in love with, he has invited the most respected persons of aristocratic society. But the evening ends badly: Madame Verdurin proceeds to set Morel and Charlus at odds, resulting in a veritable amorous failure for the latter. Charlus seems to replay a game here that Charles Swann had already lost long before in the framework of the Verdurin assemblage. But his failure will be much more devastating than it was for Swann!

In contrast, this concert will be a fundamental stage for the Narrator in his attempt to "overcome" his love for Albertine. Days earlier, he used everything to dissuade her from going to it, fearing that she would meet up with Mlle Vinteuil. Spurred on by jealousy, he has decided to go there himself to see if Mlle Vinteuil truly had the intention of attending[48] (but she remained in the countryside). He has come to Albertine's place, substitutes himself for her, and infiltrates a becoming-woman rather than continuing to resist her. Hence a veritable reversal of the situation: his hostility towards Mlle Vinteuil transforms into admiration for the musicographical work that she has accomplished with the help of her homosexual friend. In fact, both of them have partially reconstituted a Septet by Vinteuil which is presented for the first time at this concert; it is undoubtedly the masterpiece of one already considered by many as "the greatest composer of the century" (III, 241/V, 221).

Despite his hesitations and reticence, Vinteuil's Sonata has provided Swann with an invaluable assistance to extract himself from the black hole of passion, or at least to establish a compromise with it. In contrast, the Narrator has remained almost completely insensible to it, but he welcomes the Septet with fervor. This revelation thwarts the neurotic motivations which had attracted him to this concert.

This assemblage develops in the following directions:

—the atrophy of two branches of the rhizome:

• that of Charlus, which marks the failure of the masculine homosexual "attempted escape";[49]

• that of living together with Albertine, which demonstrates the impasse of a certain type of conjugality (*The Prisoner*);

—the broadening of the range of matters of expression. From the point of view of its conception as well as its orchestration, the Septet represents a considerable qualitative bond in relation to the Sonata, and it prepares the refrain's escape outside the musical field;

—the conversion of the refrain into a group of trans-semiotic leitmotivs.

1. The atrophy of two branches of the rhizomes

The failure of Swann's love led to the "launch" of two parallel attempts to take up the same problematic:

—the first, from Swann's way, with the loves of the Narrator for Gilberte, the daughter of Swann and Odette, and for Albertine;

—the other, from Guermantes' way, with the love of Charlus for the violinist Morel.

It is on condition of surpassing such personological stratifications, such drive determined destinies, that the refrain which harbors becoming-woman and creation can hope to take flight. It was thus necessary, in one way or another, to finish with these two attempts, to empty them of their substance, to show that they would never lead to anything.

Swann remained disarmed in front of Odette's power, without recourse save the anxiety-producing black hole of passion. Charlus and the Narrator, at least at first, keep from slipping down such a slope; they intend to exercise an absolute power over their partner's smallest actions and slightest thoughts. Yet this type of possession of the other (or by the other) can lead to anything: to domestic tyranny, to conjugal solitude like hopelessness, to neurosis, but in no way to an authentic creation. The liquidation of this type of micropolitics within the couple is indissociable for the Narrator from a reevaluation of "high society power" and from a decompartmentalization of the "categorized" libido, whether about of young maids and/or princesses; the elevator boys and/or handsome officers… All throughout, it is the separation between the sexual components vectorized from "Swann's way" and the aristocratic literary components vectorized from "Guermantes' way" which are found to be overcome.

2. The broadened range of matters of expression

The Sonata was the extreme point of a finished classical artwork, whereas the Septet opens up to a fully renewed world of rhythms and sounds. The timbres of the chamber orchestra bring forth a universe of colors and lights which initiate the junction between musical creation, pictorial creation, and writing.[50] Whereas the little phrase of the Sonata was associated with a limited part of Botticelli's fresco, to a self-enclosed "detail"—Zipporah's face—here the accent is placed on the colorful productions generated by brass instruments, open in all parts to the universe of sensations. The reference is displaced from the work to the creator himself, while Vinteuil, "painting his great musical fresco," is compared to "Michelangelo on his ladder, head down, launching tumultuous brushstrokes against the ceiling of the Sistine Chapel."[51]

The movement of the Sonata was linear, but it was broken into "short calls"; the Septet "brings scattered fragments back together into an indivisible armature."

In short, let us say that here we pass from discontinuous machinic indexes to a trans-semiotic machinic plane of consistency.

3. The association of becoming-women and the scriptural component

The Septet is the result of two "re-attachments":

—that which Vinteuil brings about by transforming the Sonata's linear sequences into fragments articulated in the same armature;

—that which results from the work of his daughter and her friend, which reconstitute the piece from scattered works.[52]

These two operations are assigned to *Vinteuil's name*, in the asignifying Vinteuil machine. Passing from the father to the daughter, from the little phrase to the leitmotivs of the Septet, this name is "charged" with a new libidinal energy and a diagrammatic power with incalculable consequences.

What is the meaning of the introduction of the component: Mademoiselle-Vinteuil-and-her-friend? The scene of the oedipal profanation of the father's face, doubly fixed by death and photography, constitutes the "nymph" phase of the transformation of the black hole and the shedding of the component of becoming-woman. In order to cross the threshold which will lead to the feverish rewriting of the masterpiece harboring the machinic essence of creation,[53] everything happens as though it shall have been necessary to return to the sea of Montjouvain to recover a mysterious key, or rather to break a secret lock, to bust the window frame through which the Narrator child contemplated this mute scene, paralyzed with horror, but from which he has never managed to detach himself, to break the frame of the photograph, to undo the familiar arrangement of the paternal face intolerably fixed in memory. One had to go to the very end of the scandal of death, silence, to what is buried in the past and force the cadaver to howl with pain. That which was closed off in traumatic "infantile fixations" is henceforth taken up by the writer. He will turn it into a war machine against inertia, the passivity of reminiscence, *machinic block of childhood* which will transform memory into imagination and perception into creation.

The perverse sea of Montjouvain represents the focal point of the *Recherche*'s black hole of passion. But, as seems evident by now, it is now no longer a question of a passive[54] black hole, associated with a powerless hate, like what Mlle Vinteuil felt toward her father and perhaps what the Narrator child secretly felt towards his parents, nor an empty, inhibitive black hole, like Swann's love. The sea of Montjouvain is alive; it is inhabited by representations, characters, matters of expression conveying quanta of potentialities, emitting signs-particles capable of interacting with the most diverse semiotic components. Until the intervention of the writing component by way of Mlle Vinteuil, this life has remained frozen, speech remained prisoner, gestures ritualized, phantasms whirled around as in a nightmare, and the libido remained subordinate to a Manichean Superego with devastating effects. Now everything has changed, the writing which is about to be born will no longer have anything to do with the pretty style à la Bergotte, but with an inventiveness of a wild ambition, the liberation of a multi-headed refrain playing itself out in time, space, and substances of expression. In the Swann assemblage, Odette's faciality formed a screen over the black hole; in "the Narrator assemblage," when Albertine was snatched by the diabolical field of Montjouvain, her faciality traits proliferate, her character multiplies, and the black hole itself, in counterpoint, finds its functioning profoundly redirected. It is not centered on a "face." Faciality participates in its own intrinsic machinism. A literary machine is substituted for the face and the black hole which drives characters, faces, and affects in the living rhizome of the work in progress, whose job is precisely to neutralize and abolish every black hole effect.

4. The conversion of the refrain into a trans-semiotic group of leitmotivs

The "degeneration" of the character of Charlus, the being of flight which affirms itself with Albertine's character, the broadening and proliferation of matters of expression, and the development of the creative machine are correlative to an essential mutation of the abstract machinism which must lead it to the promotion of a creative becoming-woman. Later I will return to the entire evolution of this becoming-woman associated with the refrain. Also, here I will only examine the "introduction" of the group of leitmotivs which are substituted for the refrain.

A description of the preparatory (or exploratory) phases in this mutation will be sketched out in relation to other subjective assemblages deviating from the norm: a scarcely evoked becoming-animal and a slightly more sustained becoming-child.

a) the Septet's matters of expression, besides the affects of light and color, produce a shrill song, simultaneously ineffable and squawking, a sort of "*mystic cock-crow.*" In contrast, the Sonata seems dull, and its refrain reflected the murmuring of a dove (III, 250/V, 229). Proust does not take a becoming-animal of the refrain further than this. He remarks that, in this domain, differences establish themselves in the same way as animal species with their cries and their specific bellowing (III, 256/V, 235). Musics assimilate with living beings. Thus we can consider that there are two varieties of the "Vinteuil species," two heterogeneous assemblages:

—one tied to the miserable and resigned Vinteuil of "Swann's way";

—the other tied to becoming-woman such as it has been reworked by Mademoiselle de Vinteuil and her friend.

It is only in this direction of a becoming-woman that the phylum of the *Recherche* could evolve in a creative way. The path of a becoming-animal, for example of the type Kafka explored, would have led Proust nowhere. Animality allows an escape from the dominant significations of the human condition. But it remains too totalizing, too individuating; it lends itself too easily to signifying recuperations. No, to be constituted, Proust's creative machine must pass through life itself. It required sacrificing the loved object for that, definitively renouncing to totalize it, to reify it, to "iconize" it. This will only be possible when the Narrator will unreservedly accept the deterritorialized being—faciality in perpetual movement, fugues, dreams—of Albertine. He will have to "juggle" not only his slightest gestures but also his existence. The power of the writer over his character is substituted for the power of the Creator. It is only when he gets to the end of Albertine, when he will have killed her, resurrected her, and made her disappear again by dispersing even the letters of her name, that he will manage to find the "collective side" that was present at the beginning and is now regained (his) love for the young girls of the little gang, "long undifferentiated among them, and, only briefly associated with the person of Albertine during the last months which had preceded and followed her death" (III, 596/V, 560).

b) This becoming-woman-creator somewhat "ebbs" towards a *becoming-child*. For example, the Narrator imagines that Vinteuil was inspired by the scene of his sleeping daughter for the "gentle and familial domestic phrase of the Septet." He himself has frequently tried to "defuse" Albertine's evil power by contemplating her for a long time while she slept. Despite invoking Schumann here—the musician who has injected the strongest charges of becoming-child imaginable into the occidental musical phylum—Proust does not manage to extract himself from the most insipid childishness:[55] Albertine is his "little baby;" he never stops playing the fool, for example, by reconstituting the ritual of the maternal kiss from that night in Combray.[56]

Nevertheless, the same movement of the Septet's music will carry him further away from such familialist evocations, such relapses into territorialized modes of amorous possession.[57] In fact, the abstract machinism which he presently carries within him now capable of "traversing," at every moment and in all directions, people, faces, impressions, epochs...

The abstract feminine presence adjacent to the little phrase of Swann's love is increasingly made into the ally, confidant, or enemy of Odette, but in reality never stopped being under her control, as though it were the satellite around the black hole whose support was Odette's face. With the Septet, it has lost its unicity and its fixity: it has become multiple and dancing. The Narrator evokes in his account a group of fairies, dryads, and familiar divinities (III, 259/V, 238).[58] Some of them, who remind him of the Sonata, form a circle around him during this matinee at the home of the princess Guermantes-ex-Verdurin. One in particular, *whose face he does not see*, breaks from the group and transforms into a sort of mysterious *call* which has already appeared at the beginning of the Septet. A different abstract-musical-feminine entity, but "sorrowful," almost "organic" and "visceral,"[59] then begins a battle with the first. On this point, Proust speaks of a "wrestling-match of pure energies" ("for if these beings struggled against each other, it was without the encumbrance of their bodies, their outward appearances, their names") (III, 260/V, 239). The "joyous motif" which rises victorious from this "immaterial and dynamic battle" and which seems to simply be an avatar of the Sonata's "little phrase," is very different from the latter, so different that it can be "an archangel of Mantegna robed in scarlet blowing into a mighty trumpet," "a sweetly grave Bellini angel playing the theorbo" (III, 260/V, 239). Proust tells us that this triumphant call promises the Narrator supraterrestrial joys of the type that he had experienced during his life, each separated by lengthy intervals, and which have served him as guideposts to orient himself along the path of the *Recherche* (for example, the deeply felt impression before the steeples of Martinville, or in front of a row of trees in Balbec).

But will this writing machine, whose existence at the moment seems to be of the order of the possible, respond to this call? Will the Narrator finally take up action? In other words, will this new version of the deterritorialized refrain be more capable than the others of endeavoring "the construction of a veritable life" (III, 261/V, 240)? The subject of the scriptural enunciation is disindivuated; it has become multiple and transsexual: will this be enough for the machine of expression to become *effectively trans-semiotic*?

Here we have returned again to the question we started with: has the assemblage of enunciation acquired a sufficient degree of machinic consistency? "And thinking once again about the extra-temporal joy caused by the sound of the spoon or the taste of the madeleine, I said to myself: 'Was this the happiness which the sonata's little phrase offered to Swann, which he was unable to find in artistic creation and therefore mistook by assimilating it to the pleasure of love; was this the happiness I had felt as a presentiment, even more supra-terrestrial than the little phrase of the sonata, of the mysterious, glowing appeal of the septet which Swann had not been able to recognize, being dead like so many others before the truth made for them can be revealed to them? And anyway, it would not have been any use to him, for *the phrase could easily symbolize an appeal, but not create the powers* to make Swann the writer he was not'" (III, 878/VI, 186).

Ninth Assemblage: from the musical refrain to the abstract machinism of creation

Two stages of "becoming-invisible," which transform the refrain into a pure unconscious machinism, must be distinguished before approaching certain traits that characterize the creative assemblage which is substituted, at the end of the *Recherche*, for the musical and refined assemblages examined up to now.

1. Two stages on the path of the refrain's "becoming-invisible"

a) Albertine and the crank of the pianola.

Isolated, infantilized, "re-educated," Albertine is little by little transformed into a sort of mechanical doll perfectly adapted to the Narrator's domestic life. The Narrator's attachment is based more on the jealousy that she stirs up in him, rather than any real love. Furthermore, his first concern paradoxically seems to be to liberate himself from his "Prisoner." His goal is not to keep her with him but to extract her essential substance. And here we would do best to compare her less to a marionette than to an enigmatic formula whose solution is of vital interest for him. She has become like one of those equations which we are required to add to a mathematical corpus to solve a problem and which we deduct from the end of the calculation.[60] This is precisely what Proust does by making Albertine's character die in a quasi-experimental way, whereas elsewhere he evokes the fact that she could have just as easily not existed, and he examines the consequences of such a hypothesis.[61]

We are shown a particularly significant stage of this transformation of Albertine with the scene where the Narrator reduces her to being nothing more than a cog among other cogs in a curious musical desiring machine. Ten times, twenty times he asks her to turn the same roll of music on the pianola until he is saturated by it and, upon finishing, he can shout: "one less piece of music in the world for me, but one truth more" (III, 373/V, 344).[62] Once compared to a musical instrument, Albertine is now reduced to the state of simple piece detached from a musical machine of encoding, a machine to ingurgitate, to internalize the syntax and the most deterritorialized machinic articulations of music.[63]

b) a Sunday on All Saints' Day in the Bois de Boulogne: the machinal little phrase.

The banalization of the little phrase for Swann, its reduction to the state of an obsessive old song, was correlative with the appearance of a black hole of anxiety and jealousy. The oppresive character which it had assumed was only attenuated by Swann's entrance into married life. The Narrator adopts a completely different attitude in its regard. He actively semiotizes the refrain to the point that it manages to be incorporated in its own mode of relation to the world, to belong to itself, and even to become invisible and inaudible for him. This loss of phenomenal appearance takes part in a process of deterritorialization which I must point out, does not at all imply its disappearance from the real. On the contrary, the abstract machinism which it conveys will be so much the more powerful to the extent that it has passed below facialized consciousness. Not minding one's feet while descending stairs, or looking at the dashboard from the corner of your eyes, does not signify that the stairs or the automobile are abolished or that, through distraction, we must inevitably misstep or crash into a wall. Behavioral segments are simply integrated machinically with the assemblage.

The "little phrase" has become machinic for the Narrator the moment when it entered what Proust calls "its second chemical phase," characterized by the fact that it is no longer in relation with a black hole effect, that it is no longer the cause of "oppressing the heart with anxiety" (III, 559/V, 524). The decisive phase of the decomposition of Albertine and the "Young Girls," "stardust of the galaxies" (III, 561/V, 526), corresponds with its complete disappearance: "When the little phrase, before entirely disappearing, disintegrates, and floats around for a moment as it dissolves into its various elements, it was not, as it had been, for Swann, a messenger informing me of the disappearance of Albertine. The little phrase did not awaken quite the same association of ideas in me as it had in Swann. I had been particularly moved by the variations, experiments, repetitions and *'becoming' of a phrase*,[64] which played in the sonata a role like that played in the course of my life by my love. And now, as I came to realize how far, day by day, another element of my love was drifting away, my jealousy or other aspects of my love gradually returning in a vague memory as the piece quietly started, I thought I saw my love dispersed or even dissolved in the little phrase" (III, 559–560/V, 525).

Swann remained in the first chemical phase, in the molar compromise, in generative arrangements. On the contrary, the Narrator, by approaching this "second chemical phase," sparks a molecular process which will lead him towards a trans-semiotic metabolism, towards a transformation of the refrain into a *"becoming-phrase."* Certainly, from the moment of its first emergence, the abstract machinism of the little phrase had "seen" the solution to the problem of Swann and the Narrator. But he could only realize this intuition through a long process involving the processing and experimentation of all kinds of matters of expression—artistic, but also worldly, sexual, economic, political… The "Swann complex" was important only during this process. At the beginning, he was nothing but a symptom among others; he has only become dangerous with the enrichment and explanation of the components to which he led. In order to face the fundamental questions of Time, Creation, Death…, Swann had no other recourse than to a system of machinic propositions existing in a closed economy: a face, a same old song, classical art, high society people, the "little worker girls"… Under pressure from the unconscious machinic field in full mutation within which he evolves, an implosion phenomenon has threatened the consistency of his assemblage of enunciation. He only provisionally manages to escape from it through a molar compromise which consists in letting this potential semiotic volcano die out, and in renouncing to use its incredible energy.

The Narrator operates in an open economy. His modes of semiotization are infinitely richer and more consistent. He is capable of producing his own "weapons." He depends on no one. He has no need for faces-icons and stereotyped characters. Whereas everything tended to be ritualized in Swann, everything tends to be semiotized in the Narrator. To the point that Albertine, rather than being inscribed like Odette in the conjugal code, passes directly into the hyper-deterritorialized code of the *Recherche*'s writing. She becomes pure molecular flight and, as such, more difficult to seal off; she becomes a being of untruth, pretense, and treachery.[65] There is also no compromise with her: the dilemma cannot be overcome. She will lead the Narrator to his destruction,[66] or she will herself have to disappear by being incorporated into the creative process.

In its terminal phase, the refrain not only will no longer be associated with the *Young Girls*, it will furthermore leave the musical terrain behind. This does not mean, as a number of commentators have claimed, that Proust was henceforth disinterested in music, or even that he was only interested in it to "exemplify" the *Recherche*.

Quite the contrary! With the revelation of the creative machine, then of the last matinee in the home of Princess Guermantes—ex-Verdurin—it is writing itself that becomes musical. Music traverses the notes, sounds, walls...[67]

The assemblage of enunciation of this new music will no longer just be a little pianist, like that of Swann's love, a violinist like that of the love of Charlus, the ensemble of the young girls like that of the Narrator's love, but the play of two uneven paving-stones, the sound of a spoon, as well as the taste of a madeleine. The world itself has become a sort of gigantic organ, and writing a music traversing the sonorous universe from everywhere. The taste of the madeleine is articulated with images of Combray; the Narrator's stubbed toe on a poorly paved road with the two uneven paving-stones of the baptistery of Saint-Marc; the sound of the spoon clanking against the dinner plate combined with that of a worker's hammer banging on the wheels of a train... (III, 866–68/VI, 176–178).

2. The conditions to which the trans-semiotic creative assemblage must respond

In order to work together and go beyond a simple function of index, as was the case with the little phrase at the beginning of Swann's love, in order to mobilize an energy of change, to produce a new music and inscribe it in the center of the subjective being, the diagrammatic figures, which Proust calls "signs in relief" (III, 879/VI, 187), must enter into a double process of deterritorialization by decompartmentalization and concatenation.[68] It is on this condition that they find their efficiency[69] by inscribing themselves on a sort of "complicated and florid *spell book*," whose "characters are forged within and not traced" by man (III, 879, 880/VI, 187, 188), and to the aid of which two types of chemistry will become possible:

—a chemistry of the analysis of the real occulted shrouded appearances,

—a chemistry of the synthesis of new realities, new matters, new intensities.

The signs of this spell book are not logical algorithms but abstract entities, machinic propositions in direct contact with the most deterritorialized articulations of the components of the real and thus, in a sense, more real than the real.[70] These abstract, diagrammatic machinisms of art not only involve energetic, biological, and socio-economic-spatio-temporal dimensions, but also the transitory or ephemeral modes of temporalization, fleeting intuitions, "minuscule impressions," everything that stems from the "extreme part of sensations." They allow us to access the virtualities of the real, a hyper-reality which involves the most profound dynamism of things, not simply time passed and time emerging in the present, but also all the modes of temporalization to come.

The supplementary dimension or relief that the refrain acquires with the Septet corresponds to the acquisition of a new dimension of deterritorialization, a deterritorialization which is not composed in gaps, voids, or as an absolute in a black hole, but in expansion, conveying abstract quanta of potentiality. The Guermantes hotel revelation introduces a generalized subversion of the coordinates connected to dominant significations. From the moment it will enter the field of this abstract refrain, every matter of expression employed in an assemblage, every emergence of a component of expression's deterritorialized fringe will be affected by a new consistency of existence. The trans-dimensional refrain will thus also manifest itself by way of a musical sequence as well as the play of two uneven paving-stones, figures traced by moving bells, the fragrance of a geranium…

Two series of "machinic propositions" specific to the Proustian machine must be involved for such a capture of existential consistency to become possible:

—the first concerns the discernibilization of matters of expression,

—the second concerns their concatenation and the generation of new components (the trans-duction and pro-duction of components).

The function of the discernibilization of matters of expression

"This labor of the artist, this attempt to see something different beneath the material, beneath experience, beneath words, is the exact inverse of that which is accomplished within us from minute to minute, as we live our lives heedless of ourselves, by vanity, by passion, intellect and habit, when they overlay our true impressions, so as to hide them from us completely, with the repertoire of words, and the practical aims, which we wrongly call life" (III, 896/VI, 204–205). The ordinary signs of language make us miss the essential realities. The play of signs organized in the "spell book" of the *Recherche* is not at all comparable with those of "conventional" language. Signifying semiologies simultaneously lack the natural and artificial means. They lack the natural because they trap us in everyday evidences, dominant redundancies, everything which stems, according to Proust, from the world of *habit*. They are not artificial enough because to rediscover the true "resistance of the material," it is necessary to forge semiotics which are much more machinic than can be compared to those of science: "An impression is for the writer what an experiment is for the scientist" (III, 880/VI, 188). The function of discernibilization thus implies, at the same time, a greater passivity, a greater abandon to fortuitous encounters and to the bareness of the real,[71] and to a greater sophistication of the mode of semiotization. The empirical apperception of the Kantians or the eidetic reduction of phenomenologists will have to be "armed." The semiotic machines of discernibilization will have to be able to accelerate or condense time, distend or contract space, produce composite faces, or even derive them from one another...

"The writer's work is only a kind of optical instrument which he offers the reader to enable him to *discern* what, without this book he might not perhaps have seen in himself" (III, 911/VI, 220).

But the misunderstanding begins when it is a question of determining the nature of this instrument. When the Narrator shows several outlines of the *Recherche* to his friends, they tell him that he has established a sort of *microscope*; to which he replies that he has, on the contrary, used a *telescope* "to make out things which were indeed very small, but only because they were situated a long way away, each of them a world in itself. In the place where I was trying to find general laws, I was accused of sifting through endless detail" (III, 1041/VI, 350–51). The release of such a component of discernibilization within an aesthetic pragmatic field completely overturns the traditional references to good taste, to the elegance of style, to the symmetry of parts, to the construction and harmonious development of an entirely preconceived work perfectly mastered from the moment of its conception. The readers of the *Recherche* are anticipated: they do not read a book, they use a tool: "With the result that I would not ask them to praise me or to denigrate me, only to tell me if it was right, if the words they were reading in themselves were really the ones I had written (possible divergences in this regard not necessarily always originating, it should be said, in my having been wrong, but sometimes in the fact that the reader's eyes might not be of a type for which my book was suitable as an aid for self-reading)" (III, 1033/VI, 343).

The criterion of the beautiful has become the joy of the "real regained." The intensity of desire associated with the emergence of deterritorialized objects, which will have had no chance of reaching existence, or supporting themselves here under the "normal" conditions of semiotization, have thus been raised to the rank of a veritable aesthetico-ontological "argument."

The functions of translation and generation of matters of expression

Discernibilization reduces the "semiotic entropy" relative to "impressions;" it makes it possible to construct universes founded on objects, relations, hyper-deterritorialized intensities. "Only the impression, however slight its material may seem, however elusive its trace, can be a criterion of truth" (III, 880/VI, 188). But the existential consistency of these universes depends on the nature of the assemblage that articulates them. Reality has lost its ontological uni-dimensionality. It must be worked on at the level of its modes of semiotic efficiency. It is no longer simply to the creation of new beings which this experimentation of sensations, memory, affects, and fantasy will lead, but equally to *new modes of being*.

Because "degrees of existence" have become a parameter among others, an object, a relation, or an intensity only exists to the extent that it is found at the crossroads of various matters of expression. Failing such a diversity, dreams, for example, only allow access to a very precarious[72] "Time regained." A dream is only valuable if it is translated—not interpreted—but translated into a more consistent matter of expression. Everything can be transposed.[73] "The writer's task and duty are those of a translator" (III, 890/VI, 199). The decisive existential turn of the refrain corresponds to the moment when Mlle Vinteuil and her friend transform into *translators* of Vinteuil's text. Have we here stopped at the technique of "fac-simile," evoked during the second assemblage? No, what is repeated is not the impression as such, nor a mental schema, but certain matters of content and expression. One does not interpret a content, one searches for it by way of the signifying paradigm, one makes it work in another matter. One thus reveals in it new possibilities of the "never seen," of the unprecedented.[74] This content is not reducible to a universal essence. In the last instance, it is resolved by a pragmatic field, a knot of machinic propositions, a certain manner of assembling singular modes of subjectification and conscientization. As we have seen, the ultimate transformation of the little phrase ends in its exhaustion, its automation—in the sense that one speaks of a mental automatism—in order to render it silent and invisible and in a way that it is integrated into the *Recherche*'s unconscious mode of semiotization.

A certain poetic passivity, a certain abandon in matters of expression, a certain necessitous modesty of the transcriber unlocks the paths to creation. The machinic rhizome does the rest, it guides the hand, reveals rhythms and intensities… This passivity, in the context of dominant phallocratic values, will be lived through by Swann as femininity. It is not at all self-evident that such an equivalence corresponds with reality and the aspirations of the feminine condition! That being pointed out, the refrain can be defined as the operator of a becoming-woman-creator. It manages, at present, to truly *beat time to the feminine*. Universal Time is abolished in favor of a thousand assemblages of temporalization, corresponding with infinitely varied styles of deterritorialization. One never bathes in the same impression twice as soon as the micropolitics of assemblages of enunciation leads to the liberation of living, heterogeneous and singular matters of expression. The translator artist is nothing more, as an individual, than the catalyst of such an assemblage. "Normal" time is outpaced by the "creative" deterritorializations proliferating from this becoming-woman that overtake "natural" deterritorializations. It is no longer a question, as in Swann's era, of putting oneself back into the ambiguities of synesthesias, into the aesthetic syncretism of natural memory. Nothing is left to chance, neither the so-called free association of psychoanalysts nor the "objective chance" of the surrealists. To "recapture" an impression, it will sometimes be advisable to return to it fifty times in a row.[75] And yet this relentlessness must be viewed as involving no will to power.[76] The *Recherche* has become correlative to a renunciation of power formations, an abandonment to the state of things, indeed even a disintegration of bodies: "let us leave our body to disintegrate, since each new particle that breaks away from it comes back, now luminous and legible, to add itself to our work, to complete it at the price of the suffering of which others more gifted have no need, to increase its solidity as our emotions are eroding our life" (III, 906/VI, 215).

3

Machinic Territorialities

The Trajectory of the Faciality Component in the *Recherche*

Due to its association with the refrain the faciality component never ceases to undergo profound transformations all throughout Proust's work. It is also impossible to assign a constant role to certain faciality traits traversing the various apparent systems of identification among characters (example: "the passage" from the Narrator's mother and grandmother to Odette, Gilberte, Albertine...).

In the course of this essay, I have attempted to establish that the "transversalist" drift of faces can in no way be assimilated with a drive-based sublimation, to a drifting of the libido towards non-sexual goals. It is true that in the end literary activity seems to be purely and simply substituted for the system of amorous facialitary capture which characterized the beginning of the *Recherche*. But the different assemblages put into play, the interactions of components, and the general movement of deterrorialization of matters of expression, have ended up promoting a creative abstract machinism that appears to have attracted a libidinal energy to it which was previously fixated upon territorialized imaginary formations. I would not insist so much on the fact that when such a machinism is qualified as abstract, this does not mean that it resulted from the play of formal abstraction: it is so in the sense that it makes abstraction of a certain number of stratifications; the abstract is thus synonymous here with hyper-deterritorialization. In their functioning, abstract machinic propositions include components of all types, and particularly those of a sexual nature. As corporeal and territorial as they are, these components are carried beyond themselves into domains far removed from the biological and the imaginary. There is no sublimation here for all that, nor overcoming, but simply the crossing of a continuum of components, the translation of matters of expression. The abstract machinism of Proustian creation drains out deterritorialized faces, musical refrains, sexual "partial objects," and a thousand other idiosyncratic traits, such as the taste of the madeleine of Combray, the vision of the steeples of Martinville, the affects tied to the sea of Montjouvain... The writing machine has not replaced sexuality; it is superimposed on it and develops in its extension. It is also legitimate to consider that it is itself essentially sexual, musical, social, etc., on condition of not envisaging sexuality, music, and the socius as eternal entities irreducibly separated from one another. It is through these means that the initially too formal and too Manichean division between the good way—the literary and sophisticated way of Guermantes—and the bad way—the sexual and familialist way of Swann and Montjouvain[1]—of the *Recherche* is overcome in the end.

We shall now let us return to the general movement of deterritorialization that affects the faciality component, and reexamine a certain number of the *Recherche*'s stages, sometimes simple landmarks which appear characteristic in this regard.

1. The goodnight kiss in Combray

"Everything had been decided at the moment when, unable to bear the idea of waiting until the next day to set my lips on my mother's face, I had made my resolution, jumped out of bed, and gone, in my nightshirt, to stay by the window through which the moonlight[2] came, until I heard M. Swann go" (III, 1044/VI, 354). The first "black hole complex" of the *Recherche* becomes fixated on the face of the Narrator's mother: the hostility of the father, who finds this ritual absurd; the educational rigidity of the mother; the quasi-neurotic tyranny of the child Narrator who has turned the ceremony of the "goodnight kiss" into a daily test of strength with at times catastrophic results. One night when Swann is visiting, a crisis which looks to be particularly difficult for the Narrator as leads to a happy, almost miraculous ending: instead of being harshly reprimanded, as he expected, in order to be relieved, he receives the support of his father who judges his wife's attitude toward the child as too harsh ("you'll end by making him ill, and that won't do us much good!" I, 36/I, 36). He even asks his wife to sleep in the same room as the child this night so he can be reassured and consoled. This "fruitful moment" will profoundly mark the Narrator's subjectivity: he will continue to feel his entire life the sobs which have risen from his chest ("like those convent bells covered so well by the clamor of the town during the day that one would think they had ceased altogether but which begin sounding again in the silence of the evening" I, 37/I, 37). Here let us limit ourselves to the beginning of two systems of connections which will undergo important later developments:

• *the "intrusion" of Swann and the little catastrophe* experienced by the Narrator. It indicates that the "facelessness" and impossibility of a "knowledge acquired by the lips" of the feminine presence are only seemingly tied to a paternal prohibition; they result, in fact, from a black hole effect that the *Recherche* will "attach" to Swann in order to semiotize him.

• the mechanism of *escape from the black hole* and *literature*. In effect, the Narrator and his mother have consecrated their "night of love" by reading one of George Sand's books.[3]

2. The faciality/black hole/refrain complex of Swann's Love

Because of the Narrator's taking charge of the "Swann complex" (which appears legitimate to me in the synchronic perspective I evoked above), we can include Swann's love for Odette in this trajectory of faciality. It is Proust himself who suggests so much when he evokes Swann's experience concerning the "well intentioned mediators" apropos of the goodnight kiss (I, 31/I, 32). The previous development of this faciality/black hole/refrain complex frees me from having to return to it here. I will only recall its consequences:

• a withering and isolation of iconic and musical components by impoverishing their matter of expression,

• a subjection of the feminine component to Odette's faciality,

• Swann's progressive isolation via a folding of the socius onto the "private," onto the "intimate."

However, it is on the basis of this complex that quanta of deterritorialization will be emitted from abstract machines whose vector will be the little phrase.

3. The first facialitary revolution

This affects the faces of the males present at the concert at the Marquise de Saint-Euverte's home, and it leads to the dissolution of Odette's face in the dream of "the young man wearing a fez." It leads to a reworking of the double process inherited from the two preceding assemblages, namely:

• a territorialization which takes us from Swann's intrusion in the ritual of the maternal kiss to the face of lover-mother-wife Odette;

• a deterritorialization which begins a "musical" escape for Swann and a "literary" escape for the Narrator.

Faciality traits lose their usual "framework" here. The black hole is emancipated from the feminine component and develops into the series of monocles (the latter seems to be embodied by the character of Charlus); the black hole no longer results from a simple rupture of inter-component connection, from a semiotic collapse, but from a complex phenomenon of facialitary resonance, of identification. Anxiety is "projected" on the socius, or to speak like psychologists, it is "socialized." But this consciousness-based facialization is accompanied by an emission of deterritorialized faciality traits able to work with the artistic and literary components adapted to the *Recherche*.

4. The dissimulated smile and Gilberte's indecent gesture in Tansonville

It will take decades of the *Recherche* for the Narrator to manage to decipher the meaning of the first look Gilberte sent him when they met in the park of Tansonville. What he took for indifference and insolence (I, 141/I, 144)—as Gilberte, who slightly embarrassed, will confess to him at the beginning of *Time Regained*—was in reality nothing but an insistent invitation to join her in the dark ruins of the Rousainville dungeon, where the village children were often met together. Staying too close to the direct sense meaning of words, as well as following social codes and manners too strictly, the Narrator's love for Gilberte will take on the same "fatality" as Swann's for Odette—Gilberte's parents—leading him also towards a serious melancholic depression (I, 499/II, 73).

It is worth noting the existence of a dissymmetry between the component of faciality and that of the refrain when it is a matter of "discriminating" Albertine from Gilberte. After the latter has revealed the meaning of her first look, the Narrator becomes aware that it is not only in this distant era of his childhood that he has "lacked" the truth concerning looks and faces, but also during the rest of his life, particularly during his relation with Albertine: "And suddenly I thought that the real Gilberte and the real Albertine were perhaps those who offered themselves in a single glance, one by a hedgerow of pink hawthorn, the other on the beach" (III, 694/V, 655). It is completely different in regards to the musical "discrimination": Vinteuil's Sonata remains indexed to Gilberte whereas the Septet is "carried" towards Albertine. ("Starting out from Gilberte, I could have as little imagined Albertine, or the fact that I would love her, as the memory of Vinteuil's sonata could have enabled me to imagine his septet" (III, 502/V, 469)).

Gilberte's character will function as a *component of passage*. In certain aspects, it continues to belong to Swann, to the impasse of the black hole, to the incommunicability of components and, in others, it already involves us in the conglomeration of the *Young Girls*, and leads towards the fascinating universe of "feminine trans-sexuality"—the Roussainvile dungeon being very close to the sea of Montjouvain (I, 158/I, 161). It is through Gilberte, through her parents, that the Narrator yields to Vinteuil's music and sees the doors of aristocratic salons opened to him. Music, sex, faces, and the socius are all already present on the same scene; they are waiting for an assemblage to make them work together.

5. The profanation of Vinteuil's face

Gilberte's sexually "charged" look is the *index* of a beyond of appearances and good manners. It seems to designate the ulterior stage of the specification of the black hole which constitutes the silent scene next to the sea of Montjouvain. The various components of expression are always separated from one another: in particular, the visual component functions in an autonomous way via the mode of voyeurism. In a way, we have passed from the feminine-maternal face of Odette, which massively explodes in *a dream*, to the masculine-paternal face of Vinteuil, who is profaned in a very elaborate *fantasy scenario*. But this isolation and autonomy are only so in appearance. The fantasy is not a pure powerless contemplation; it is the support of a diagrammatic process in an embryonic stage. The Narrator's gaze, substituted for the child Gilberte, has become an "armed" gaze. And silence seems to be more pronounced in this scene because it appears to serve to warding off—by distancing it—the charge of musical deterritorialization which Vinteuil's name encloses. The silent scene of Montjouvain constitutes a sort of musical implosion, of the "eye of the storm" in the heart of a cyclone whose effects are still unforeseeable. From the brutal explosion of the black hole—in Swann's version—only a vertiginous descent into madness, or a resigned return to marital faciality and its stereotypes could be the result. Madness is imagined and exorcised, as in "normal" familialist neuroses. But no oedipal key will unlock the secret of this little scene of profanation. Moreover, Proust does not at all attempt to explore Vinteuil's or his daughter's past to try to find explanatory elements. The fantasy, in question here, stubbornly resists any attempt at psychoanalytic anamnesis: the *Recherche* is not directed towards this type of past, but towards a construction of things to come, towards a proliferation of the future in the act of creation. Vinteuil's photo, his humiliated face, his deformed, destroyed features are only a stage on the path which will make a deterritorializing machine of the *name Vinteuil* itself. The profanation announces future transfaciliatary passages towards new matters of expression, towards a multiplication of characters and affects which will constitute so many materials to be integrated in the *Recherche*. In short, if what is profaned is indeed the face of *a* musician, what is promoted is a new music conveying a mutant faciality. The Verdurin salon and Odette's face had served as a cage and prison for this music; the question posed now is to illuminate an assemblage of expression adapted to its new functions: this is the role that will be given to the *Young Girls* who seem to emerge in the extension of Gilberte's first "perverse" look.

6. The "Young Girls in Flower" conglomeration

The *Young Girls* have a very particular and very specific power: they can deterritorialize visual perception: "The men and youths, the old or middle-aged women, in whose company we think we take pleasure, we conceive of as shallow beings, existing on a flat and *insubstantial* surface, because our only awareness of them is that of unaided visual perception; but when our eye ventures in the direction of a young girl, it is as though it acts *on behalf of all our other senses*: they seek out her various properties, the smell of her, the feel of her, the taste of her, which they enjoy without the collaboration of the hands or the lips; and because of *desire's artful abilities in transposition, and its excellent spirit of synthesis*, these senses can draw from the color of cheeks or breasts the sensations of touching, of savoring, of forbidden contact, and can rifle girls' sweet succulence, as they do in a rose garden when plundering the fragrances of the flowers, or in a vineyard when gloating with greedy eyes upon the grapes" (I, 892-893/II, 471). After reading this precise and rigorous text, is it conceivable to claim, as some commentators have, that the Young Girls were, for Proust, only a substitute for young people, only a way of dissimulating his homosexuality to the reader? There is no literary process there, and, in my view, the only question posed here is to clarify the relation between Proust's becoming-woman—expressed throughout the *Young Girls*—and the deterritorialization of strata, the refrainization of faces, characters, and landscapes, such that they are implicated in his becoming-creator. No doubt, we are in the presence of a factual given which does not call for general explication.[4] However, another very significant passage of *In the Shadow of Young Girls in Flower* can shed some light on this question for us and specifically on the very particular position which the *Young Girls* occupy in relation to matters of expression.

Proust describes in them a sensitive period which renders them able to grasp faciality traits, vocal traits, manners of speaking, intonations, expressions, etc., not only in the familial milieu ("the family heirlooms") but also in the *"matter imposed by the original province"* (I, 910/II, 488).

It is indeed a question of a sort of imprint phenomenon, because it stops at a given phase of development: "As infants possess a gland whose secretions help them digest milk, which grown-ups no longer have, the lilt of the girls' light voices struck notes that women's never reach" (I, 908/II, 487). After this part of the text, Proust abandons this first ethological type of rapprochement on behalf of a comparison between the Young Girls and musical instruments. The Young Girls—becoming-woman—do not function to represent, to illustrate a landscape or a country. It is even the opposite: *these are the intrinsic qualities of a matter of expression which "uses" the faces and voices of the Young Girls*, as sensitive plates, as instruments of creation: "Whenever Andrée gave a sharp twang to a deep note, she could not prevent the Périgourdine string in her vocal instrument from singing its little provincial song, in harmony with the south-western purity of her profile; and Rosemonde's perpetual pranking and skittishness were a perfect match for her regional accent, which could not help shaping the northern *substance* of which her face and her voice were made. My ear enjoyed the bright dialogue between the province of origin and the temperament producing each girl's inflections, a dialogue that never turned to discord. Nothing can come between a girl and the part of the country from which she hails: she is it. Such reaction of *local materials* on the genius of the one who exploits them, and

whom it invigorates, does not make the outcome less individual…"
(I, 910/II, 488).

7. The first kiss to Albertine and the crossing of faces and identities

Before transformed into a becoming-creator, the becoming-woman passes through several stages: the *Young Girls* become refrain, leit-motiv, trans-semiotic dryads… These stages are characterized by a general process of the disindividuation of the object of desire, the effect of which is to transpose its investment successively:

—on a group of people ("a love created by its dispersal among several young girls") (III, 505/V, 471);

—on a person who has become multiple ("Albertine was several people" (III, 338/V, 311)); "Do we believe her to be unique? She is everywhere. And yet she is consistent and indestructible before our loving eyes…" (III, 503/V, 469).

—then of dissolving itself with its object: "… was it not natural now that the waning star of my love in which they were condensed should be once again dispersed into this scattered stardust of the galaxies?" (III, 561/V, 526).

At the beginning, the existence of the *Young Girls* was tied to a system of visual aesthetic values. The Narrator manages to access them by unlocking Elstir's universe, and their first appearance irresistibly evokes an impressionist canvas: "… and there, still far away along the esplanade, where they made a strange mass of moving colors, I saw five or six young girls, as different in their appearance and ways from all the other people one was used to seeing in Balbec as the odd gaggle of seagulls…" (I, 788/II, 370).

From five or six girls, we quickly pass to three young girls and, after a few hesitations, the Narrator's love is solely fixated on Albertine. But the "collective side" of the beginning of this love (III, 596/V, 560) does not lose its rights for all that, the invested object's nature of multiplicity being, in some way, transferred from a group to an individual. The traversing of faces is thus found prolonged and deepened by the traversing of an identity, that of the unhappy Albertine, who will be observed, tested, and dissected like a lab animal.

An essential mutation of Proustian faciality appears with the Narrator's first kiss to Albertine. He seems to "recover" that of Swann to Odette (I, 233/I, 242), but his approach is much more "studied," it is accompanied by various close-up and slow-motion effects (II, 361/III, 357). It leads to the exfoliation of three Albertines who were assembled, until this point, through different matters of expression:

—that of the first encounter in front of the beach, simply visual, almost theatrical;

—that, well socialized, which can only be arrived at through a strict respect of the applicable codes (Proust compares her to an inedible jade raisin that is used as a table decoration!);

—and that which is in the reach of the lips, a miraculous synthesis of the previous two, since all the while appearring *real* as in the second, it also provides one with *facility* of access like in the dream of the first (II, 361/III, 357).

But the miracle only lasts a fraction of a second: at the end of this approach, through successive planes and semiotic magnification, the semiotization process gets carried away and ends by missing its goal "… now what I saw, in this brief trajectory of my lips toward her cheek, was ten Albertines; because this one girl was like a many-headed goddess…" (II, 365/III, 361). The visual and olfactory components shatter, while the assemblage is reorganized around a shrill, hyper-lucid[5] consciential component, which brutally reestablishes a subjective distance tinged with bitterness and revulsion: "suddenly my eyes ceased to see, and my nose, in turn, crushed against her cheek, no longer smelled anything, so, without my efforts' bringing me any clearer notion of the taste of the rose I desired, I discovered, from these abominable signs, that I was finally in the process of kissing Albertine's cheek" (II, 365/III, 361). The assemblage which was tied around a desire of "knowledge acquired by the lips" has "rebounded" on a feminine component with several faces to then return to a more deterritorialized form of multiplicity, comparable to that of the first encounter.

This new assemblage then only draws its relative consistence from redundancies of resonance and from a consciential micro black hole effect: the possibility of a veritable diagrammatic opening is provisionally lost. It will be necessary that all the other deterritorializing components—musical and scriptural—be set in play for the Narrator to finally manage to access the essence of becoming-woman.

Let us point out that this micro black hole, unlike what happened with Swann's love, has not "absorbed" the sexual component properly speaking. In effect, the latter has conserved its autonomy, which is demonstrated by the fact that the Narrator managed to secretly indulge his "pleasure" during this embrace with the complicity—if not satisfaction—of his partner. The process of libidinal idealization is thus not fixated, as was the case with Swann, on the loved face, while sexuality is not ritualized in an inter-personal relationship. Such a process will only be stimulated by the entry of the feminine homosexual component; but the assemblage of enunciation will by then already be deeply taken up by the transformation of becoming-woman into becoming-creator.

Subjective Components: the Facialization of Time and Refrainization of Faces

During the previous developments, the interactions between various musical and scriptural components and the faciality component have been envisaged insofar as they make the latter evolve successively towards a deterritorialized becoming-woman and a trans-semiotic becoming-refrain. The processes leading to the implementation of a literary creation machine—inseparable from a machine to change the perception of the world—are not linear at all. Throughout the *Recherche* it is developed via approximations, advances, and retreats; it has made forward leaps in certain semiotic registers while also e having neglected others. (This is notably the case of Vinteuil's music which is talked about in the last part of the novel.)

In my view, the origin of these zigzags, these solutions of continuity, resides in a problem which never stops haunting the *Recherche*: that of the promotion of a new type of assemblage of enunciation. The Proustian exploration of components of expression can only be understood if it is not related to this continual attempt to illuminate a mode of subjectification breaking with the world of "habit,"[6] in direct contact with matters of expression proper to the creation of another reality, not only for what concerns the present but also the past. The subject refuses being passive with regard to his or her past. As actual intensities, memories must be folded onto the work of creative semiotization. Every evolutionary phase, every mutation of components, every generation, every transformation is only important because it contributes to the perfection of such a new assemblage. When Proust has extracted the maximum from a component, he does not linger on it; he directs himself towards the index, the line of flight that will make it possible to dig, deepen, and deterritorialize the assemblage in formation an extra notch, to the point that he will be able to make it cross the threshold of its affective enactment, its diagrammatic stimulus. His politics in regard to characters is the same way. He takes them and leaves them to the chance development of the rhizome of subjectification. Albertine is "liquidated" because at some point she barely serves for anything but cranking the pianola; she is taken out at the same time as a certain refrain. Madame Verdurin "resurrects" in the character of the Princess of Guermantes because, as we shall see, a new type of refrain requires the functioning of an assemblage of enunciation which reunites the qualities of the first Verdurin salon and a sophisticated salon like that of the marquise of Saint-Euverte. The assemblage always primes components and characters. Under these conditions, every "normal" genealogy, every oedipal generation must be refuted *a priori*. The *Recherche* can and must be read in all directions: from the end towards the beginning, but as well as diagonally by traversing spaces,[7] times, faces, characters, intrigues. The Narrator is the son of Swann and Charlus, but these two are just as much "developments" of the Narrator. We can "deduce" Gilberte from the Narrator's mother and Albertine from Gilberte, and nevertheless accept the idea that each of these characters illustrates a different aspect of the same becoming-woman of the Narrator. Whereas statements are drawn out in time and space, the enunciation is hollowed out layered, and differentiated on the basis of the same assemblage. And the key to all the synchronies assembled here is obviously the dimension of Time regained.

One still needs to establish, contrary to what Proust suggests, that this is in no way a question of a hidden dimension, of a world of essences whose discovery is to be carried out in the manner of an explorer, but of a fundamentally micropolitical dimension leading to a subjective "reversal" and which involves the entry of a new type of refrain that works to empty the dominant redundancies of their content and deterritorializes and disindividuates the enunciation.

Let's examine the different phases of this subjective reversal.

1. Cosmic polyphony

The Narrator's arrival at the last matinee given in the Guermantes home develops in counterpoint to that of Swann, decades earlier, in the home of the Marquise de Saint-Euverte. Here we rediscover the same sort of "fermentation" of sensations, the same effervescence of memories. But while Swann, an aesthete, a dilettante, gathered his impressions along the way, like someone moving quickly through the rooms of a museum, the Narrator immediately adopts the attitude of a "professional." He pauses at every semiotic schizz to study the phenomenon in depth. It is in no way a sort of "past-time" for him. He is aware that this access opening before him to the profound reality of Time is inseparable from his own finitude and that his involvement in the *Recherche* implies an unreserved acceptance of his death and an irrevocable renunciation of all worldly life. ("This idea of death established itself permanently within me, in the way that love does" (III, 1042/V, 352).)

Furthermore, it is a mortal reminder that will trigger the ultimate revelation. Arriving at the court of the Guermantes hotel and not noticing a car coming towards him, as the driver shouts out, he abruptly steps back and stumbles on an uneven paving-stone (III, 866/VI, 175). While he regains his balance on a slightly lower stone than the other, he is flooded by an extraordinary succession of evocations, which will lead him to the baptistery of Saint-Marc, where, by putting his foot on two uneven rockslabs, he realizes that he had already experienced this type of phenomenon. He will repeat the movement of his foot ten times, then twenty times just until he manages to perfectly define his multiple impressions, to "clarify them in their utmost depths." Here the novelty does not reside in the nature of such phenomena. Since he was a child he never stopped exploring them, indexing them. But due to the fact that he thus manages to release them at will for the first time, he has passed from the stage of passive observation to that of experimentation. This cobblestone under his foot functions as the pedal of a sort of cosmic organ with which he will finally be able to compose the music to which he aspires. This discovery is so overwhelming that he no longer worries about what happens around him, with what people may think in observing him there: standing blocked, motionless like a catatonic. His relation to the world, art, music, and creation are definitively put into question by this revelation. In fact, he will not even attend the concert given at the Princess's home; he will remain behind the scenes in a nearby library where he will continue to experiment with his new method by reading George Sand's *François le Chanpi*, which refers us to one of the first components of his literary vocation.

He is now able to overcome his anxieties and battle his old inhibitions regarding this vocation. The creative instrument no longer rests upon one or several semiotic components; it involves the entirety of the subjective assemblage which constitutes it. The goal to reach is no longer an object, a technique, nor a style but the subject itself. Beginning from impressions, memories, representations of any nature, it is a question of producing "something of a subject" a new type of subject. This process of the discernibilization of matters of expression has no other finality: the clang of a spoon against a dinner plate (III, 868/VI, 177), the vibrations of a flow of water, the evocation of the noise of a hammer against the wheel of a train on the way to the station are so many instruments of transformation of the subjective assemblage of enunciation: "all my discouragement vanished in the face of the same happiness that, at different points in my life, had given me the sight of trees I had thought I recognized when I was taking a drive round Balbec, the sight of the steeples of Martinville, the taste of a madeleine dipped in herb tea, and all the other sensations I have spoken about, and which *the last works of Vinteuil had seemed to me to synthesize*" (III, 866/VI, 174–75).

Vinteuil's music had "seemed to synthesize" these various sensations. But that is where the trap resided. The question was precisely not of synthesizing the sensations; or if so, then only from Swann's perspective who sought to merely taste them. The Narrator wants to create from them a music closer to the deterritorializing subject. Unless music is itself the subject, if we come to consider it as music in the process of being created, below instruments and partitions, i.e. a music of deterritorialized refrains.

As of the turn of the century, a few science-fiction authors had proposed the hypothesis that the human brain was not at the origin of thought, but was only a sort of condenser of an ambient cosmic thought circulating everywhere in a diluted state. Some of this is relevant here. The subject—individuated, collective, or machinic—captures refrains within fields of all sorts, assembles heterogeneous matters of expression beginning from which it produces times, spaces, significant redundancies, and above all else the components of subjectification and conscientialization *which, furthermore, are at its foundation.* Vinteuil's "little phrase," like a minuscule spaceship, has completely overwhelmed Swann's molecular universe and, in piercing it, has deployed another type of universe.

What remains of the refrain after it had been analyzed, fragmented, deterritorialized, "processed" on the pianola until its mystery is completely revealed? It can reintegrate the plane of pure recurrent potentialities. Vinteuil's music has had its day! Even the Septet is presently too territorialized in relation to the musics to come, to the future facializations of times and refrainizations of faces. It will remain marked by the compromise it has made with the pragmatic fields of an era: *Swann's way* and *Guermantes way.* The Narrator is liberated from the oedipal mystery of Montjouvain. This does not mean that he is "cured"! On the contrary, he has taken the side of madness, but one mad with creation, mad with a music at the root of all other music. His problem is no longer that of Form, of good taste, "the harmony of parts," but that of rhythms and intensities. How do we make rhythms proliferate? The question of the refrain is stepped up to infinity.

Before definitively cutting with the world, to finally get to work, one last confrontation with the faciality of the "people of the world" will give him the opportunity to elucidate the relations between two pairs which have now become essential:

—time lived passively and creative time,

—alienated subjectivity and subjectivity that creates itself.

As I have tried to show, the modalities according to which subjects articulated themselves in ordinary time depends on the matters of expression of components such as those of faciality and refrains. New machinic time and creative subjectivity are also based on them, but the relationships it has with them are profoundly modified.

At the conclusion of this essay, we shall examine the three lines of deterritorialization that preside over these changes and which lead to the fact that:

—faciality loses its substantial function of support from signifying semiologies;

—refrains are liberated from preformed encodings (which depend on natural, social, aesthetic formations, etc.);

—assemblages of enunciation produce modes of disindividuated, transversalist subjectification distancing themselves from the dominant socio-spatio-temporal systems of enslavement and setting themselves in direct contact with the phylum of abstract machinisms.

2. The search for a machinic consistency

"I was going to try to find the objective reason why it should be precisely and uniquely this kind of sensation which led to the work of art, by continuing the thoughts which had come to me in such rapid sequence in the library; for I felt that the impetus given to my intellectual life was now strong enough for me to be able to continue as successfully in the drawing-room, among all the guests, as alone in the library; it seemed that, from this point of view, even in the midst of this large gathering I should be able to retain my solitude" (III, 918/VI, 226). Until now, the method I qualified as "cosmic polyphony" has only been applied to objects, impressions, and memories. How would it work with subjects who have their say about what happens to them, who are constantly assailed by time and death? Will it resist the test of faciality? To tackle this problem, Proust stages what he calls a "coup de théâtre"—though it is only barely dramatic, since it is too obvious in its didactic goals—which is supposed to raise the "greatest objection" to the Narrator's project. It is a question of showing with the maximum force that an endeavor to explore Time regained could only be compromised by the avatars of everyday time, such as they are revealed by the wear and tear of faces and bodies.[8]

This "coup de théâtre" prolongs the parallel (which I evoked concerning the incident of the "uneven paving-stone") between Swann, in his escape from the black hole of passion, and the Narrator at the outset of his literary conversion. Upon entering the salon of the Marquise de Saint-Euverte, Swann became fascinated with the series of black holes-monocles disfiguring the faces of his friends. On the other hand, in the dream of the "young man in a fez," he had seen the face of Madame Verdurin become deformed and he was filled with the desire to tear out Odette's eyes. Upon entering the salon of ex-Verdurin princess Guermantes, after the end of the concert which he had not attended, the Narrator is astounded when he realizes that all the faces of the people he formerly knew have become unrecognizable. He starts to imagine that he has returned, without noticing, to a dress-up party, or even that his friends have been the object of "metamorphoses analogous to that of insects" (III, 932/VI, 242). Why these hypotheses, then, when it is obvious that the burlesque and even grotesque aspect of this spectacle has no other cause than the ravages worked by time on the people of his generation? We will not grasp the meaning of such a detour unless we accept the necessity of a synchronic approach to the *Recherche*; unless, as the Narrator wants, we set our goal to "describe man... as possessing the length not of his body but of his years" (III, 1046/VI, 355); unless we endeavor to extract ourselves from a "flat psychology" (III, 1031/VI, 341); unless we propose to go past the masks to "enjoy the essence" of beings. If not, we will not manage to comprehend the relations instituted between words and things, between names and faces (III, 923/VI, 233). The designations founded by power formations impose false individuations, false identities: "The features of our face are little more than expressions ingrained by habit" (I, 909/II, 487). But, "if they change, if they form a different ensemble, if their expression habitually alters more slowly, [they] take on a different meaning with their different appearance" (III, 925/VI, 233). When names are removed from their familiar faces, a whole world of new words will finally be able to appear: "I understood the meaning of death, loves, the pleasures of the mind, the use of suffering, a vocation, etc. For while names had lost their individuality for me, *words* were yielding up their full meaning. The beauty of images lies behind things, the beauty of ideas in front of them" (III, variant 932/VI, 240).

Is this to say that this defacialized world, this "behind of things," is a world without images? Must the becoming-invisible of faces, such as it seemed to be implied by the transformation of becoming-woman, cover every faciality? In fact, what is abolished here is only a certain *territorialized faciality* based on dominant significations. In contrast, what emerge are *asignifying faciality* traits, figures of expression which allow us, beyond trans-sexuality, to access a trans-subjectivity. It is no longer a question of removing faces from sexes, but of making them pass from one individual to another. Hence the importance of the portrayal of the faces of the elderly: not only do the faciality traits arising from this subjective revolution resist the translations of desire, but they manage to traverse the ages of life and, to a certain extent, the threshold of death. Time Regained is thus not simply populated with empty gazes and universal refrains. On the contrary, all the singularities of faciality and refrain find with it their true field of activity. Such is the meaning of the Narrator's second revelation, then of that Guermantes matinee: the alteration of faces proposes "something much more valuable than an *image* of the past," and, by offering all the successive images of an individual, it makes it possible to *externalize time* (III, 924–925/VI, 234).

To extract time from subjectivity: is this not a much more radical operation than that, arising from the first facialitary revolution of the *Young Girls in Flower*, which consisted in composing a new sort of music from a whole gamut of intensities, memories, and images? It is a question, in fact, of two complementary times assembled in such a way that the absence of one renders the other impossible. On a first level of *extensive deterritorialization*, becoming-woman generates a sensitive plate capturing the most heterogeneous matters of expression. The faciality of young girls secretly menaces the dominant significations right at the point where they could let irreversible points of deterritorialization emerge. But this sensitive plate reaches its limits in that it is not able to reassemble a process of subjectification by itself. It disconnects components at the risk of releasing a black hole effect of the Odette-Zipporah type; it brings new matters of expression to light; it makes a hundred faces quiver on the same young girl, or it passes them on from one person to another, but always in the respect of a certain pre-established unity of individuals. Elstir's art, Vinteuil's music, and the Narrator's first manner of writing lead to a similar type of impasse. As long as the question of a transformation of the subject and time, of an *intensive deterritorialization*, of a mutation of the assemblage's nucleus, will not have been posed in its radicality, not only will we not manage to bypass it, but we will see it resurge under increasingly tyrannical forms: at the end of the unfolding of the *Young Girls*, Albertine, depleted of all substance, thus becomes so "over-individuated, so mechanized" that the novelist is forced to eliminate her by any means possible.

The faciality of Time Regained no longer has much to do with that of men, women, young girls, or everyday reality. The model Proust suggests is that of superimposed puppets "bathing in the immaterial colors of the years," puppets "externalizing Time, the Time which is normally remains invisible to us," and which, "seeks out bodies in order to become them and wherever it finds them seizes upon them for its magic-lantern show" (III, 924/VI, 233).

This machinic faciality can no longer be affected by the individuals "controlled" by dominant institutions and significations; it is essentially articulated in infra-individual, pre-personal, pre-identificatory[9] singularities and in the social and material realities which cannot be circumscribed on an individual level. The time it articulates is simultaneously before the abstract time of the "cogito" and after. It is the result of multiple refrains, multiple processes of refrainization, the former objective and the latter subjective. Also, when the Narrator proposes to extract "a bit of time in its pure state" (III, 872/VI, 180) or to "cradle Time" (III, 1025/VI, 335), is it not his goal to unify the different components of temporalization, to make them fall under the same reductive rhythms! What he seeks is simultaneously "the distance and continuity of time," the setting in continuum of heterogeneous times, and the setting in heterogeneity of seemingly continuous times. In other words, for him it is a matter of attaining a certain consistency of *machinic time*, inarticulable time, indecomposable from the plane of machinic consistency. It is on condition of discernibilizing such an abstract machinic consistency of time that heterogeneous components could succeed in holding together, working together, assembling, on the one hand, the world of thought and affects and, on the other, that of "external reality." For the novelist, it will no longer be a question of representing "certain individuals not as outside but as inside us, where their least acts can entail fatal disturbances, and to vary the light of the moral sky, according to the differing pressures of our sensibility..." (III, 1045/VI, 355) With this new faciality-refrain, he will no longer have to worry about the risks of the black hole.[10] Introspection, folding upon oneself no longer leads to a contemplation of the void and powerlessness: the subject's search has become the construction of a new subjectivity; it opens up reality in its diversity and illuminates the diagrammatic articulations between the realities of the "outside" and those of the "inside." The lover is able to manipulate objective and subjective intensities at will—for example, he will be able to "make the rain sing gently in the middle of the room and to make the bubbling of our tisane..." (III, 1045/VI, 355) Furthermore, he can treat the composition, the subjective "chemical reaction" of his "characters," with the same mad freedom. In being installed at the core of subjective realities, the writing machine, establishes countless passageways between the subject of enunciation and the subjects of the statement. It does not operate a single splitting of the ego; it does not double a one and only Narrator attached to Time Regained: there are as many Narrators as characters, modes of temporalization and crystallizations of desire.

This multi-headed subjectivity has lost not only its individuation, but also its transcendence. It is emptied of the redundancies of resonance which kept expressive interactions at bay. Its existence no longer precedes the matters of expression; it is exactly contemporaneous with the assemblages that actualize it. The abstract machinisms which occupy everywhere, all the while ballasting it with irreducible singularities and territorializing it in history and the socius, cast it through the past and the possible and lead across all personological thresholds. To arrive at such a degree of subjective creativity, it is undoubtedly necessary to perfect an assemblage that operates a sort of *"reduction,"* not eidetic but machinic. All the situations of the *Recherche* and particularly the salons constitute so many approaches of this assemblage that are to make it possible for this creative work to "take off." The triggering of "sensation-calls," such as tripping on a paving-stone, the constitution of blocks of memories on the basis of involuntary memory, impressions of "déjà vu" of "déjà ressenti"[11] only become important the moment when they function within the framework of such an assemblage. The little miracles, the "fruitful moments"—*the madeleine*, the steeples of Martinville...—will become common occurences. But such a subjective chemical reaction will not remain limited to metaphorical or metonymic approximations. Here literature implies a sort of scientific and technical work of extraction and concatenations of abstract machinisms which have, up until now, functioned, each for themselves, within strata of coding and components of semiotization, "on this side" of the individual or beyond, on the side of the socius and material assemblages. The same gamut of machinic propositions—which furthermore never cease to transform themselves—the same set of quanta of possible, works on the sophisticated salons and the amorous involvements, exalts the becoming-woman of creation, sets a certain constellation of faciality traits into relief, detaches a certain refrain from the musical environment. At this level, it is no longer possible to establish hierarchies and priority levels between metabolisms proper to the socius and those of the most secret desire. Swann could not have received the machinic message of Vinteuil's little phrase if the Narrator had not "preliminarily" succeeded in bringing back to life the refrain of the little doorbell from the entrance to the house of Combray, whose "echoing, ferruginous, inexhaustible, piercing and fresh" sound never stops ringing in him from his childhood onward, conferring to his whole existence its most secret consistency (III, 1046/VI, 356). But the narrator himself would not have managed to extract such a machinic assemblage of enunciation if, following Vinteuil, he had not been able to access the trans-semiotic refrains of the white Sonata and the red Septet...

Notes

Part I: The Machinic Unconscious

1. Introduction: Logos or Abstract Machines?

1. René Thom, *Mathematical Models of Morphogensis,* trans. W.M. Brooks and D. Rand, Chichester: Ellis Horwood Ltd (1983).

2. Against a very widespread belief, Jacques Tonnelat has established that the second principle of statistical thermodynamics did not imply any necessary bond between an increase in entropy and disorder. The definition of entropy accounts for the distribution in space of the basic elements considered and their energy levels; however, a variation of entropy can only relate to a modification of the latter. Moreover, the realization of a state of equilibrium, far from corresponding to the "ordering" of a system, implies, on the contrary, that it is the most disordered possible and thus that it supports the appearance of local singular situations. The appearance of structured bodies in living beings, concludes Jacques Tonnelat, is therefore not absolutely in contradiction with the second principle of thermodynamics. Jacques Tonnelat, *Thermodynamique et Biologie*, Maloine-Doin, 1978, and the article in *La Recherche*, No. 101, June 1979.

3. Cf. note 26 on page 343.

4. Although I wrote them alone, these essays are inseparable from the work that Gilles Deleuze and I have carried out together for many years. This is why, when I am brought to speak in the first person, it will be indifferently with that of the singular or plural. Let one not see there especially a business of paternity relating to the ideas which are advanced here. There as well as here it is all a question of "collective assemblages." Cf. our book in collaboration: *A Thousand Plateaus*, trans. Brian Massumi, Minneapolis: Minnesota UP, (1988).

5. This annex, which is presented in the form of an axiomatics (or rather a "machinics"), in fact constitutes the central element of this essay and, for that reason, the reader should refer there often.

6. We shall specify during this essay how schizoanalysis can be considered as a case in point of such analytical pragmatics.

2. Escaping from Language

1. See *Langages*, Sept. 72, No. 27, p. 72, titled "Generative Semantics."

2. Cf. Bar-Hillel, "Out of the Pragmatic Wastebasket," *Linguistic Inquiry* LL, No. 3, p. 71.

3. Cf. note 7 page 355.

4. Concerning the "combinatory latitudes" freed from the construction of minimal signs (morphemes and monemes) on the basis of figures (phonemes), Nicolas Ruwet writes that the utilization of these unexploited possibilities for creative ends remains very exceptional, even in poetry. "We can rightly cite Lewis Carroll's 'Jabberwocky' or *Finnegans Wake*, or certain of Michaux's texts; but the least we can say is that this type of creativity only has extremely remote relations with the creativity that is at work in the ordinary exercise of language." *Introduction à la grammaire générative*, Plon, (1970).

5. Cf. the nature of the colonial campaign that has imposed the "language of the Republic" on "savage France," such as it has been inaugurated by the Jacobin period of the Revolution. Here one finds the same slogans that will criss-cross the Colonial Empire: "roads and school teachers": "Thus, with thirty different *patois* for language, we are still on the tower of Babel, while for liberty we represent the avant-guarde of nations." Rapport Grégoire to the Convention, cited in *Une politique de la langue. La Révolution française et les patois*, Michel de Certeau, Dominique Julia, Jacques Revel, Paris: Gallimard (1975), p. 302.

6. Natan Lindquist declares that linguistic novelties can fall upon important centers "like paratroopers" in order to afterwards radiate to neighboring domains. Cited by Malmberg, p. 98: *Les Nouvelles tendances de la linguistique*, P.U.F. (1966).

7. Ferdinand de Saussure, *Course in General Linguistics*, trans. Wade Baskin, New York: McGraw-Hill (1966).

8. And we do not have the impression that linguists are about to let go of it so soon when we see, for example, that same Françoise Robert to be frightened by her own audacities regarding the ideas which she advances about a "community grammar," and to fear that such a conception could lead to a notion of competence dislodging the sacrosanct concept of language. *Langage*, no. 32, December 1973.

9. *Langage*, no. 32, 1973, p. 90.

10. Perhaps, however, it would have been beneficial to reclassify them in relation to their "degree of introjection" of capitalistic machinisms, which include: a position of overcoding scriptural components in relation to verbal components; a general tendency toward the collapse of prosodic traits; a contraction of the range of figures of expression and content, etc…

11. One could make a parallel remark concerning Freud's first "machinic" models, around the time of *Project for a Scientific Psychology* (1895).

12. S.K. Saumjan opposes Chomsky's system of linear concatenation with a system of abstract objects founded on the operation of application (A.G.M.: Applicative Generative Model); but his formalization does not help account for the modelization of language proceeding from actual instances of power. Cf. *Langages*, March 1974, no. 33, p. 22 and 54 for Hjelmslev's influence.

13. Abbreviation of "Sentence."

14. Until Marxism, capitalist political economy has also claimed for a long time to pass as the general grammar of all economy, but linguistics still has not found its Marx and Engels who would reset it on its feet.

15. We shall see in what follows that indeed certain components of bird songs are innate. But, artificially separated from the rhizome of behavioral assemblages, they appear unable to reconstitute specific, veritable songs.

16. Cf. J.L. Dillard's study *Black English*, New York: Vintage (1973).

17. In this domain, the ethological weight concerning factors in early pregnancy is probably preponderant as it indicates the simple fact that a four-year old child educated in an environment of musicians can come to acquire a strong competence in musical reading and interpretation.

18. Herbert E. Brekle, *op. cit.*, p. 94–104, and W.C. Watt, who is equally oriented towards an "abstract performative grammar," have made an account of the functionality of what they call "mental grammar" in its relations with perception, memory, etc…

19. Different types of syntactic, semantic, and pragmatic problems are relevant to each of these levels.

20. The distinction proposed by Julia Kristeva within the process of signifiance between a level called the "semiotic chora" and a symbolic level could have constituted a breakthrough for linguistic semiologies, but, as it universalizes and eternalizes the signifier, it also has the inconvenience of again shutting diagrammatic transformation in on itself, again making it a sort of underlying structure, a sort of arche-writing. With Kristeva, the innateism of universals leaves the symbolic in order to emigrate to semiotics. Under these conditions, pragmatics risks being bogged down in an interminable textual practice (comparable to psychoanalytic practice) and infinitely wandering between a symbolic phenotext and a semiotic genotext. In order to be delivered from the personological polarities of communication, we must refuse to be imprisoned by the hypothesis of a self-enclosed signifying unconscious subjectivity.

21. The notion of "enslavement" should here be understood in a cybernetic sense.

22. In such a perspective, while engaging with the Anglo-American tradition, pragmatics should stop being considered a great suburb of syntax and semantics; while engaging the Franco-European tradition, it should stop being considered a sub-discipline of linguistics. In fact, on the contrary, signifying semiologies would become a particular case of a more general pragmatics.

23. Pierre Clastres, *Society against the State*, tr. Robert Hurley, Brooklyn: Zone (1989).

24. The first expressions of a child are, for the past tense, past participles ("parti," "tombé") and for the future, infinitives. After this they develop periphrases ("je vais aller") and only in the last place inflexions. Cf.: "Le changement linguistique et sa relation à l'inquisition de la langue maternelle," E. Traugott, *Langages*, no. 32, 1973, p. 47.

25. Cf. Robin Lakoff, *Language and Women's Place*, Harper and Row, New York, 1975.

26. Louis Hjelmslev, *Prolegomena to a Theory of Language*, trans. Francis Whitfield. University of Wisconsin: Madison (1961).

27. Hjelmslev defines language as a "semiotic into which all other semiotics can be translated, every language as well as every semiotic structure conceivable."

28. As René Lindekens writes: "the semiotic relation of absolute interdependence characterizing the bond between the planes of expression and content—that from which the denotative power of sign systems arises—and what Hjelmslev calls relation of solidarity, must be considered as exclusively contracted by these two forms, from one sign plane to another." *Hjelmslev*, Hatier, (1975).

29. This expression of linguistic "abstract machine" begins with Chomsky. Cf. *Dictionnaire encyclopédique des sciences du langage*, Oswald Ducrot and Tzvetan Todorov, p. 59.

30. Louis Hjelmslev, *Essais linguistiques*, Paris: Éditions de Minuit (1971), p. 58.

31. Christian Metz, *Essai sur la signification au cinéma*, Klincksiek (1967); *Langage et cinéma*, Larousse (1971).

3. Assemblages of Enunciation, Pragmatic Fields and Transformations

1. Cf. annex p. 205 and 207.

2. According to Greimas, the superiority of linguistic semiologies over what he calls "communicative gesturality" would hold that only the former would come to make a syncretism between the subject of the enunciation and the subject of the statement. But this is also perhaps what constitutes the wealth of nonverbal semiotics, on condition that this semiotics is conceived as capable of "hitting" upon abstract machinisms of the machinic unconscious.

3. Each side of the semiological triangle is, in effect, "loaded" with assemblages highly differentiated from the point of view of their capacity of semiotic "exploitation," and each side calls for responses that are at least at their "height":
    —on the side of the signifier: power assemblages that are diagrammatic, scientific, economic, etc…;
    —on the side of the signified: "ideological apparatuses," State facilities (education, hygiene, etc…),
    —on the side of the semiotics of the referent: systems of enslavement of the modes of perceptive encoding, mass-media, etc…
Example: we do not perceive objects of consumption except in the sense that 1) monetary semiotics give us the authorization to comply with them ("purchasing power"); 2) the public points them out for us; otherwise, we pass by their aspects

without noticing or only imagine them. Cf. Jacques Fontanel, *L'anti-publicité*, Université des Sciences Sociales de Grenoble.

4. Cf. especially the developments concerning diagrammatic components, p. 217.

5. Cf. table p. 51.

6. Cf. developments p. 52.

7. It would be advisable to establish distinctions between the different possible modes of translation according to whether they have a scientific proposal or a statement of daily life as an aim, according to whether they are carried out by an aesthetic machine or a revolutionary social machine, etc… Each case, each situation is marked by a machinic formula related to a particular type of intrinsic consistency. It would be illusory to believe, for example, that the structure given to musical forms in the Baroque period "potentially" contained the axiomatic of the development of romantic music. We can return to the constant and logical correspondences of one period to another, but the real transitions are always of a different nature. Multiple factors always have to be taken into account on technological, scientific, economic, and political levels, etc… No formal structure hangs over the various semiotic layers, except in the minds of art theorists or epistemologists. Even if styles and theories manage to be imposed like dogmas and seem to mark the era of their publication, the true mutations in fact result from the crossing of components overflowing the considered structure from all sides.

8. In that it escapes any system of coordinates.

9. Cf. annex p. 199–210.

10. On this point we must distance ourselves completely from Hjelmslev, who has never completely relinquished a "linguistico-centrist" perspective, by retaining only the case of a complementarity between content and expression similar to that between front and back, i.e. the case of a total reversibility between the form of expression and the form of content. In fact, no kind of semiology or semiotics could claim to establish a perfect isomorphism between the formalism of its contents and the formalism of its expression. Unlike Hjelmslevian form, the inclination of abstract machines is by no means to render congruent the systems of coding and modes of formalization, but to engender trans-semiotic metabolisms connected with singularity points and generators of surplus-value of code and machinic surplus-value.

11. Cf. his introduction to the translation of Searle's book, *Les Actes de langage*, trans. Hélène Pauchard, Paris: Hermann (1972), p. 25.

12. Relative to the speech acts that in and of themselves constitute "the performance of an act." J.L. Austin, *How To Do Things with Words*, Oxford: Oxford UP (1976).

13. In the terminology of C.E. Brazell, here we should instead speak of non-grammatical statements. Indeed, this author establishes a distinction between agrammatical statements and non-grammatical statements; the former, like the phrase "he seems sleeping," would be susceptible to being rearranged and retranslated

into "normal" statements, for example in "he seems to be asleep;" but the latter, like the phrase "colorless green ideas sleep furiously," do not "lack" anything and are not relatable to any signified crystallization or to any recognized correspondent and would themselves escape from eventual correction. But this distinction seems to me completely relative: it exists from repressive intermediaries between the grammatical "correction" by the teacher and the incorrigible segregation of mad speech by psychiatry. Cf. *Langage*, no. 34, June 1974.

14. We end up with the following formula: $C = \{A \leftarrow \rightarrow D \ / \ B \leftarrow \rightarrow D\}$

15. Cf. Hjelmslev, *La stratification du langage, op. cit.*

16. Cf. Herbert C. Brekle, *Sémantique*, Armand Colin, (1974), pp. 54–60.

17. Like that, for example, of the Dogons studied by Marcel Griaule and Germaine Dieterlen.

18. Information theorists define signification as "an invariant during the convertible operations of translation." B.A. Oupenski, cited by Iouri Lotman, *La structure du texte artistique*, Paris: N.R.F. (1973), p. 69.

19. Alain Rey, *Langage*, Dec. 73, no. 32. J.C. Chevalier writes that the "language of 'General Grammar' is inscribed in processes of assimilation and repression; with the middle-class, the predicative schema and its metalanguage, syntax (and the preeminence of syntax is an ideological decision); with the people, technical vocabularies and a spoken language abandoned to an indifferent freedom" (*Id.* p. 118).

See also Iouri Lotman: "In the process of transcoding, the more distant mutually leveled structures are from one another, the more their nature will differ and the more the act of commutation of one system into another will be carrying content." Iouri Lotman, *La structure du texte artistique*, Paris: Gallimard (1973). (Content for Lotman is synonymous with the signified.)

20. This Symbolic has nothing to do with the pragmatic field which is in question here. In fact, it is a question of the signifier.

21. Don C. Talayesva, *Soleil Hopi*, preface by Claude Lévi-Strauss, Terre Humaine, Plon.

22. Paul Ricoeur opposes the possibility of translating the sense of an instance of discourse to the impossibility of translating the signified of a sign system: "This logical function of sense carried by the entire phrase should not be confused with the signified of each of the signs set to work by the phrase. Indeed, the signified of the sign is interdependent with a given system of language; on the contrary, the sense of a phrase, what we could more justifiably call the 'intended' than the signified, is a global content of thought which can be proposed to be stated otherwise within the same language or translated into another language; thus, the signified is untranslatable and the intended is highly translatable." From "Signe et Sens," *Encyclopaedia Universalis*, 1975.

23. In Hjelmslev's terminology: the figures or glossemes of expression.

24. The development of a semiotic of syntheses would be fundamental on this point: how can we see sounds, hear colors, incarnate words... Concerning "inter-

sensory transpositions," Merleau-Ponty wrote: "The senses translate one another without any need of an interpreter, and are mutually comprehensible without the intervention of any idea." Maurice Merleau-Ponty, *Phenomenology of Perception*, trans. Colin Smith, Routledge: London, (1962), p. 273.

25. See the differences in the semiotization of jealousy and vengeance between the Crow and the Hopi, related by Lowie and signaled by Lévi-Strauss in his preface to *Soleil Hopi, op. cit.*

26. On a possible multipartition of deixis according to space, time, and the socius, cf. Elisabeth Traugott, *Langage*, Dec. 1973, p. 39–52.

27. In this regard, these three pragmatic fields could be characterized:
—in level a, by a territorialized human actualization
—in level b, by an abstract institutional actualization
—in level c, by an experimental diagrammatic actualization

28. In following the works of J.L. Austin and John Searle, Oswald Ducrot has begun to decisively criticize a definition of language such that it would claim to reduce language to nothing but a means of communication.
J.L. Austin, *How To Do Things with Words*, Oxford: Oxford UP (1976).
John Searle, *Speech Acts: An Essay in the Philosophy of Language*, Cambridge: Cambridge UP (1970).
Oswald Ducrot, *Dire et ne pas dire*, Paris: Hermann (1972).

29. I repeat that taking Chomsky's terminology in the opposite direction is quite deliberate here. According to this author, what is primary are the basic syntactic systems that make it possible to *generate* the structure of formally correct sentences which are *transformed*, secondarily, into effective statements through the entry of semantic, phonological, and phonetic components. On the other side, pragmatic transformational components are first compared to the "generative" components of the effects of signification and subjectification, although in the context of this essay they are directly put to work on the level of deterritorialized asignifying figures while "propelling" abstract machines that produce machinic sense "with the same reality" (passage from the machinic redundancies to the redundancies of resonance). To say this in a formula: the allegedly profound structure of syntax is brought back to an affair of power (pouvoir), while the allegedly superficial fermentation of phonemes and graphemes is an affair of machinic force (puissance).

30. The vectorization of the components in this table can be progressively inverted to the point where it would be the interpretive generations that would affirm their supremacy over non-interpretive transformations.
We would have, for example, vectors:
→
A-C, corresponding to hysterical fields
→
B-C, corresponding to paranoic fields
→

A-D, corresponding to phobic fields

→

B-D, corresponding to obsessive fields

(Also notice the subject of the qualification of these fields on page 213 concerning figure 9.)

31. Cf. the particular position which in Hjelmslev the level of collective appreciation occupies in relation to socio-biologial levels and the physical levels of substance of content and substance of expression.

32. Thus, significative feelings will be engendered by the "return to": return to infancy, return to nature, return to primitive semiological fields. In reaction to capitalistic pragmatic fields, semiological fields of artificial reterritorialization are deployed around questions of nation, nationality, religion, race, etc.

4. Signifying Faciality, Diagrammatic Faciality

1. Cf. the myths of the double, the faceless man, etc. and the fact that all significations are modified when "psychotics" fail to recognize their own faces.

2. Cf. annex p. 199.

3. Cf. the description by René Spitz of the functionality of a "Gestalt-sign" in infants constituted by "the eyes, forehead and nose in movement." In the second month, the infant follows the mobile face of the adult with its eyes and while nursing it continually fixates upon the mother's face. It smiles at a face (or a mask), but solely on the condition that it is *seen as a face*. René Spitz, *De la naissance à la parole*, Paris: P.U.F. (1968).

Cf. also the effect of inter-subjective resonance resulting from the exchange of glances in the infant stage in: *The role of eye-to-eye contact in maternal-infant attachment*, Kenneth S. Robson J., *Child Psychiatry*, Vol. 8, pp. 13–25, Pergamon Press.

Cf. Isakower, "Contribution à la psychopathologie des phénomènes associés à l'endormissement." *Nouvelle Revue de Psychanalyse*, no. 5, 1972 and Lewin, "Le sommeil, la bouche et l'écran du rêve," *Ibid*.

4. By supposing that these imprints themselves are fixed, ethologists want to make us believe it, too.

5. Jacques Lacan, "The Mirror Stage as Formative of the *I* Function as Revealed in Psychoanalytic Experience," trans. Bruce Fink in *Écrits*. New York: W.W. Norton and Co. (2006). 75–81.

6. Guattari is punning on the French here, since *personne* can mean "person" or "nobody": "Personne! C'est personne en personne!" [Tr.].

7. In this chapter, faciality will essentially be brought under this angle in the micropolitics of molecular fields.

8. The current "retro" phenomenon should not be considered a passing fashion. It has always existed, although to a lesser degree in the framework of societies engaged

in processes of the acceleration of history, i.e. the acceleration of the process of deter-ritorialization; the Romans, for example, were fascinated by the survival of the Greek and Egyptian past.

9. The universal and ahistorical cogito of Western philosophy in fact results from a very particular type of social assemblage; it is not only marked by the preeminence of decoded flows, but also by a white, male, heterosexual, hegemonic faciality... the human world and the intimate world thus do not arise from a formal ontology or from the phenomenology of a "buried eideticity," to borrow an expression from Ger-ard Granel, but from concrete machines (such as faciality traits) and from socially and historically located pragmatic fields.

Granel writes in his article on "Husserl" in the *Encyclopaedia Universalis*: "In any event, this is to say that whether we want it or not, whether we know it or not, we are on the verge of unifying the Earth and the people that it holds under the infinite pro-duction of reason in its 'purity' and consciousness in its 'proper sense.'" The whole question is knowing if it is only a matter of taking control of the capitalistic crusade of the unification of modes of subjectification, or if it is better to put oneself at its ser-vice, in the name of an unadulterated metaphysics of being and universal truth, which would have to be thus: "a question, a place of combat and decision."

10. Correlative to a deterioration of "networks of dependence," to return to an expression of Philippe Ariès, and a closure of the conjugal family. Philippe Ariès, *L'enfant et la vie familiale sous l'ancien régime*, Paris: Seuil, (1973).

Isaac Joseph, Philippe Fritsch, Alain Batteguay, "Disciplines à domicile, L'edi-fication de la famille," *Recherches*, no. 28, Nov. 1977.

11. Frances Yates, *The Art of Memory*. Chicago: University of Chicago Press (2001).

12. It is possible that faciality as such has not had the same importance in archaic societies. It seems that through the use of tattoos and masks faciality was at the time less individuated and less universal. At the limit, the only facialities that were recog-nized were those that characterized a tribe or an ethnicity. Let us add that such a collective faciality can never be separated from other diverse systems of marking bodies and territories, of dance and music, components of postural, vocal, ritual, warlike, "economic," expressions, etc. Let us again remark that this semiotic syn-cretism, far from ending in a confusion of genres, on the contrary preserves the specificity of the matters of expression of these components.

13. The Kleinian resurgence of the superego before Oedipus changes nothing. Super-egoistic consciousness, by being detached from father's mustache to the bad objects of the mother, does not bring us an inch closer to the real givens of social repression.

14. As Basil Bernstein writes, "When a child learns its language, or, in the terms which we shall use here, when she learns the specific codes that determine her ver-bal acts, she learns at the same time the urgencies of the social structure in which she is inserted: her experience instead is transformed by the apprenticeships of exercises more than her own discourse, spontaneously appearing, makes her realize." *Langage et Classes sociales*, Paris: Éditions de Minuit (1975).

15. Here mechanism is opposed to creative machinic assemblages.

16. "I had always striven, when looking at the sea, to exclude from my field of vision not only the bathers in the foreground but the yachts with their sails as excessively white as beach clothe—indeed, anything that prevented me from having the feeling I was gazing upon the timeless deep, whose mysterious existence had been rolling on unchanged since before the first appearance of mankind." M. Proust, *A la recherche du temps perdu*, (I, 902/II, 480–481).

17. Rather than being content with preaching against ethnocentrism, ethnologists could work more towards an anti-ethnology that would allow "primitives" to give their point of view on whites of whom they speak amongst themselves that they find them sad, inhuman, corpselike…

18. It does not seem that in antiquity there existed a "racism of skin" strictly speaking.

19. The good sense of Descartes which is, as it takes hold of everyone, the most widely distributed thing in the world.

20. In the sense that mathematics today elaborates a "fuzzy logic." Theories of fuzzy subsets are not content with refining mathematical structures based on a logical binary framework. They go further than multi-valued logic or the system of Łukasiewicz who admits a non-denumerable infinity of truth values. Unlike aleatory objective evaluation, *fuzzy evaluation* remains irreducibly subjective. This is what forces it, against the traditional mathematical ideal of an integral formalization, to adopt everyday language in its definitions: "true, totally true, more or less true, somewhat true, not true, false, not totally true, and not totally false, etc." Cf. "Logique et mathématique du flou," account rendered in Arnold Kaufmann's book "Introduction à la théorie des sous-ensembles flous," Ed. Masson, 1977, by Hourya Sinaceur, *Critique*, May 1978.

21. This is particularly visible in the case of a faciality of power: "The Director seems to take things lightly. But does he really laugh? On the other hand, if I remain too serious, then he will think such and such of me…"

22. It would be necessary to make a distinction here between:
    —an invisible monotheistic faciality of reference relatively localizable in familial coordinates;
    —and an invisible "bureacratistic" faciality of reference (of the Kafkaesque type) which is immanent to all social institutions.

23. Jacques Lizot, *Le cercle des feux: faits et dits des Indiens Yanoami*, Paris: Seuil (1976). Biocca Ettore, *Yanoama: récit d'une femme enlevée par les Indiens*, Paris: Plon (1968).

24. In this regard, look at the way tribunal judges presiding over flagrante delicto cases literally judge the accused "according to the client's face," Ch. Hennion, *Chronique des flagrants délits*, Stock (1976).

25. There are good and bad precedents: the face of the Pope on TV during his travels has been a good precedent; but the notion of the face of a bishop prowling Saint-Denis street or of a president of the Republic fleeing at night has been a bad one.

26. Cf. René Thom, *op. cit.* "It is important to understand that this quantification of information is completely independent of the signified contents of the message; it rests upon the implicit hypothesis that the message appears as if it were drawn to fate starting from a ground of equiprobable events (for example, as if the message were typed by a monkey), i.e. the fact that Shannon's theory, departing from his theoretical framework of communication through a physical channel, is practically incapable of specifying it, even though it is through the message's form that we shall recognize its *a priori* signification." "The same objection applies to the probabilistic definition of information and its identification with negentropy: (...) the concepts of thermodynamics are hardly of interest for closed systems, *which exclude morphologies from the emission and reception of communication*," *ibid.* p. 187.

27. In the unit of a bit (binary digit) according to the general formula: $H=n\mathrm{Log}2N$, N being the length of the message, n the number of elements. Let us remark that this formula is only applicable when the occurrence of signs is equiprobable: it will have to be corrected in relation to every different possibility.

28. Cf. note 7 page 355.

29. An "appreciation" in the Hjelmslevian sense.

30. Example: the Indian "Shabono" habitat which redistributes everyday and ritual objects, limits of the territory, points of cosmic location, spirits, etc. in a concentric way.

31. Example: the passage from a becoming-animal to a machinic becoming-imperceptible through the play of two ping pong balls in Kafka's novella *Blumfield*.

32. We can only follow Greimas here when he proposes to stop considering the extra-linguistic world as an absolute referent and stop treating it as a set of more or less implicit semiotic systems. A.J. Greimas, *Du sens*, Paris: Seuil (1970), p.52.

33. Cf. Christian Houzel, "Les mathématiciens retournent au concret." *La Recherche*, May 1979, p. 507. According to this author, mathematicians could be amenable, due to the introduction of computers in their field, to distinguishing three types of propositions: 1) theorems relating to "short" demonstrations; 2) undecidable propositions; 3) propositions uniquely demonstrable through gigantic calculations with the means of computers.

34. The elaboration of a fuzzy mathematics to which we previously alluded could be able to go in this direction. Hourya Sinceur evokes elsewhere, in her article, the possibility of construing *fuzzy computers*, i.e. which would no longer rest upon the principle of sequential machinic assemblages (p. 520).

35. Certain biochemists, for example, call into question the presuppositions concerning thermodynamics and information theory in the description of evolution: "If the purely chemical evolution of a prebiotic soup is described, we do not see where the fundamental categories of biology will be introduced which are the replication and the transfer of information. If prebiotic systems are represented by means of informational language, it is not clear how we will be able to escape from a mathematical treatment of a new property such as motricity. More precisely, it is not

excluded that we can reveal properties which at first glance seem outside the conceptual field of initial description, but on condition that they are looked for explicitly. However, *we need an instrument that would help us see the unsuspected, because the intermediate states of the organization of matter could very well obey logics* entirely different from the logic of an actual living being." Jacques Ninio, *La Recherche*, No. 66, April 1976, p. 325.

36. Which Jacob von Uexkull distinguished between Innenwelt/Umwelt: *Mondes animaux et mondes humains*, Trans. Paul Muller, Paris (1956).

37. Annex p. 199.

38. Jean-Paul Sartre, *Being and Nothingness*, trans. Hazel E. Barnes, New York: Washington Square Press (1984), p. 346.

39. Jean-Luc Parant, *Les yeux MMDVI*, ed. Christian Bourgois (1976). "The work that these large builders of EMPTY holes that constitute the eyes WITHOUT WHICH NEITHER THEY NOR THE EYES COULD FLY OR SEE AND THE EYES HAVE DUG HOLES IN ALL THE WALLS SIGHT HAS COMPLETELY EMERGED as the pioneers of the space OF THE VOID which would have cleared the path to life while digging in the night and the consistency WHICH ENCLOSED US LIKE SKIN until finding the EMPTY day and this emptiness THIS EMPTINESS without which EYES we could neither FLY to move nor see and the eyes are entirely submerged in space and never go up to the surface except when covered with their tough and crumpled EYELID membranes."

5. The Time of Refrains

1. Cf. *Histoire de la musique*, Encyclopédie de la Pléiade, tome I, p. 1168.

2. For example, with the Bambara, circumcision is always practiced by the blacksmith. Dominique Zahan, *Societies d'initiation Bambara*, Mouton, (1960), p. 110.

3. C. Sachs has remarked that 26 varieties of sound on the same scalar height could be played by a learned zither musician. Cited by R. Francès, *La perception en musique*, Paris: Vrin, (1972), p.18.

4. Cf. page 47.

5. Pierre Clastres, *Society against the State*, pp. 107 and on.

6. "What is important is the existence of an intermediary relay between perception and image, which is at the same time concrete if the machine is considered and abstract if the representation is considered. The concept of a third world thus becomes more clearly situated between matter and image, not a natural universe but a manufactured one, involved at the same time within various forms and within the concrete and the imaginary." Pierre Francastel, *La Figure et le Lieu*, Gallimard: Paris (1973), p. 68.

7. "Josephine the Singer or the Mice People," in *The Complete Stories*, New York: Shocken (1995). Also let us relate from this point of view that, for John Cage, a politics of sound should not be an obstacle to silence and that silence should no longer

be a screen with regard to sound. He considers a sort of "recovery" of nothingness, as the following extract of one of his discussions with Daniel Charles shows, *Pour les oiseaux*, John Cage, Belfond, 1976:

John Cage.—This nothingness is still just a word.

D. Charles.—As silence it must overcome itself.

J.C.—And by that one returns to what it is, i.e. to the sounds.

D.C.—But don't you lose something?

J.C.—What?

D.C.—The silence, the nothingness…

J.C.—You see well that I lose *nothing*! In all that it is not a question of *losing* but of *gaining*!

D.C.—To return to the sounds is thus to return, *before any structure*, to the sounds "accompanied" by nothingness… (p. 32).

Cf. also the comparison that John Cage establishes between the surpassing of what is called music and what is called politics: "politics is the same thing. And I can then rightly speak of the 'non-political' as one speaks a propos of my 'non-music'" (p. 54).

8. Cf. the very beautiful homage by the musician Jacques Besse: "Robert Schumann est interné," *La Grande Pâque*, Belfond, 1969.

9. In certain African music, for example, a phrase is drummed out without being verbally articulated.

10. I will attempt to show in the following essay on Proust that facialized consciousness can coincide, in certain cases, with refrainized consciousness.

11. Or the "effects of percolation," to borrow from the new language of physicists.

12. René Thom, *Structural Stability and Morphogenesis*, trans. David Fowler, Westview Press: Boulder (1994).

13. "Spectacular" example: that of the peacock, whose courting phase consists in staying at a distance and fascinating a female which comes to peck at imaginary food, precisely at a focal point of subjectification determined by the concavity, slightly tilted forward, of its tail-end black eye hole. Although the existence of orgasms in animals is denied, can it sometimes happen to them other than in this instant? A "courteous" orgasm attaches itself to the partner with a lure and probably releases the hormonal components necessary for the following events.

14. This absolute polyvocality is "guaranteed" by the plane of consistency of all abstract machinic possibles.

15. "Early development of female sexuality," Ernest Jones, *Papers on Psychoanalysis*, Baillière, Tindall & Cox: London (1912).

16. In this respect, I will not follow Michel Foucault in the *History of Sexuality* when he appears to consider that a general tendency of sexual repression and the rise of capitalism were not concomitant. Undoubtedly, there is always about "as much sexuality" from one age to another, but the question of repression is very different. It

relates to the nature of the desire associated with this sexuality. The contemporary expansion of discourses relating to the sexuality Michel Foucault justifiably emphasizes does not at all constitute an attenuation of this repression, quite the contrary. It is correct today that all power formations are increasingly worried about sexuality: but it is precisely in order to better subject it to capitalistic codes, in order to miniaturize and internalize its repression. The whole difficulty here stems perhaps from the fact that Michel Foucault never poses these questions in terms of desire but only in terms of sexuality. Michel Foucault, *History of Sexuality: An Introduction.* trans. Robert Hurley. Vintage: New York (1990).

17. Including when this vitality takes on the form of behaviors spoken under submission, which are, in fact, among others only components of "machinic *élan vital*," since they are related to the collective assemblages of the species and not simply to individuals.

18. Example: the current coexistence (far from peaceful) of the vestiges of communal neolithic territorialities from inherited social relations appears in a straight line through "Asian despotism" and "wandering" migrations in the form of massive population displacements. For the best as for the worst, the crucial social transformations always seem to find their "origin" in singularity points, in history's "accidents" (technological discovery related to writing, armaments, navigation, agriculture, invention of religions).

19. Eibl Eibesfeldt, *Ethologie-Biologie du comportement*, NEB, p. 154.

20. Rémy Chauvin, *Entretiens sur la sexualité*, Collectif, Plon: Paris. Cf. the references gathered by Eibl Eibesfeldt, op. cit., pp. 158–59.

21. *Op. cit.*, pp. 323 and 450.

22. It would have been necessary to find a better formulation in order to distinguish this faciality-corporeality of faciality components properly speaking. In effect, it is not simply a question of an animal proto-faciality. Faciality-corporeality in mankind coexists with the diagrammatic triangle of faciality (example: the global face and profile of a CRS (French riot control police officer) such as those on the posters of May 1968 which have been restored for us). Conversely, the specific faciality traits of a particular part of the face are found on every "rung" of the animal ladder.

23. "Every study of animal behavior (one could say as much about human behavior) initially implies the determination of norms for the species considered living in its natural environment or the conditions reproducing them as accurately as possible... Whereas wild rabbits live in a society and express complex sexual manners, rabbits in cages limit themselves to a vegetative activity. No comparison is possible between the behavior of a free wild rat and that of a living white rat confined to a narrow cage. Man has selected the softest individuals, the least similar to 'rodents,' and created a being whose psychic level is, compared to that of the wild rat, the same as that of an idiot mongoloid compared to normal man. When we think about the fact that the immense work accomplished by American zoopsychologists,

using labyrinths and other tests, is founded *exclusively* upon the reactions of this moron which the white rat of the Winston race or any other exemplifies, we are at the very least disconcerted…" Pierre P. Grassé, "Zoologie," *Encyclopédie de la Pléiade*, volume I, p. 251.

24. The first "quantitativistic" studies by primatologists (Washburn, de Vore) leading to the hypothesis of a direct relation between the rigor of hierarchical dominance in monkeys and the degree of adaptation to life in the savanna have to be reoriented. What is highlighted is no longer simply the quantity of social relations (delousing, etc), but the quality of their diverse assemblages and their order of appearance. Example: the graph with sequences of four assemblages between two baboons (one dominating and one dominated): 1) combat, 2) presentation of the backside, 3) rise in sexual character, 4) social delousing. *La Recherche*, no. 75, Dec. 1976, pp. 10–12: "Le comportement social des singes," by Hans Kummer.

Each arrowed line describes a succession of phases for 9 pairs of male gelada baboons. In a random mixture, there would have been 20 inversions of this order of succession instead of the one that appears in the bottom on the right. The durations indicate at the end on average how long a stage is attained.

25. On this subject, we will reconsider further the use, for example in birds, of specific refrains for sexually "enclosing" a species (cf. Eibl Eibesfeldt, p. 24, p. 104) and of the more fundamental relations that appear to exist between semiotizations of rhythm and semiotizations of territory.

26. *La Recherche*, no. 73, Dec. 1976, *op. cit.*

27. Choices that are elaborated starting from the material semiotics of the dream (a privileged field, as it were, of faciality and refrains) are sometimes freer than those stemming from a well constituted propositional logic. Let us notice that traditional hermeneutics—and moreover also Adlerian psychoanalysis—had understood that oneiric semiotization engages the future at least as much as the past.

28. Example: the training techniques of driving an automobile, playing a musical instrument, etc.

29. J. Nicolai, *Vogelhaltung und Vogelplege*, Das Vivarium, Stuttgart, 1965. Cited by Eibl Eiblesfeldt.

30. In particular, they are comprised of imperceptible phases of raised eyebrows and dilated pupils which do not last more than 2 to 3 tenths of a second. These expressions, filmed at 48 images a second and broken up image by image, are found in the Solomon Islands, New Guinea, France, Japan, Africa, as well as in the Indians of the Amazon, etc. (cf. Eibl Eiblesfeldt, pp. 436–442).

31. Could the "urgency" of signs and tools have been greater in certain animal species than in man? The paradox is only apparent because, in effect, it is mankind itself which is, as such, submitted to a process of accelerated "machinization."

32. Human facialitary deterritorialization can be characterized from a phylogenetic point of view by:

—the anatomic freedom of joints, the muscular mobility of the mouth (correlative to the development of phonatory devices);

—the protrusion of the eyes, the mobility of oculo-motor muscular systems (correlative to the laterality of the gaze), orbicular eyelids, frontal and arching brows...

Let us note in passing that these partial, morphological "detachments" equally play a fundamental role in components of sexual expressivity.

33. This facialitary "concentration" is also localizable on an onto-genetic level, for example in studying the formation of the smile. This concentration for the infant sets in play not only the ensemble of facial musculature, but also arm and leg movements, tensing of the hand muscles, an acceleration of respiratory rhythms, the emission of various noises... whereas in "normal" adults it no longer concerns anything but the basic muscles of the face. Cf. J.L. Laroche and F. Tcheng *Le sourire du nourrisson*, Louvain, 1969.

34. Concerning the critique of mechanically "progressist" phylogenies, here we can do no better than to return to what François Dagognet has written and to transpose it from botanical taxonomies onto zoology: "simplicity cannot be valued as an index of primitiveness or ancestrality. In fact, it is not excluded that the flower was first of all polycarpic and multipetaled (cycadoidienne theory) as the oldest documents of the lesser Cretaceous seems to suggest (the Bennettites). Conversely, monocotyledons also derive from dicotyledons and not the other way around, as an additive theory of evolution had believed *with the regular passage from one to two*. It is true that certain paleobotanists are content to admit branched and ramified lines beginning from a unique complex, but this is still a way of refuting the conception of a rectilinear or progressive course. And these remarks show well enough *the traps of a phylogeny overly conceived as a transition from the simple to the composite*, whereas abundant, spiral, and non-coned forms can translate a previous situation." *Encyclopedia Universalis*, vol. 15, p. 764.

35. Paul Géroudet, *Les Palmipèdes*, Delachaux and Niestlé, (1959), pp. 22–40.

36. Paul Géroudet, *Les Echassiers*, Delachaux and Niestlé, 1967, pp. 31–40.

37. Paul Géroudet, *Les Passereaux*, book II, pp. 88–94.

38. Concerning this topic, we have spoken of an "irregularity" in sociability. Thus, the Swiss have sometimes been submitted to veritable invasions of bramblings (*Fringilla Montifringilla*). In 1945–1946, a "dormitory" in Ajoie gathered 27 millions birds; whereas in 1950–1951, 100 million finches united near Thoune. Cf. Paul Géroudet, *Les passereaux*, book III, p. 212.

39. *Ibid.*

40. In approximate forms, a courting ritual is found referring to "nest-building" in certain fish. For example, a male of the grey tilapia clears a space for itself with twigs so as to produce a decorative effect that will attract females (cited by Eibl Eibesfeldt, p. 126).

41. I. Nicolai has studied the conjoint evolution of Veuves (Viduinea) and the birds upon which they parasite (different species of Bengalis, Astrilds, etc.) According to

this author, this evolution has been "piloted" by the setting in common of refrains resulting from the parasitical imitation of the host's song: "it is strongly probable that traditional bonds of Veuve birds with their host species, which are maintained through the imitation of the host's song, led to the evolution of different subspecies of this group" (cited by Eibl Eibesfeldt, pp. 162 and 194).

42. Eibl Eibesfeldt, pp. 130 and 136.

43. This ritual is composed of assemblages:
—of dance: the neck is drawn down, partners turn their beaks in alternation, face to the side in such a way that the beak touches the shoulders held high;
—of fencing with their beaks, which "imitates" the young's search for food;
—of clacking their beaks, which evokes a danger;
—of cries toward the sky, instead evoking an appeasement;
—of smoothing the feathers of the partner's shoulders (always punctuated with a clacking of beaks).
And at the end of each sequence, whose order is not very rigorous, the two birds mutually incline themselves on the ground and emit "two sonorous syllables" in order to seal a sort of "nest-building contract."

44. Paul Géroudet, *Les Passereaux*, book II, p. 10.

45. *Ibid.*, book III, p. 133.

46. A whole rubric of animal play should equally be explored. Eibl Eibesfeldt describes, for example, an extraordinary game of cricket between two Galapagos finches which alternatively pass a small worm through the crevice of a branch within which they have previously inserted it.

47. K. Immelmann has shown that mottled diamonds, which have brightly colored plumage, maintain a certain distance between one another, whereas the white subjects of the same species will huddle close together (cited by Eibl Eibesfeldt, p. 151).

48. Even at this level of biological fascination which constitutes the imprint, certain kinds of degrees of freedom or optional matters will continue to exist, as this is indicated by the fact that diamonds raised by females of the Munie family will only perform the courting ritual with the latter *even when other choices are available*. If they are forced, on the contrary, to cohabitate with a female of their species, they will seemingly again become "normal"; they will court with her and couple with her as if the imprint had not existed. This later fact, in sum, seems to impose its effects above all upon the order of desire.

49. From the work of K. Immelmann, cited by Eibl Eibesfeldt, p. 241.

50. Cited by Eibl Eibesfeldt, p. 54.

51. It should be noted that the techniques of mathematical data analysis have resorted in the last few years to methods of transcription precisely calling upon elementary faciality traits. Thus, in Chernoff's method, the parameters are represented by the mouth, the nose, etc., and physiognomies are compared in order to compare the

objects studied. Cf. "l'analyse de données," by Edwin Diday and Ludovic Lebart, *La Recherche*, No. 74, Jan. 1977.

52. According to them, all or part of the behaviors of negation, appropriation, reception, flirtation, arrogance, intimidation, triumph, submission, rage, etc. will arise from hereditarily transmitted encodings. Cf. Eibl Eibesfeldt p. 440 and on.

53. Let us recall that these are not "centers" that neurosurgeons locate, but merely points of resection which result in disorganizing the components in question. Everything leaves one to think, in effect, that each real act of memorization—in particular concerning long-term memory—brings into play the electric potentials of *an entire population* of neurons which is not at all "localizable" but which is "selected" from every part of the brain. W. Penfield, B. Milner, "Memory deficit produced by bilateral lesions in the hippoccemphal zone," Archive of Neurology and psychiatry; E.R. John, *Mechanisms of Memory*, London, (1967).

54. "Rhythm is in the beat of the wings of migratory birds, in the trot of wild horses, the undulating slithering of fish; but it is also impossible for animals to trotter, to fly, or to swim to the degree that humans breathe to the time of the metronome." Ludwig Klages, *Expression du caractère dans l'écriture*, Delachaux and Niestlé, 1947, p. 41.

55. Rhythms in a period of 24 hours play a role that proves to be increasingly important to the extent that they are studied on the level of cellular biology, pharmacology, the physiology of tissues, organs, functions as well as ethology. The majority of rhythms in a longer period—like those of migrations—would result from a composition on the basis of circadian rhythms and thus, in the last analysis, on those molecular rhythms.

56. A. Reinberg, *La Chronobiologie: Une nouvelle étape de l'étude des rythmes biologiques*, Sciences, vol. 1, 1970; "Rythmes biologiques," *Encyclopaedia Universalis*, vol. 4, p. 568; *Cycles biologiques et psychiatrie*. J. Ajurriaguerra, Ed." Genève Georg V, 1968.

57. W.H. Thorpe, *Learning and Instinct in Animals*, Methuen: London, (1969), pp. 421–426.

6. Reference Points for a Schizoanalysis

1. Kurt Goldstein's "structure of the organism," Merleau-Ponty's "structure of behavior," Lacan's "symbolic structure," each in their own way, at the least presuppose a distinction between the "ontic" and the "pathic," to take up Von Weizsecker's terms again. In this author, this distinction was in addition explicitly associated with a radical opposition between the laws of the physical world and those of the vital world. "In the case of physics, he wrote that the law resides in the action of forces, in the case of organic movement it comes from form." *Le cycle de la structure*, trans. Michel Foucault and Daniel Rocher, Desclee de Brouwer (1958).

2. In *moral* languages like Latin in the classical era, such micro-refrains were codified. In modern languages, prosodic units, though less musically and rhythmically localizable, nevertheless conserve a primordial function in the refrainization, familiarization and familialization of statements.

3. An assemblage will give the impression of being solidly tucked away in a system of machinic redundancies, of being attached to the world of evidences, of making do on the spot, whereas in fact it is the seat of a sort of subterranean war between several semiotic components. Some English researchers have shed light on such interferences in spoken language between auditory components and components of faciality by modifying the text of a message via reading lips in relation to what is heard through the voice. Cf. "l'oeil écoute. BABA + GAGA = DADA." Account rendered in *Le Monde*, 26 Jan. 1977 of the works of Hang McGurls and John McDonald, "Nature," Dec. 1976.

4. Probabilities "oriented" by calculations bearing on stochastic processes do not seem to us to be incompatible with such a conception of molecular choices.

5. Ludwig von Bertalanffy, *General System Theory: Foundations, Development, Application*. George Braziller: New York, 1969.

6. This is particularly significant in Anglo-Saxon and Italian familial psychotherapy (J. Haley, D.O. Jackson, P. Watzlawick, Selvini Palazzoli, etc.: cf. *Cahiers critiques de thérapie familial et de pratiques de réseaux*, Ed. Gamma, 1979.

7. The discovery in 1793 of a "*terra incognito*" beyond Marat, according to Camille Desmoulin's expression, that is, a "social question" associated with the birth of a new *deterritorialized proletarian class*. Michelet, *Histoire de la Revolution francaise*, Bibli. Pleiade Gallimard, tome II, p. 530.

8. The Cartesian "*res extenso*:" "By the body I include anything that can be terminated by some figure, which can be expressed in some place and *fill* a place such that every other body is excluded."

9. Freud distinguished:
    1. A primary unconscious process setting in play a free energy of specific mechanisms of displacement, condensation, overdetermination, hallucination, etc.
    2. A secondary conscious or pre-conscious process setting in play an energy bound to mechanisms of inhibition, control, attention, focused thought, etc.

10. "Let us dare to say it and repeat it incessantly: there is nothing amazing in the phenomenon of thought, or at least nothing that proves that this thought is distinct from matter, nothing that makes us certain that matter, elaborated or modified in some way, can produce thought." Sade, *Juliette*, New York: Grove Press (1994).

11. R.W. Braly has shown for example that the "natural" immediate perception of complex forms was considerably influenced by an apprenticeship leading to an unconscious perceptive memory. R. W. Braly, "The influence of past experience in visual perception" (cited by R. Frances) *La Perception de la musique*, Vrin, 1972, p. 52.

12. Gilles Deleuze and I have tried to show how an author such as Kafka, in order to explore the coordinates of a new type of bureaucratic capitalistic unconscious, had begun to resort to animal becomings, to musical deterritorializations, perceptive deterritorializations, etc. In the second essay of this book, supported by the prodigious analytic work which constitutes Proust's oeuvre, I will try to examine the incidences of certain capitalistic mutations of amorous love at the beginning of the century.

13. And consequently of reserving its exploration to specialists of psychoanalytic "passwords."

14. Life has crossed such thresholds of consistency, has "taken off," by setting off from chains of carbon atoms rather than, for example, chains of silicon atoms. A multitude of physico-chemical, planetological conditions, etc. have delimited such a choice concerning which nothing prohibits thinking, in the current state of our knowledge, that it could have been very different!

15. Certain converters seem to partake in an elementary simplicity—like, for example, the "magnetic effects" described by E.V. Holst which impose the domination of a rhythm onto a set of other rhythms. Others, like the "decision-making operators" of the human brain, partake in a complexity that scientific research is undoubtedly still far from being able to comprehend! In particular, how do we conceive that a selection of schemes and rhythms, paradigmatized on deterritorialized mental objects, themselves articulated via an expressive combinatory of an unlimited richness, manages to "enter" into systems that induce "acting one to act"?

16. F. Oury, J. Palin, *Chronique de l'école-caserne*, Paris: Maspero (1972).

17. Little Hans does not speak of *the* penis, but of a concrete machine, the "peepee-maker" (*Wiwimacher*).

18. Cf. fig. p. 181, the rhizome of the progressive circumscription of "Little Hans," Freud's first edition monograph related to the psychoanalysis of children.

19. Renouncing the simplifications that would tend to reduce genetic encodings and evolution to a capitalization of information and to a statistical selection where the most complex levels would support an "arborescent" dependence in relation to the most elementary levels, certain theories currently envision being able to produce transferences of genetic information through viruses and in some sense that evolution can "return" from a more evolved species to a less evolved species or one that generated the former. "If such passages of information should reveal themselves as having been very important, certain geneticists declare it would be introduced to substitute *reticular* schemata (with communication between branches after their differentiation) for schemata in bushes or trees which serve to represent evolution." "Le rôle des virus dans l'évolution," *La Recherche*, (March: 1975), p. 271.

20. S. Freud, *Three Essays on the Theory of Sexuality*, New York: Basic Books, (200).

21. "Babillages… Des crèches aux multiplicités d'enfants," Liane Mozère, Geneviève Aubert, *Recherches* 27 (May: 1977). Anne Querrien, "L'ensaignement," *Recherches* 23 (June: 1976).

22. Pierre Clastres, *Chronique des Indiens Guyakis*, Plon., 1972, and *Society against the State*, trans. Robert Hurley, Brooklyn: Zone Books (1989). Jacques Lizot, *Le Cercle de feu*.

23. *La société psychiatrique avancée. Le modèle américain*, Françoise Castel, Robert Castel, Anne Lovell, Grasset, (1979).

24. This term is here understood in the sense that I have originally given it not in the one psycho-sociologists gave it afterwards. Cf. *Psychanalyse et Transversalité*, Paris: Maspero (1972).

25. Thus they simultaneously escape from sense and signification, even if we were to assimilate, as Brekle proposes (cf. Brekle, *Sémantique*, A. Colin, 1974, p. 44), the former to the intentional content of a concept attached to a signifier and the latter to its extensional aspect. But in a "machinic" (and not simply logical) perspective, sense would mark the establishment of a diagrammatic connection independent from any representative and significative system.

26. Cf. figure p. 180.

27. Like in Jacques Prévert's "Page d'écriture," where the flight of the "bird-lyre" liberates not only the semiotics repressed by the school (singing, dancing…), but also all the other modes of encoding and stratification: "And the windows again become sand, ink again becomes water, desks again become trees, chalk again becomes hillside, quill-holder again becomes bird…" (*Paroles*, Paris: Gallimard (1949)).

28. In the framework of quantum physics, a "tunnel effect" makes it possible to describe the passage from one physical system of an "authorized state" to another "authorized state," through a succession of intermediary "prohibited" states.

29. Individual, dual, collective, social, machinic to various degrees… Here I am omitting the question of the side and also the possible recuperation of some of the technical aspects of psychoanalysis and current psychotherapies.

30. A child running away, for example, will be able to be envisioned from radically different angles according to whether we will be situated from the perspective of the law, "the families' interest," psychology, the educator, an anti-establishment movement or different modes of the child's subjectification in question. The selection of a psychotherapeutic point of view is not a choice *alongside* other choices. It is imposed necessarily as a micropolitical option implicating all the assemblages of enunciation having a determinant relation with this child.

31. There is thus no question of characterizing a schizoanalytic process according to stages of development, initiatory phases akin to the "castration complex," the entry into the "symbolic," "alliance with a homeostatic tendency of a system"…

32. Example: which type of machinic nucleus was able to transform the minority constituted by the Russian working class at the beginning of the century into a "motor" of the political and social history of all of Russia for a long time? Cf. "La coupure léniniste," *Psychanalyse et Transversalité*, Paris: Maspero (1972).

33. After the war, when Fernand Deligny launched the mutual-aid network called "La Grande Cordée," he had decided to accept whichever lifestyle a young person could formulate to him without discussion. It was next up to him to experiment by himself with the objective and subjective consistency of his project. The Network was only there to assist him and not to direct him or judge his behavior.

34. The order of presentation we have adopted to enumerate these three dimensions does not correspond to any particular hierarchy but perhaps to the difficulties that an analytic assemblage can encounter when approaching them.

35. Cf. the annex, p. 206.

36. In our study of the faciality and refrains of *In Search of Lost Time*, we will endeavor to rediscover these three dimensions within the creative Proustian assemblage:
    —that of components of passage (perceptive, affective, etc.) which open up time, faces, landscapes and authorize all possible crossings;
    —that of assemblages of enunciation which collaborate in the "ungluing" of these components of passage, through the extraction of a block of childhood or a social group of singularity points and abstract machinisms. (Example: the faciality traits of the Narrator's mother semiotized from the repetitive scene of the "good-night kiss," Odette's faciality traits which Swann sifts from Botticelli's Zipporah; certain "manufactured" refrains from salons like Mme Verdurin's…);
    —finally, that of the writing machine of the *Recherche* as simultaneously ruptured and continuous, which emerges at the intersection of various branches of the literary and artistic phylum which has marked Proust.

37. It is not for nothing that various fascisms have never stopped laying claim to them!

38. We could transpose verbatim what we say here about psychoanalysis onto the professional militant upon whom it falls to "effectuate" the working-class-as-motor-of-history, even when it has given in, become worn out, or complicit with the dominant order—like in certain bastions of capitalism—or, better still, when it does not exist practically on the ground, as is the case in a number of Third World countries.

7. Annex: The Molecular Transition of Signs

1. At this stage, I will indifferently employ assemblages and components as interchangeable terms. There is no obligatory hierarchical relation between components and assemblages. Some assemblages reunite with components but, conversely, some assemblages can so to speak enter an element within a component. The distinction will only find its relevance when it will be a question of differentiating micropolitical assemblages starting from their machinic nuclei. Cf. p. [45].

2. However, this does not consequently imply that the referent itself be real. Reality's character of consistency only bears upon the *relation* of f to the referent, which can itself be virtual or imaginary. The question for example will be of knowing, when I desire to introduce a word for the representation that I have of a mythical beast, if the word "*licorne*" fits well, if I'm not mistaken in my choice, if I'm not intending something a little different. At the same time, when I consider the English word "unicorn," I seek to assure myself that it is simply a question of a good translation and of knowing up to what point does the English word more or less speak of the same things the French one does. The degree of consistency of a sign-referent designation is only absolute in logic or mathematics; otherwise, it pertains to virtual objects. It is then a question of establishing that such a relation

really exists between such *irreal* objects (which I shall call: absolutely deterritorialized objects).

3. Which will be converted into semiological systems in the redundancy of morphemes of the referent.

4. The "contact of the universe" which, according to Einstein, is established by photons represents a machinic inertia and a serial time of encoding bordering on zero. At the other extreme, certain material stratifications can represent a machinic inertia and a time of encoding bordering on infinity.

5. If a component of semiotization is specified by the existence of one or several components of passage, it falls to us to employ one expression for another.

6. According to François Jacob, the linearity of a mode of encoding enables a much more rigorous control of the linking of encoded sequences, *Critique*, March 1974, no. 322, p. 202.

7. Discrete: constituted from distinct units and in a limited number; example: phonemes.

   Digital: translatable into information units, into bits (binary digits) corresponding to an elementary binary choice; example: Jakobson's distinctive traits.

8. Symbol-reference-referent. C.K. Ogden and I.A. Richards, *The Meaning of Meaning*, London: Routledge and Kegan (1946).

9. Types II and III are born from the division of semiotic redundancies.

10. The redundancies of designation only have a virtual existence within signifying semiology. Indeed, in this type of assemblage, signifiers cannot directly communicate with the referent; they must make a "detour" through the signified (the acoustic figures of the signifier and the concepts and representation of the signified take part in the same "mental world"). In order to be virtual, this semiotization of the referent is no less perfectly defined from a semiotic point of view. What Roland Barthes says of denotation, which constitutes only the "first of the meanings" (*S/Z*), can be transposed here by the designation which never determines anything but realities among others ("degrees"of reality). This no longer functions in the same way when we pass to a diagrammatic semiotics whose figures of expression "deal" directly with the referent. (For example, in the case of a computerized system.) Is this to say that now we would be dealing with "true" reality? No doubt we find degrees of consistency here, but in a techno-scientific order that no longer returns to the same play of relations of social forces.

11. Incident: from this perspective, iconic polytheism is not established "before" monotheism, but "after," against, in reaction to it. Monotheism, which today sells us liberating virtues with great reinforcement of publicity, as the religions of deterritorialized flows, constantly threatens the interior of every so-called "primitive" religion which, let us note, *always* requires a monotheistic component. Notice that Judaism, Christianity, and Islam equally constituted themselves in reaction to what

could be a pure monotheistic religion; they do not cease, in effect, to reterritorialize the divinity in a revealed text, in the history of an ethnic group, in all sorts of incarnations.

12. Here we leave aside the philosophical "abuses" which consist in only accounting for one type of consistency and which ends up for example: in naïve realism, Platonic realism, nominalism, or realism of interiority…

13. In the sense that Pierce speaks of sign-ocurrences in opposition to sign-types.

14. The idea of fixed matter, inert such that it is produced by signifying semiology, does not correspond to any reality, especially to the surface of the earth where matter and life are inextricably tied and, more generally, because the state of matter is only the result of particular cases of energetic interaction.

15. In the sense that David Cooper uses this word in *Grammaire pour l'usage des vivants*, Le Seuil.

16. In this regard, the diagrams proposed here must only be considered as hyper-simplified, even simplistic reductions of the abstract machinisms at work in real assemblages. The pragmatic analysis of the most elementary icon or index within a concrete situation will *inevitably* lead to a much more complex cartography or rather to an "open" complexity, in the sense that Umberto Eco speaks of the "open work."

17. The "linguistic superego" is undoubtedly today much more demanding and selective than it was in pre-capitalist societies. Perhaps it is less apparent—one judges people less on their language, and yet, one is not so sure—but it has insinuated itself within the center of behaviors and modes of subjectification in a much more molecular way.

18. He opposes the stability of acute resonances to the instability of fuzzy resonances.

19. ("Can we not admit (…) that factors of phenomenological invariance which create in the observer the feeling of signification come from *real* properties of external objects and manifest the *objective* presence of formal entities bound to these objects of which we say that they are 'vehicles of signification?'") René Thom, *op. cit.*, p. 197.

20. One or several particular types.

21. Diagrams are here dissociated from images, whereas in Charles Sanders Peirce they were ranked with the latter under the same general category of the Icon. Charles Sanders Peirce, *Collected Papers*, Belknap Press Harvard-Cambridge, 1965.

See also: Bettini and Casetti who rightly discern the contour of diagrammatic signs, without however shedding light upon their specificity. Bettini and Casetti, *Sémiologie des moyens de communication et le problème de l'analogie*, Cinéma, Klincksieck, (1973), p. 92.

22. Unlike Freudian psychoanalysis, which relates this passion of abolition to a pulsional agency [*instance*] on a metapsyhological order—Thanatos opposed to Eros—schizoanalysis simply considers it as the degree zero of machinic desire

which can moreover coincide with its point of maximum intensity. Desiring-machines are thrown into confusion, their codes and their structures threatening to be decomposed at the same time as a question of crossing thresholds of intensity is posed for them.

23. Which results in the miniaturization of the basic technical components of data processing as well as in the speed of expansion of the "dromocratic revolution" whose effects Paul Virilio has studied. *Speed and Politics*, trans. Mark Polizzotti, New York: Semiotext(e) (2007); *L'insecurité du territoire*, Stock; *Popular Defense and Ecological Struggles*, trans. Mark Polizzotti, New York: Semiotext(e) (1990).

24. "Sense always becomes the substance of a new form and does not have any possible existence except as the substance of an unspecified form." *Prolegomena to a Theory of Language*, p. 57.

25. The fact that the deterritorialized possible can manifest itself under the form of quanta does not thereby signify that it is measurable in the manner of an abstract quantity.

26. For the definition of the six fundamental linguistic levels in Hjelmslev, see *Dictionnaire encyclopédique des sciences de langage*, Oswald Ducrot an Tzvetan Todorov, Le Seuil, p. 39.

27. Cf. *Le Capital comme integrale des formations de pouvoir*, "Echafaudages," Collectif of the CINEL, Éditions Récherches, 1979.

28. Cf. Korzybski's considerations on language as map. Alfred Korzybski, *Science and Sanity*, International neo-Aristotelian Library, 1933; E.T. Belle Numerology Baltimore; J. Royce, "The Principle of Logic," *Encyclopedia of the Philosophical Sciences*, Vol. I, Logic, London, New York. Also remember in Borges the idea of a map which recovers a territory. *Collected Fictions*, trans. Andrew Hurley, London: Penguin (1999).

Part II: Refrains of Lost Time

1. Swann's Love as Semiotic Collapse

1. Maurice Merleau-Ponty, *Phenomenology of Perception*, p. 245–257.

2. "As the tea had done, the multiple *sensations of light*, the *airy sounds*, the *noisy colors* which Vinteuil sent us from the world in which he composed, presented to my imagination, forcefully but too rapidly for it to take in, something which I could compare to the *perfumed silk* of a geranium. The only thing is, while in a memory the vagueness can be if not eliminated at least made more precise by pinpointing the circumstances which explain why a *certain taste* recalls sensations of light, since the vague sensations conveyed by Vinteuil came not from a memory but from an impression (like that of the steeples of Martinville), one would have had to explain the *geranium fragrance* of his music not by a material resemblance but by its profound equivalent, the unknown, multicolored festival (of which his works seemed to be disparate fragments, dazzling shards with scarlet fracture lines), the mode according to which he 'heard' and projected the universe" (Book III, p. 375/V,

346–47, Marcel Proust, *A la recherche du Temps perdu*, Gallimard: Paris, (1989)). For all the following citations, I will only mention the volume in Roman numerals and the page number in Arabic numerals. All italics in these passages will be my emphasis.

3. Proust began the writing of the *Recherche* almost around the same years that Ferdinand de Saussure gave his celebrated *Course in General Linguistics* in Geneva.

4. That which, in this essay, I tend to express by the verb "semiotize."

5. The field opened by music is not reduced to a range with seven notes, but to an incommensurable keyboard, still almost entirely unknown. Great artists discover new universes, showing us "what richness, what variety, is hidden unbeknownst to us within that great unpenetrated and disheartening darkness of our soul which we take for emptiness and nothingness" (I, 350/I, 363).

6. Proust has remarkably described the nature of the collective assemblage of enunciation of refined salons, particularly in *Sodom and Gomorrah*: "the salons cannot be portrayed in the static immobility that may have been suitable hitherto for the study of characters, which must also be as it were swept along in a quasi-historical movement" (II, 742/IV, 145). He furthermore compares them to a living organism: "As for Swann, Odette's presence did indeed add something to this house which none of the others in which he was entertained possessed: a sort of *sensory apparatus*, a *nervous system* ramifying through all the rooms and causing constant excitations in his heart" (I, 226/I, 234).

7. "The abundance of impressions that he had been receiving for some time, and even this abundance had come to him more with his love of music, had enriched even his delight in music..." (I, 223/I, 231). This renewal will be short lived for the painter; during the process, he will also fall into the black hole of semiotic collapse which will characterize Swann's passion for Odette.

8. The differential analysis of the works of Kafka and Proust, which I suggested previously, will probably lead to shedding light on a very different functioning of iconic *matters of expression* in both authors (example: in Kafka, a painting is related to a photograph and, in Proust, a photograph is instead related to a painting).

9. Essentially an extension of animal ethology, human ethology has been above all attached, until now, to the study of the most visible, most territorialized components of human behaviors. But an inversion of this relation of dependence is not inconceivable, and all doors remain open when an ethologist like W.H. Thorpe declares that fundamental characteristics as of human behavior such as structured language, the translation of numeric concepts, the use of symbols, artistic appreciation and even creation are not absent in the animal world at all. W.H. Thorpe, *Learning and Instinct in Animals*, Metheun: London, 1969, p. 469.

10. The question of the death of the loved object will be posed in an entirely different way for the Narrator and Baron Charlus. The latter had *really* envisioned murdering Morel (III, 804–805/VI, 112–114), whereas the "murders" of which the Narrator is accused only stem from the chain of circumstances which he has not managed or not

wanted to bend: "it seemed to me that through my totally selfish affection I had let Albertine die, just as I previously murdered my mother" (III, 496 and 501/V, 468). Albertine's death does not proceed from the Narrator's "criminal impulse" like what is suggested of Charlus when he demonstrates a murderous intention towards Morel; this death less concerns PERSONS than the creative PROCESS of the novel; it is required by the perspective of a radical renewal of situations and assemblages of enunciation.

11. In this essay, I will not make any explicit reference to Gilles Deleuze's book *Proust and Signs*, although I have been constantly inspired by it; but it would have called for citation of it on every page!

I have not made a reference to the work *Musique et structure Romanesque dans la Recherche du Temps perdu* (Ed. Klincksieck) by Georges Matoré and Irène Mecz because I was not aware of it until after having lead my own investigation on "Vinteuil's little phrase." It is regrettable that the authors of this carefully documented, well written work, were unable to resist the most scholarly psychoanalytic interpretations, and only propose reductionist explanations of music in the *Recherche*, which would be limited, according to them, either to a sublimatory function of Proust's obsessive or perverse drives, or to a simple illustration of his thought.

2. Nine Assemblages for a Refrain

1. Cf. Georges Painter's *Marcel Proust* (Mercure de France). The notion of "facsimile" also evokes one of Proust's "preparatory" phrases at the beginning of the *Recherche*: that of the pastiche. Pastiching an author consists in trying to undo from the inside what tends to function as a model in a particular work, in such a way as to better illuminate the singularity of its abstract machinisms through contrast. In a general way, it is all a conception of the relation of conformity between art and the dominant reality (well represented by Saint Beuve's critical method) which must be reevaluated for the *Recherche* to become possible in its creative, rhizomatic aspect.

2. This impossibility of attributing a name to the performers is certainly not fortuitous. We know that in this domain Proust left nothing to chance. It is only to the extent that people become singularized by a proper name that they can enable a fragment of the *Recherche* to proliferate. The machinic nucleus of "inspiration" and the asignifying crystals which are at the beginning of the different branches of the novel appear closely tied to the choices of these proper names, sorts of phonological and semantic cocktails that "frame" a possible direction, stimulating the attempt of new developments. We shall see for example that when Vinteuil's name will be set in circulation, it will no longer be only a question of an elliptical face-to-face between the *Amateur* and the *Work*: all the dimensions of Swann's life, the Narrator's destiny, and the Proustian writing machine will in fact be implied by this actualization of such an asignifying catalyst.

3. "Until then, as is true of many men whose taste for the arts develops independently from their sensuality, a bizarre disparity had existed between the satisfactions he conceded to one and those he conceded to the other, as he enjoyed, in the com-

pany of increasingly crude women, the seductions of increasingly refined works of art…" (I, 246/I, 255). The misogyny that duplicates Swann's feminine passions—and no doubt also Proust's—perhaps aims less at the "young maids" in question than the high society women.

4. It is only much later that the Narrator will discover the Verdurins's generosity and disinterest. Cf. the narration of their active charity in regard to Saniette (III, 324, 327, 338/V, 299, 301, 311).

5. Unlike Proust's commentators who envision the Salons as an external framework for "situating" characters, here we prefer to insist on their function of modeling the latter in what is most essential to them.

6. Who at this point we only know here under the familiar name Biche.

7. [Translation modified].

8. Let us note that the little phrase has not simply been "discernibilized" by Swann. The pianist, for example, will explicitly announce during another audition his intention of "playing the little phrase for Monsieur Swann."

9. To make Madame Verdurin "give in," her husband will propose a compromise with her: the little pianist will only play the andante (I, 206/I, 214).

10. This will furthermore concern the announcement of his death. Proust will design a proper name at the limit of a common name: Dechambre (II, 894/IV, 292). For a specialist of… chamber music (*music… de chambre*)!

11. A very tangential allusion to Charlus will reach the state of an amorous relationship that he would have had with Swann (III, 229/V, 209). But to suppose that he had spoken truthfully will have been nothing but an incidence in the development of the *Recherche*.

12. "That Swann felt as though he had encountered in a friend's drawing room a person whom he had admired in the street and despaired of ever finding again. In the end, diligent, purposeful, it receded through the ramifications of its perfume, leaving on Swann's face the reflection of its smile." (I, 212/I, 219).

13. On the contrary, the Narrator is *forced to witness* this scene due to an extremely singular situational circumstance: he is accidentally surprised by two little girls; he hides in the closet; he cannot move without attracting attention… (I, 159/I, 162–163). The discovery of Charlus's homosexuality results from a similar procedure (II, 601–612/IV, 5–16).

14. "Her profile was too pronounced for his taste, her skin too delicate, her cheekbones too prominent, her features too pinched. Her eyes were lovely, but so large they bent under their own mass, exhausted the rest of her face, and always gave her a look of being in ill health or ill humor" (I, 196/I, 203).

15. Odette always fits in with the established order, the most conservative side of power. When she and Swann marry, for example, she involves herself with the anti-Dreyfusards and anti-Semites (II, 252–252/III, 246).

16. Let us relate in passing this menace of a becoming-animal which seems to constitute an exception in Proust's work, which seems much more fundamentally marked by becoming-woman, becoming-plant, becoming-landscape (but this appreciation must be nuanced if we remember that Swann means "swan" in English!). Let us equally note that at the end of the *Recherche* Proust is tempted to make all the faces of the people present at the last reception in the Guermantes' home enter into a "becoming-insect." But it is hardly a question of a fantasy! (III, 923/VI, 232 and page [328] of the present work).

17. Each of Odette's visits "renewed the disappointment he felt at finding himself once again in the presence of that face whose details he had somewhat forgotten in the meantime and which he had not recalled as being either so expressive or, despite her youth, so faded; he felt sorry, as she talked to him, that her considerable beauty was not the type he would have spontaneously preferred" (I, 197/I, 204).

18. It is self-evident that the "little phrase" does not "fabricate" this revolution by itself. It is just the most concrete manifestation, the catalytic operator of a virtual mutation of the assemblage. During the course of history, certain refrains, certain icons, certain predications have thus taken on a singular relief: Christ's resurrection, but also Giordano Bruno's option in favor of the infinite nature of the Universe. Along with a new conception of charity, a certain "cosmic modesty" leading the earth to turn around the sun can be felt as a danger to social order. The same goes with new ways of organizing mathematical signs, physical relations, sonorous objects, plastic spaces...

19. "So that for some time, the order he had followed the first night, when he began by touching Odette's throat with his fingers and lips, was not changed, and his caresses still began this way each time; and much later, when the rearrangement (or the ritual simulacrum of rearrangements) of the cattleyas had long since been abandoned, the metaphor 'make cattleya,' having become a simple phrase they used without thinking about it when they wanted to signify the act of physical possession—in which, in fact, one possesses nothing—lived on in their language, commemorating it, after that forgotten custom" (I, 234/I, 242–243).

20. After their marriage, Odette will refuse to wear a scarf that Swann offered her due to her resemblance to a Virgin painted by Botticelli, and he recommends to the Narrator not to make the comparison which he believes is revealed between the movement of Odette's hands and that of this Virgin: "Be sure not to mention it to her! One word—and she'd make sure it wouldn't happen again!" (I, 618/II, 193).

21. "And this disease which was Swann's love had so proliferated, was so closely entangled with all his habits, with all his actions, with his thoughts, his health, his sleep, his life, even with what he wanted after his death, it was now so much a part of him, that it could not have been torn from him without destroying him almost entirely: as they say in surgery, his love is no longer operable" (I, 308/I, 320).

22. This latent homosexuality is illustrated by the fact that Swann will attempt to form an alliance several times with his rival, Forcheville (I, 315/I, 327).

23. "Poor Swann, what a role they make him play: they make him leave so that she can stay there alone with her Charlus—because it was him, I recognized him!" (I, 142/I, 145).

24. An allusion to this Odette-Charlus relation is made in the dream of the "young man in a fez" (cf. p. [281] of this book).

25. The people of the highest nobility will not abandon Charlus in his distress. For example, the queen of Naples will help him when he is excluded from the Verdurin salon (III, 322/V, 297).

26. Let us note in passing that the theme of the "little worker girl" detaches from Swann to emigrate to Odette, with that of the "little-retired-dressmaker-on-her-fifth-floor." Thus the fundamental theme of feminine homosexuality has begun. (But there is nothing spectacular at this stage: Swann vaguely imagines that he could seem to be the lover of Odette's old dressmaker after being able to meet with the latter everyday.) (I, 319/I, 331)

27. Proust himself will make an ulterior reference to this notion of *machinism* concerning the monocle on a face: "the part of the machinism this monocle introduced into Bloch's face" (III, 953/VI, 261) [Translation modified].

28. What could be called its "sufficiency."

29. We will rediscover this theme of setting fire in the dream of the "young man in a fez" and in the "colorless flames" of the sixth assemblage.

30. The refrain component has distanced itself from the most sensual forms of the sexual libido. Let us note however that Swann is still tempted to grasp it in a kiss: "he involuntarily made the motion with his lips of kissing its harmonious fleeting body as it passed" (I, 348/I, 361).

31. In fact, with the following assemblages it will instead be organized like a grapheme.

32. The two functions of moonlight, that of "dematerialization" and the antiblack hole, which are rediscovered in *The Fugitive* (III, 480/V, 446), do not coincide with a process of deterritorialization; the first tends instead towards a neutralization and the second towards an activation. (The same thing applies to the "Moonlight Sonata" as a substitute for Vinteuil's sonata.) However, other times the moon indeed has a deterritorializing and diagrammatic function. Example: "the moonlight... duplicating and distancing each thing by extending its shadow before it, denser and more concrete than itself, had at once thinned and enlarged the landscape like a *map* that had been folded and was now opened out" (I, 32/I, 33). This double function of the moon would itself deserve specific study (cf. I, 27/I, 27; I, 208/I, 216; etc.).

33. III, 116–128/V, 102–115. This passage is situated thirty pages before the actual return of Vinteuil's sonata, which we shall examine in the following assemblage.

34. Which furthermore appears to be a "piece related" to the *Recherche* as was previously written.

35. III, 93/V, 81 and III, 435/V, 403.

36. Proust himself references writing on a palimpsest concerning war stories (II, 109/III, 106). See Gerard Genette's analysis of the simultaneous metamorphoses which the individuals of the *Recherche* experience and of the synchronic nature of Proustian time. *Proust palimpseste*, Figure 1, 1976.

37. After the Verdurins' soiree at the Raspeliere in *Sodom and Gomorrah*, Vinteuil's Sonata is evoked but is not played, and at the end of the novel, after the reception at the Guermantes hotel (while the Narrator will have the revelation of Time regained and of his literary vocation), there will no longer be any allusions to Vinteuil's music. (III, 865–991/VI, 165–358).

38. Cf. for more on the opposition between redundancy of resonance and redundancy of interaction, see page [49] of this work.

39. "In short, when I thought about it, the raw material of my experience, which was to be the raw material of my book, came to me from Swann…" (III, 915/VI, 223).

40. Cf. page [192] and [193] of this book

41. The Narrator and his mother; Swann and Odette; the Narrator and Gilberte; the Narrator and Albertine; Charlus and Morel; Mlle Vinteuil and her friend.

42. "One reasons, that is one wanders off the track, each time that one does not have the strength of mind to force oneself to make an impression pass through all the successive states which will lead to its stabilization and its expression" (III, 882/VI, 190). But already at the beginning of the *Recherche*, Proust expressed the same concern "to go to the end of his impression" (I, 179, 180/I, 183, 184) op. cit. [242].

43. When Vinteuil introduced a dance into his last works, the little phrase "remained trapped in an opal" (III, 259/V, 238).

44. The Narrator believes to have discovered a commonality between Wagner and Vinteuil: the same "Vulcanesque skill." But was not Vulcan, before being assimilated by the Romans with Hephaestus as the blacksmith god of the Greeks, foremost the protective god of blazes? The refrain seizes fire from the black hole to forge a sign machine unlocking new matters of expression.

45. There will be no more allusion to this displacement of the "little phrase" in the *Recherche*, and we will be given no other indication, apart from the previously cited passage, about the nature of the movement of the Sonata to which it is related. When he has to localize the "little phrase," Proust will use such paraphrasing as: "*the part* of Vinteuil's Sonata with the little phrase that Swann had once loved so much" (I, 529/I, 103–104). This probably stems from the fact that he must avoid a too narrow association of the Narrator and the Sonata, so as not to re-stimulate the mechanism of the reterritorialization of the refrain on the loved one's faciality.

46. Concerning this passage: cf. page [323] of this book.

47. "Enjoying the essence of things..." (III, 871/VI, 180). "Making an impression pass through all the states that end in its stabilization..." (III, 882/VI, 191).

48. Charlus had unconsciously set a trap for Swann by having him go to Mme de Saint-Euverte's reception. Here we again find the same kind of trap; but it is the Narrator who has set it for himself. He has no need of a homosexual "companion." He himself assumes his own becoming-woman.

49. The sadomasochistic and voyeuristic practices associated with this attempt only occupy a relatively marginal place throughout the rest of the novel.

50. Concerning the trans-semiotic nature of the Septet's music: the comparison of Elstir's universe with Vinteuil's music which "extended, note by note, touch by touch, the unknown, priceless colorations of an unsuspected universe..." (III, 255/V, 234). Music transposes depth into the order of sound; the sonata was flat in relation to the Septet which deploys itself on three dimensions (III, 257/V, 236). Music is a unique example of what could have been the "communication of souls" without the invention of language, the formation of words, the analysis of ideas (III, 258/V, 237).

51. Botticelli's fresco is also situated in the Sistine Chapel. But to the extent that it is in a "normal" position, i.e. on a wall, we can consider that it is "flat," that it does draw on the third dimension deployed on the ceiling, which was reserved for Michelangelo.

52. Unlike Swann, Charlus and the Narrator are perfectly capable of reading music. But with Mlle Vinteuil and her friend the scriptural component crosses a new frontier because they are both capable of writing and recomposing music.

53. At these depths, Vinteuil's creative effort "attained its proper essence" (III, 256/V, 235).

54. In astrophysics, a black hole is anything but an energetic "void"; the gravitational point of collapse which constitutes the black hole results, on the contrary, from an energetic hyper-concentration.

55. Proust evokes two pieces of Schumann's Kinderszenen: "Bitten des Kind" and "Der Dichter spricht." But he reverses the meaning of the title of the former when he translates it by "sleeping child" instead of "pleading child." Overall, Proust's contemporary French music does not operate on the basis of the refrains of childhood. Certainly, there is a lot about childhood and nostalgia, but in a different way, less "basic" than German music. It concerns more the form of content than the form of expression. One simply dreams in Debussy's "Children's corners," in the "Boîte à joujoux," in the role of childhood in "Pelléas et Mélisande" or in Ravel's "L'enfant et les sortileges." In my view, what specifies the position of infancy in works like these is the fact that it functions more as a redundancy of resonance than as a diagrammatic catalyst. Frequently moreover, Claude Debussy only characterized the content of his works *after the fact* by giving them an expressive title; which perhaps explains

why his references to childhood are something "superimposed"; it is only a question of a childhood facialized by the adult world.

56. Other attempts of detaching a becoming-child in the *Recherche* will not have a more spectacular future. Cf.:
  —the Narrator's contemplation of little girls in the street (III, 138/V, 123);
  —the little girl whom he attracts to his home, an event which caused him to be investigated by the police (III, 432 and 443/V, 400);
  —the fact that Morel "seduces" little girls for Albertine (III, 600/V, 564).

57. "And yet, I said to myself, something more mysterious than Albertine's love seemed to be promised by the beginning of this work, by those first dawn cries. I tried to put aside the thought of my friend so as to concentrate on the musician" (III, 253/V, 232).

58. One also thinks of the guardian nymphs of Wagner's "Das Rheingold."

59. In each of his retakes, we no longer know if it is a "theme" or "neuralgia."

60. It dawns upon Swann to compare Albertine… to a time-table (III, 360/V, 341) or even to an "algebraic remainder" (III, 441/V, 408). But, according to Charles Sanders Peirce, an algebraic equation can be assimilated to a diagram!

61. "All it would have needed was for Mlle de Stermaria, the evening when I was to dine with her on the island of the Bois de Boulogne, not to have called it off. There was still time then for this fear of the imagination, which enables us to extract from a woman a notion of the individual so special that she appears to us to be unique in herself as well as predestined and necessary for us to have been focused on Mlle de Stermaria" (III, 501/V, 468).

62. We know that Proust himself made musicians come visit him, sometimes late at night, to play the quartets which inspired him to write on Vinteuil's music (Marcel Proust, *Les années de maturité*, Mercure de France, 1966, p. 303). There is a parenthesis in a passage of the *Recherche* concerning this precise scene that the pieces played on the pianola were often by Vinteuil. But because this parenthesis was not kept in the text reviewed by Proust, we can assume that during the course of its terminal development, the *Recherche* was brought to distance itself more and more from Vinteuil's music. Let us note however that there are several allusions to it in this same passage.

63. The rolls of the pianola, the primitive equivalent of the punch cards of a computer, constitute a rudimentary form of the machinic diagram.

64. [Translation modified.]

65. Even so far that Albertine's name itself, after her death, is deterritorialized and transformed into that of Gilberte (III, 656/V, 619–620).

66. "I did not, alas, have the nobility of young Werther. Without for a moment believing in Albertine's love, I had twenty times wanted to kill myself for her" (III, 909/VI, 218).

67. The revelation takes place when the Narrator waits in a library next to the salon where the concert is being held.

68. "The gesture, the simplest action remains enclosed as if within a thousand sealed vessels each one of which would be filled with things of a completely different color, odor and temperature; quite apart from the fact that these vessels, arranged across the full length of our years, during which we have never ceased to change, even if only our thoughts or our dreams, are placed at quite different heights and give us the sensation of extraordinarily varied atmospheres" (III, 870/VI, 178).

69. They will pass from an efficiency of resonance to an efficiency of interaction.

70. "Art is the most real thing there is" (III, 880/VI, 188).

71. The first characteristic of the reminiscences which serve as support for the signs of this spell book is, Proust explains, that the Narrator is not free to choose them, that he is given them as they are (III, 879/VI, 188).

72. The semiotic transformations brought about by dreams make operative seem sometimes to provide us access to lost Time; but this is only an illusion (III, 912/VI, 221).

73. "With my eyes shut, I would say to myself that everything can be transposed, and that a universe made up only of sound could be as varied as any." (The same intuition occurs in Kafka the day when he discovers that "everything can be written.")

74. "And I noticed in passing that, in the work of art that I now, without having made any conscious resolution, felt close to undertaking, this would pose great difficulties. For I would have to execute its successive parts in *slightly different materials*, and would need to find one *very different* from that suited to memories..." (III, 870–71/VI, 179).

75. To interpret such repetitions in terms of obsessive neurosis is simply foolish!

76. The child Narrator considered the grasping of an impression as an affair of will (I, 179/I, 183) or chance. "And seeing on the water and on the face of the wall a pale smile answering the smile of the sky, I cried out to myself in my enthusiasm, brandishing my furled umbrella: 'Damn, damn, damn, damn'" (I, 155/I, 158). "But was this really what reality was? When I tried to ascertain what actually happens at the moment when something makes a particular impression on us, whether as on the day when, crossing the bridge over the Vivonne, the shadow of a cloud on the water had made me exclaim 'Damn!' and jump for joy..." (III, 890/VI, 198).

3. Machinic Territorialities

1. "The two ways were not as irreconcilable as I had thought" (III, 693/V, 654).

2. See page [284] of this book.

3. It is due to the quality of their style that the Narrator's grandmother has offered him the books of George Sand. Nevertheless, we cannot help but think that the "feminine emancipation" side of this author played a certain role in Proust's choice. (Although the four novels in question here form part of the so-called "country" series at the end of George Sand's life.) Let us also note that one book called *La Mare au Diable* [The Devil's Sea] seems to evoke the sea of Montjouvain.

4. There is always the risk of falling into psychoanalytic, structural, even medical explanations. Have there not been attempts to discover the origin of Proust's long phrases in... his asthma attacks!

5. Of absolute deterritorialization. Cf. page [220] of this book.

6. What Proust calls: "The speed that accompanies habit" (III, 897/VI, 206).

7. For example, it would be necessary to study in detail the different sorts of stairs that appear in the *Recherche* (that of Combray where the child looks for his mother; that of the revelation of Charlus's homosexuality; that of the hotel of Saint-Euverte; that of the "little dressmaker"; that of the Guermantes hotel, etc.). One realizes that there is no linear series between any of them, no "geneticism," but that they constitute machinic series, diagrammatic operators whose function is to set heterogeneous components into interaction and to release surplus-values of code which synchronically irrigate the entire novel.

8. "I discovered this destructive action of Time at the very moment when I wanted to begin to clarify, to intellectualize within a work of art, realities whose nature was extra-temporal" (III, 930/VI, 239).

9. "It is simply, as I had often had reason to suspect, that what seems unique in a person whom one desires does not in fact belong to her. But the passage of time was giving me a more complete proof of this since, after twenty years, spontaneously, I was trying to find, not the girls whom I had known, but those who now possessed the youth that the others had had then" (III, 987–988/VI, 297).

10. Rather than continuing, as is usually done, to add features to the face of a passer-by, in the place of her nose, cheeks and chin, the Narrator will allow *an empty space* to appear upon which at very most "the reflection of (his) desires" will play. Instead of the black hole of faciality, a *surface of creation* opens to desire (III, 1045/VI, 355).

11. Literally "already felt." [Tr.]